BESTSELLING
BOOK SERIES

# Cocoa® Progr...
## for Mac OS® X Fo...

## Useful Cocoa Internet Resou...

### Apple Developer

`developer.apple.com`

Your Cocoa research online should begin at the Apple Developer site. This is the mothership of all Cocoa programming, where you can find the full Cocoa documentation, dozens of code samples, tips, tricks, and advice from the creators of Cocoa.

### Borkware Quickies

`www.borkware.com/quickies`

The Borkware Quickies Web site provides readers with numerous code snippets that demonstrate how to perform many different Cocoa tasks. The insights here are practical, concise, and pertinent. If you need to know how to do something rapidly, try one of the Quickies!

...gs that deal with Cocoa subject material. A ...gs gives you instant access to the rantings and ..., and philosophical views aplenty.

...d Cocoa discussion groups, and book reviews, .... You'll visit this site frequently.

...grammer. Staffed by some well-known Cocoa ...als representing different aspects of Cocoa ...know how to perform a task step-by-step.

FL-28-2

...ok Series for Beginners

# Cocoa® Programming for Mac OS® X For Dummies®

Cheat Sheet

## Xcode Keyboard Shortcuts

| Shortcut | Action |
| --- | --- |
| ⌘+Q | Quit Xcode |
| ⌘+Shift+N | Create a new project |
| ⌘+N | Create a new file |
| ⌘+F | Find text in the foremost document |
| ⌘+Shift+F | Find text in a project or framework |
| ⌘+B | Build |
| ⌘+R | Build and Go |
| Option-double-click | Look up any definition by Option-double-clicking its keyword in the code |
| ⌘+? | Open Xcode's Help |

## Interface Builder Keyboard Shortcuts

| Shortcut | Action |
| --- | --- |
| ⌘+Q | Quit Interface Builder |
| ⌘+N | Create a new NIB file |
| ⌘+R | Test the interface in the Cocoa Simulator |
| ⌘+Shift+L | Open the Library window |
| ⌘+1 | Open the Attributes Inspector |
| ⌘+5 | Open the Connections Inspector |
| ⌘+6 | Open the Identity Inspector |
| ⌘+? | Display Interface Builder Help |

## Data Types

| Type | Represents |
| --- | --- |
| NSString | String of Unicode text |
| NSAttributed String | Stylized text string |
| NSCalendarDate | Date |
| NSColor | Color |
| NSNumber | Number |
| NSRange | Beginning and endpoint of a numeric range |
| NSImage | Graphics image |
| NSArray | Array |
| NSDictionary | Collection of key-value pairs |

## Components of a Cocoa Project

| Group Name | Contains |
| --- | --- |
| Classes | Source code files for user-defined classes |
| Other Sources | main.m; additional source code files |
| Resources | NIB file, InfoPlist.strings file, icon files, documentation files, image files, and audio files |
| Frameworks | Cocoa frameworks; libraries that define how Cocoa works |
| Products | Application you're building |

# Cocoa® Programming
## for Mac OS® X

## FOR
# DUMMIES®

# Cocoa® Programming for Mac OS® X

## FOR DUMMIES®

by Erick Tejkowski

WILEY

Wiley Publishing, Inc.

**Cocoa® Programming for Mac OS® X For Dummies®**

Published by
Wiley Publishing, Inc.
111 River Street
Hoboken, NJ 07030-5774

www.wiley.com

Copyright © 2009 by Wiley Publishing, Inc., Indianapolis, Indiana

Published by Wiley Publishing, Inc., Indianapolis, Indiana

Published simultaneously in Canada

For general information on our other products and services, please contact our Customer Care Department within the U.S. at 877-762-2974, outside the U.S. at 317-572-3993, or fax 317-572-4002.

For technical support, please visit www.wiley.com/techsupport.

Wiley also publishes its books in a variety of electronic formats. Some content that appears in print may not be available in electronic books.

Library of Congress Control Number: 2009920903

ISBN: 978-0-470-43289-1

Manufactured in the United States of America

10 9 8 7 6 5 4 3 2 1

WILEY

# About the Author

**Erick Tejkowski** is a freelance author and software developer. He is the author of *Cocoa For Dummies, Mac OS X Tiger Simplified,* and *Mac OS X Panther: Top 100 Simplified Tips and Tricks,* among others. He has also served in editorial and writing roles for popular Macintosh publications, such as *MacTech, MacWorld,* and *RB Developer.* When he's not computing, he enjoys spending his free time with his wife, Lisa, and their children, Mercedes, Leopold, and Emil.

# Dedication

This book is dedicated to Maria Paredes, PhD. Good job!

# Author's Acknowledgments

Thank you to Greg Croy, Dennis Cohen, and especially Rebecca Senninger for editing this book. The quality of the final transcript can be attributed to their suggestions, recommendations, and editing expertise.

Thank you to Mixi, Mister, and Emil for inspiration.

## Publisher's Acknowledgments

We're proud of this book; please send us your comments through our online registration form located at http://dummies.custhelp.com. For other comments, please contact our Customer Care Department within the U.S. at 877-762-2974, outside the U.S. at 317-572-3993, or fax 317-572-4002.

Some of the people who helped bring this book to market include the following:

### Acquisitions, Editorial, and Media Development

**Project Editor:** Rebecca Senninger

**Executive Editor:** Gregory S. Croy

**Acquisition Editor:** Katie Mohr

**Copy Editor:** Jen Riggs

**Technical Editor:** Dennis R. Cohen

**Editorial Manager:** Leah Cameron

**Editorial Assistant:** Amanda Foxworth

**Sr. Editorial Assistant:** Cherie Case

**Cartoons:** Rich Tennant
(www.the5thwave.com)

### Composition Services

**Project Coordinator:** Erin Smith

**Layout and Graphics:** Samantha Allen, Reuben W. Davis, Melissa K. Jester, Sarah Phillipart, Christine Williams

**Proofreaders:** David Faust, Toni Settle

**Indexer:** Broccoli Information Management

---

**Publishing and Editorial for Technology Dummies**

    **Richard Swadley,** Vice President and Executive Group Publisher

    **Andy Cummings,** Vice President and Publisher

    **Mary Bednarek,** Executive Acquisitions Director

    **Mary C. Corder,** Editorial Director

**Publishing for Consumer Dummies**

    **Diane Graves Steele,** Vice President and Publisher

**Composition Services**

    **Gerry Fahey,** Vice President of Production Services

    **Debbie Stailey,** Director of Composition Services

# Contents at a Glance

# Table of Contents

# Introduction

W elcome to *Cocoa Programming for Mac OS X For Dummies.* This book shows you how to create applications for Mac OS X, complete with beautiful Aqua interfaces and advanced functionality. The best part is that Cocoa provides you with programming skills that you could only dream of a few short years ago.

## About This Book

*Cocoa Programming for Mac OS X For Dummies* is a newcomer's guide to Cocoa programming for Mac OS X. This book guides you through the basics of Cocoa application development, so you can finally realize the full potential of your Macintosh. Although Cocoa isn't the easiest thing on earth to figure out, it's easy enough that beginners can create applications. Furthermore, even beginner projects can have features that rival professional applications. You'll be surprised at how easy it is to add complex features — features that would have taken an army of engineers to build in the past.

This book won't make you a certified Cocoa expert, but it will give you a good start on your way to becoming proficient with Cocoa. From the beginning of the book to the very end, you'll explore Cocoa programming by using it. Each chapter guides you through the process of creating at least one simple application that illustrates the features presented in that chapter.

*Cocoa Programming for Mac OS X For Dummies* covers the fundamentals of Cocoa programming as well as advanced features. The weird thing about Cocoa is that you sometimes can't tell which is which. In Cocoa, the simple is complex, and the complex simple. You'll gasp in awe as you add sophisticated graphics, multimedia, and professional typography to your application in minutes. Then you'll turn around and bang your head against the wall trying to remember how to create a simple list of items in Cocoa. The great part about Cocoa is that after you get the hang of the basics, you can build applications with high-quality features that would've been near impossible for a beginner to achieve in the past.

# Conventions Used in This Book

This book guides you through the process of building Cocoa applications. Throughout, you create interfaces and make them functional with the use of Objective-C code. The code examples in this book appear in a monospaced font. For instance:

```
#import <Cocoa/Cocoa.h>
```

Objective-C is intimately connected to the C language, which is a case-sensitive language. Therefore, it's a good idea to enter the code that appears in this book *exactly* as it appears in the text. Some capitalization may not be mandatory, but until you're familiar with the rules, it's best not to stray from the text. If you're ever uncertain about case sensitivity, you can always use the source code on the *For Dummies* Web site, at www.dummies.com/go/cocoafd. All URLs in this book appear in a monospaced font as well:

```
www.apple.com
```

# Foolish Assumptions

To begin programming Cocoa applications, you need a Macintosh computer, a copy of Mac OS X (preferably 10.4 or higher), and the Developer Tools, which Apple offers for free as a download. If you're not sure how to install the Developer Tools, the appendix can lead you through the steps necessary to prepare your Mac for Cocoa development.

In addition to the computer and software, you'll also need some computing skills. For starters, you should be familiar with using the Macintosh operating system. You should know how to launch applications, save files, work with Finder, and use the Internet.

You should also have at least a passing knowledge of some computer language. Ideally, you should have working skills in the C programming language. Even a passing experience with an object-oriented language, such as C++ or Java, would also be beneficial, but it's not an absolute must. This isn't to say that you'll be completely lost without these skills. Different computer languages tend to share many features in common. Whether you have a Pascal, a JavaScript, or an AppleScript background, you'll find that Objective-C, although strange looking at first, is easy to learn, and many aspects will feel familiar.

The examples in this book stay focused on the Cocoa aspects of programming. Although some accessory C code is necessary to make this happen, the examples are not obfuscated code that an average beginning programmer can't grasp. If you're still not sure that you're ready for Cocoa, jump on in anyway. There's a good chance that you'll understand what's going on. When you get lost, you can always refer to one of the many C language references on the Internet for extra help.

# How This Book Is Organized

*Cocoa Programming for Mac OS X For Dummies* has five main parts.

## Part I: Developer Tools

Part I introduces you to the world of Cocoa programming. You explore the tools that you need to write Cocoa software and in the process build your first Cocoa application.

## Part II: Instant Cocoa and the Objective-C Language

In Part II, you continue your quest for Cocoa enlightenment by examining the basics of the Objective-C language, the elements of a Cocoa interface, and object-oriented programming. These chapters give you the fundamental background knowledge that you need to use the features presented throughout the rest of the book.

## Part III: Putting It All Together: Cocoa Programming in Depth

Now that you have the basics behind you, it's time to dive in to the fun features of Cocoa. In Part III, you add some glitz and glamour to your applications using graphics, audio, video, Internet features, and stylized text. It's the stuff that applications are made of!

## Part IV: Advanced Cocoa Topics

Part IV takes you into the realm of advanced Cocoa programming topics. Until now, applications remained simple one-window affairs. With Cocoa, you can easily create applications with multiple documents or even other executables that aren't traditional Mac applications at all. In this part, you discover some of the more advanced features of Cocoa and find out how to use them in your own projects.

## Part V: The Part of Tens

Part V consists of useful Cocoa tips, tricks, and pointers. Whether it's advice about how to make the most of Cocoa or help for what to do when things go wrong, Part V covers some common issues you'll encounter when using Cocoa.

# Icons Used in This Book

When you see this icon, you can be sure that the code on the *For Dummies* Web site applies to the current example. The Web site contains the code for all projects in this book for those who don't feel like typing the code. Just go to www.dummies.com/go/cocoafd.

This icon indicates a useful pointer that you shouldn't skip.

This icon represents a friendly reminder. It describes a vital point that you should keep in mind while proceeding through a particular section of the chapter.

This icon signifies that the accompanying explanation might be informative (dare I say, interesting?), but it isn't essential to understanding Cocoa. Feel free to skip past these tidbits if you're a technophobe.

This icon alerts you to potential problems that you may encounter along the way. Read and obey these blurbs to avoid trouble.

# Where to Go From Here

It's time to explore Cocoa! If you're apprehensive about embarking upon this journey, relax in the knowledge that anyone can program in Cocoa. This book will show you how to get started.

# Part I
# Developer Tools

"We're here to clean the code."

# In this part . . .

Your first sip of Cocoa begins with an introduction to the Cocoa development process. Next, it's on to Apple's Developer Tools, where you'll put that process into practice.

Part I guides you through the basics of Cocoa development using Xcode and Interface Builder. These two applications form the foundation of your Cocoa experience, and you'll use the knowledge you gain from them throughout the book. To help you understand how they work, you'll build your own working Cocoa application. As you progress through Part I, you'll continue to improve that application, adding features and improving functionality as you go. After you're happy with the results, the end of Part I shows you how to prepare the final application for public consumption.

# Chapter 1

# A Brief Tour of Cocoa Development

*T*hese are exciting times for Macintosh users. When Apple unleashed Mac OS X upon the world, it ushered in a new era of computing for the Mac faithful. Besides the rock-solid stability of UNIX, Mac OS X offered functionality and features that Mac users could have only dreamt of a few years earlier. Along with this great operating system, Apple saw fit to remember Macintosh developers and have done so ever since. Principal among Apple's achievements is Cocoa, the subject of this book. This chapter introduces you to the world of Mac OS X programming and, in particular, Cocoa programming.

## Mac OS X Is a Programmer's Dream

Macintosh programming has never been as easy or as accessible as it is with Mac OS X. For starters, Apple, the friendly folks that they are, thought it'd be a great idea to give away the development tools. For free. Apple provides the Xcode Developer Tools as a free download on the Apple Developer Connection Web site. By installing the Xcode Developer Tools download, you instantly gain access to a complete collection of tools, utilities, documentations, and example source codes to get you started programming for the Mac OS. In the past, a developer bundle this comprehensive would have cost hundreds of dollars. Today, Apple provides it for no additional charge.

Some older versions of Mac OS X ship with a Developer Tools disc; newer versions don't. If you're searching for the disc and can't find it, you may have an installation of Mac OS X that doesn't include the Developer Tools disc. You needn't worry, however, because you can download the Xcode Developer Tools by signing up for a free ADC membership at Apple's developer site (`https://connect.apple.com`). In fact, even if you already have a Developer Tools disc, check Apple's developer site for updates because each version of Xcode Developer Tools is specific to a particular OS X release. ***Note:*** Xcode Developer Tools installations can total in the hundreds of megabytes, so you'll probably want a fast Internet connection to download them.

*Apple Developer Connection (ADC)* is Apple's support program for developers. You can register at different tiers (and pay different prices) for membership, which gives you varying amounts of support and other perks, such as Worldwide Developers Conference (WWDC) tickets. The lowest tier is completely free, so it doesn't cost you anything to download the Xcode Developer Tools.

Just because the Xcode Developer Tools is a free download doesn't mean that the software is second-rate. On the contrary, Xcode Developer Tools are world class. When developing software for the Macintosh with these tools, you can take advantage of the following benefits:

- ✔ Write code in a variety of programming and scripting languages: C, Objective-C, Python, Ruby, Java, or even AppleScript.

- ✔ Create beautiful interfaces that follow Apple's Human Interface Guidelines.

- ✔ Develop applications with rich features, some of which you can add to your project without writing a single line of code.

Further, because Mac OS X has a UNIX flavor at its core, you can take advantage of the decades of work by UNIX users. For example, most open-source software run on different varieties of UNIX, so you can leverage thousands of compatible source-code examples for use in your own Mac OS X applications as well.

# Why Program with Cocoa?

Cocoa is one kind of programming that you can perform with the Apple Xcode Developer Tools. Cocoa is a collection of tools and libraries (or *frameworks*) that allows you to get the most out of Mac OS X programming. Many features make Cocoa great; some include

- ✔ Modular object-oriented design
- ✔ Use of frameworks
- ✔ Visual interface design

Object-oriented programming is in common use these days, and for good reason. By programming with an object-oriented design, your code can more closely model items in the real world. This book isn't an object-oriented text; in fact, you should come to Cocoa with at least an idea of how to program in an object-oriented fashion. This book does, however, discuss the object-oriented nature of Cocoa and examines its primary language: Objective-C. Objective-C, as you might induce from its name, is an object-oriented super-set of the C language. It permits you to program in an object-oriented fashion without some of the messy baggage that C++ has. Because Objective-C is a superset of C, you can also take advantage of the C that you know. Everything that you can do in C is valid code to the Objective-C compiler.

The use of frameworks is another great aspect of Cocoa development. Experienced programmers may be tempted to call frameworks by another name — libraries. *Frameworks* are collections of classes that provide you, the Cocoa developer, with a specific type of functionality. Mac OS X ships with several frameworks for you to choose from, but two big ones stand out: AppKit and Foundation. The *AppKit Framework* provides you with scores of classes and functions for working with interfaces, and the *Foundation Framework* gives you utilitarian functions relating to data manipulation and program execution. You use them a lot when writing Cocoa software.

The object-oriented nature of Cocoa and its rich set of frameworks form an unbeatable code-reuse duo. Computer programmers can be a lazy bunch, not wanting to repeat a single task. To aid developers in their pursuit of reusable code, Cocoa offers a wide array of reusable classes. After you complete some programming tasks, you can even store the results in your own framework for use in other projects. Apple gives you reusable code out of the box, and you can reuse your own code as well. The object-oriented design of Cocoa makes this reuse possible.

Reusable code is good for a variety of reasons: It lets you create software quickly, it reduces the number of bugs in your code, and it prevents you from reinventing the wheel each time you sit down to program. By reusing the frameworks that Apple provides with the Xcode Developer Tools, you gain all sorts of great functionality without having to know how it works under the hood.

Besides the geekier benefits, you'll love many other aspects of Cocoa programming. For starters, the frameworks that accompany Mac OS X provide a rich set of interface elements that you can use to build sophisticated interfaces demanded by professional software. Moreover, Cocoa programming gives you instant access to a wide range of free classes. Whether you need an About box, a spell-checker, or QuickTime movies in your application, Cocoa has a solution for you.

# The Tools You Need

To facilitate your Cocoa development, Apple was nice enough to provide you with a large selection of tools and utilities. With these tools, you can begin creating Cocoa software from the ground up. When you're finished programming, the tools will even build the application, prepare it for distribution, and put together an installer.

To begin programming with Cocoa, find the development tools. If you installed them in the default location, they reside in the following directory on your hard drive:

```
/Developer/Applications
```

If you discover that you don't have the development tools on your system, visit `developer.apple.com` to download the latest version.

You won't need all the applications that Apple provides in the `/Developer/Applications` directory. In fact, for many tasks you can probably get away with using only two: Xcode and Interface Builder.

## Xcode

*Xcode* is the main application that you'll use for all your Cocoa projects. Xcode serves a number of roles in the Cocoa development process:

- ✔ **Xcode acts as the central repository for all the files in your Cocoa projects.** Using a familiar document approach, Xcode lets you organize the components of a Cocoa project in one easy-to-use document. Figure 1-1 shows a Cocoa project opened in Xcode.

- ✔ **You also use Xcode to write and edit Cocoa source code.** When you write code for a project, Xcode guides you by coloring the syntax, indenting code automatically, and providing auto-completion features to reduce the amount of typing (and remembering) that you have to do. It also offers convenient one-click access to all the functions in your code, as shown in Figure 1-2.

- ✔ **Your Cocoa project may have other types of files beyond code, and Xcode is prepared to help you work with them.** For example, if you want to include images in your project, Xcode lets you view them in the main project window without skipping a beat. You don't need to use another application to view those images. Xcode displays them right in the code editor, as shown in Figure 1-3.

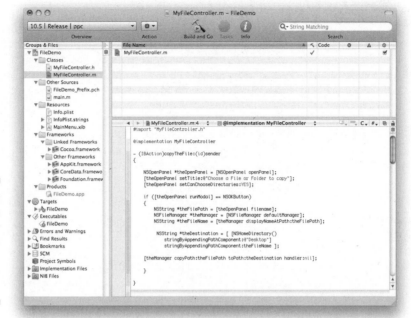

**Figure 1-1:**
Xcode acts
as your
primary tool
for writing
Cocoa
software.

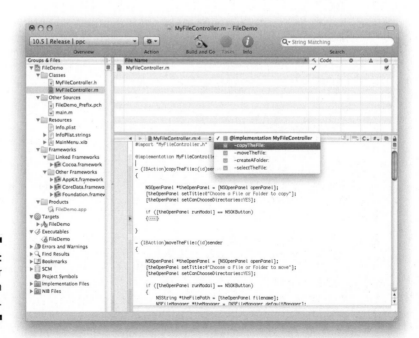

**Figure 1-2:**
Edit your
code in
Xcode.

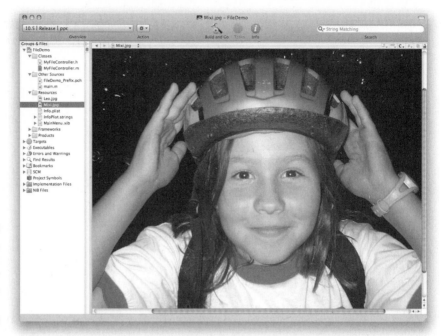

**Figure 1-3:**
You can
view other
types of files
in Xcode.

> ✔ **When you get stuck, Xcode gives you access to the complete collection
> of Cocoa, Xcode, and other developer documentation.** You can view
> and navigate the documentation with Xcode in much the same way as
> you would a Web browser. Figure 1-4 shows what the screen looks like
> when documentation is loaded into Xcode.

After you complete your Cocoa project, you use Xcode to compile, link,
and build a final application. You can then distribute the application to
friends, co-workers, and even the world (as long as they use Mac OS X).

Xcode wears many hats. If you're accustomed to other development environments, you may be surprised to discover that Xcode performs tasks
that require multiple tools in other environments. For example, Xcode
functions as a

> ✔ **Project organizer,** managing files and resources in your Cocoa projects
>
> ✔ **Code editor,** allowing you to write and edit Cocoa code
>
> ✔ **Browser,** displaying built-in documentation or other kinds of resources
> in your Cocoa projects
>
> ✔ **Compiler and linker,** spitting out a complete Cocoa application at the
> end of the development process

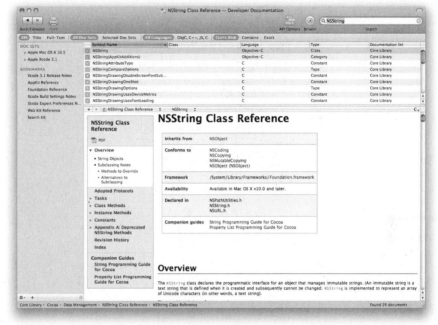

**Figure 1-4:**
You can
view
the Cocoa
documen-
tation in
Xcode.

# Interface Builder

*Interface Builder* is a constant companion to Xcode. As you can probably guess, Interface Builder's main purpose is to create interfaces. With it, you can build interfaces that adhere to Apple's interface guidelines.

Interface Builder provides a complete set of controls that you can add to your application. From windows and drawers to buttons and sliders, Interface Builder gives you drag-and-drop access to a full suite of interface elements to make your software the best it can be. Don't forget that Interface Builder is an Apple product. No one knows the Macintosh user interface better than Apple, because they created it, so you can be certain that the controls in Interface Builder follow the strictest Apple guidelines.

Figure 1-5 shows an example interface with many different types of controls available to you in Interface Builder. The interface won't win any design awards, but it does show you the range of elements that you can use in your own Cocoa software.

**Figure 1-5:**
Interface
Builder has
a complete
set of
interface
controls for
you to use in
your Cocoa
projects.

Interface Builder's features aren't limited to WYSIWYG (what you see is what you get) interface editing. You can also create classes that have no visual representation. Although you don't actually write the code in Interface Builder for your classes, you do define the basic structures and methods for them there. You can also connect the interface to your classes with simple drag-and-drop techniques, as shown in Figure 1-6.

## Do you speak the language?

Cocoa programming (like most kinds of computer programming) requires the use of a programming language. To create Cocoa applications, you need to know Objective-C, Python, Ruby, Java, or AppleScript. This book uses Objective-C because it's the "native language" of Cocoa. Objective-C is a superset of the traditional C programming language. If you have experience with C, you're well on your way to understanding Objective-C. All the C functions you know and love are available to

you in Cocoa. Objective-C, however, goes one step further and enhances C by adding object-oriented features to the language.

Objective-C has a syntax that may look a little foreign to you at first, unless you're also familiar with SmallTalk. But after you get the hang of it, you'll find that it isn't hard to understand at all. Chapter 6 goes into the details of Objective-C, but you start using it in Chapter 2 to build your first Cocoa project.

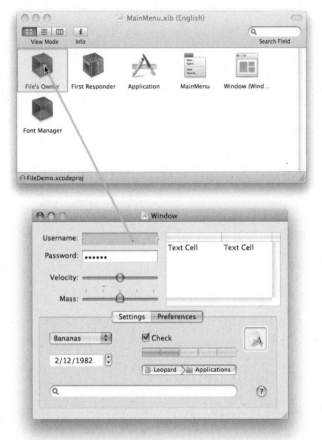

After you complete an interface, Interface Builder goes the extra mile and creates the header and implementation files for you and then inserts them into the desired Xcode project. Although Interface Builder's strongest features pertain to designing and creating great-looking interfaces, many other features make it much more than an interface-building tool. It plays a big part in the Cocoa programming experience.

# Chapter 2

# Creating Your First Cocoa Application

**In This Chapter**

▶ Attaining fame and fortune with Cocoa in six easy steps

▶ Creating a project

▶ Building your interface

▶ Adding code to the project

▶ Testing and building a completed application

*P*rogramming computers can be grueling. Apple tries to simplify that task by offering a complete set of tools, an easy-to-understand programming language, and a sophisticated object-oriented framework to help you produce great software. The complete package is so well honed that you can create an application in one sitting with only a small amount of code.

This chapter shows you how to create your first Cocoa application from scratch with Apple's Xcode Developer Tools. Whether you're building an interface, adding code to make the interface functional, or building the finished product, the Apple Xcode Developer Tools offer a professional development environment that lets you work quickly to produce amazing applications.

## Creating a Cocoa Application in Six Simple Steps

Writing your own software is a process. Much like following a recipe, you proceed through a sequence of steps until you end up with a working application. Here's the six-step process to creating a Cocoa application:

1. **Think of an application.**

   For some people, this can be the toughest step in the programming process. For others, it's the simplest. Consider a task that you want your computer to perform. Then think of a computer program that would do it. What would the program look like? How would it operate? What behaviors must it possess?

2. **Create a Cocoa project in Xcode.**

   You usually begin your Cocoa development in the Xcode application. *Xcode* is the tool at the center of Cocoa programming; it's where you create and work with the various parts of your Cocoa projects. Chapter 3 covers Xcode in depth.

3. **Build an interface in Interface Builder.**

   After you create a project in Xcode, launch Interface Builder to work on your application's interface. In traditional Mac fashion, creating an interface is as easy as dragging and dropping. Using only the tools in Interface Builder, you can quickly build attractive interfaces in minutes. Chapter 4 covers Interface Builder.

4. **Return to Xcode and add code.**

   After you create the interface, return to Xcode and add code to make the interface functional. This part of the programming process gives functionality to the interface you just created. Fortunately, Interface Builder can help the process along by laying out a basic shell in Xcode where you can enter your code.

5. **Test your work.**

   No one gets everything right the first time, especially not with something as potentially complex as programming a computer. To assist, Xcode gives you a complete set of tools for testing your application before you unleash it on the world.

6. **Build an application.**

   You've created an interface, added the code, and tested your project. Now it's time to build an application. With one click, you can build an application that you can run on almost any Mac OS X computer.

If you're using a version of Mac OS X prior to Leopard (version 10.5), you may not be able to run your application on later versions of Mac OS X. Because Apple is always improving the operating system, a time may come when frameworks from a newer version of the operating system are incompatible with an older version of the operating system. To ensure that you have the necessary frameworks to target the latest version of Mac OS X, always upgrade to the most recent version of Mac OS X and its corresponding Xcode Developer Tools.

Now that you have a basic understanding of the steps that you must perform to create a Cocoa application, it's time to create your own project! The remainder of this chapter guides you through the process of building, coding, and creating your first Cocoa application.

# Beginning a Project

To begin creating your first piece of Cocoa software, come up with an idea of what you want to create. After you establish the type of software that you want to build, you'll create a new project with Xcode to begin programming it.

## Thinking of an idea

Instead of putting you through the sometimes-arduous task of dreaming up your own idea, here's one to get started. Everyone needs a calculator. Whether you want to add your earnings from selling great Cocoa software or figure out how soon you can retire from said earnings, a calculator is a handy tool for the task. Sure, Mac OS X has a few different calculators, but no one ever said that you weren't allowed to build a better one.

One troublesome aspect of traditional calculator applications rears its head when you press an operator key (+, -, *, /) and enter another number. You can't see the first number that you entered. Your application solves this problem by always displaying the two numbers you're working with.

Unlike a traditional calculator interface, your calculator will look more like a form. You enter numbers in the various fields of the interface and press a button to calculate the result. Figure 2-1 shows what the completed application looks like.

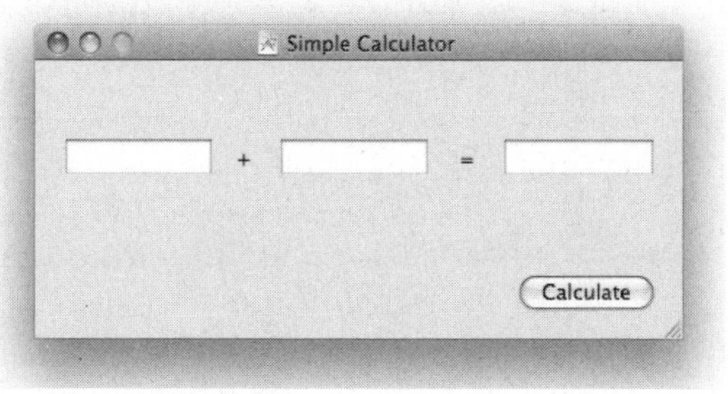

**Figure 2-1:** When thinking of an idea for an application, try to imagine what it will look like.

As you can see, you now have an idea (build a better calculator), you've thought about how to do it (with a form-like interface), and you've constructed a mental image of what it will look like. Of course, in this example, the mental image is an image of the finished product (refer to Figure 2-1). But because you can't read my mind, I provided an image of the finished product.

## Getting started with your Cocoa project

Now that you have an idea in mind, you can begin the Cocoa development process:

1. **Launch Xcode by double-clicking its icon.**

   The icon is on your hard drive at the following location:

   ```
   /Developer/Applications/Xcode
   ```

   When you first launch Xcode, a handy window may open welcoming you to Xcode, as shown in Figure 2-2. This window also offers convenient one-click access to documentation and tutorials for using Xcode. If it opens, close the Welcome to Xcode window to reduce window clutter. It opens again the next time you launch Xcode, unless you deselect the Show at Launch check box.

2. **Chose File⇨New Project.**

   The New Project window appears, asking you what kind of project you want to create, as shown in Figure 2-3.

**Figure 2-2:**
Welcome to
Xcode!

3. **Select the Application template on the left side of the New Project window.**

   On the left side of the New Project window is a list of project templates that Apple has created for you. You use the Application template for building standard Mac OS X applications. Figure 2-3 shows the Application template selected on the left.

4. **Select Cocoa Application from the list of choices on the right side of the New Project window.**

   On the right side of the New Project window is a list of application templates from which you can choose. For most applications in this book, choose Cocoa Application, as shown in Figure 2-3.

5. **Click the Choose button.**

   A Save As dialog opens.

6. **Type a name for your project in the Save As dialog.**

   For example, you can name the project My First Project, as shown in Figure 2-4.

   When you first open a Save As dialog, it may not appear like the one in Figure 2-4. Instead it may appear smaller and it may not display the expanded list of files. To expand the dialog, click the triangle button that's adjacent to the Save As field.

**Figure 2-3:**
Choose
the Cocoa
Application
option.

**Figure 2-4:**
Give your
project a
descriptive
name and
select a
location for
saving the
project.

7. **Select a location for the project and click the Save button.**

   Your hard drive buzzes and whirs for a few seconds, and then Xcode
   displays a project window. In the Finder, the project files are contained
   within a folder that has the same name as the one you designated in
   Step 6. In Xcode, the project window displays a list of elements in
   the project, grouped into folders (which, unsurprisingly, Xcode calls
   *Groups & Files*), as shown in Figure 2-5. Your project is comprised of the
   components on the left side of the project window. These components
   include class files, source code files, interface files, and images, among
   other items.

8. **Open the Resources group folder and double-click the MainMenu.xib
   file.**

   *MainMenu.xib* is the default interface file for your project. Your project
   opens in Interface Builder.

Files in your project reside in one of a handful of group folders in Xcode. You
can read all about these group folders in Chapter 3, which covers the operation of Xcode. For now, the only group folder that you need to be concerned
with is the Resources folder.

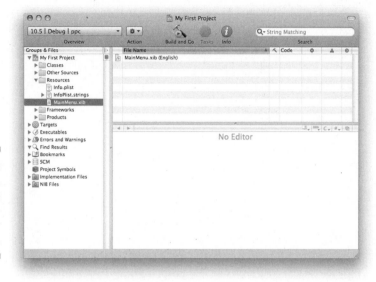

**Figure 2-5:**
MainMenu.
xib contains
the inter-
face for
your project.

# Building an Interface

When you double-click the MainMenu.xib file in Xcode, the Interface Builder application launches. Figure 2-6 shows the MainMenu.xib file open in Interface Builder.

By default, the project's main window should be open, ready for adding new controls. If you don't see an open window in Interface Builder, double-click the Window object in the XIB project window.

This window is the starting point for your application's interface. Because other people may use this application, it's a good idea to make it look as nice as possible. Begin by changing the window's title:

1. **Open the Inspector window by choosing Tools⇨Inspector.**

   The Inspector window appears, showing you properties that pertain to the window, as shown on the right side of Figure 2-7. The Inspector window can display different types of information, but when it's showing properties relating to a window, it's titled Window Attributes.

2. **In the Inspector window, change the Title property to the name of your window.**

   For example, you can change the title to Simple Calculator. The name shows up in the title bar of your window, as shown on the left side of Figure 2-7.

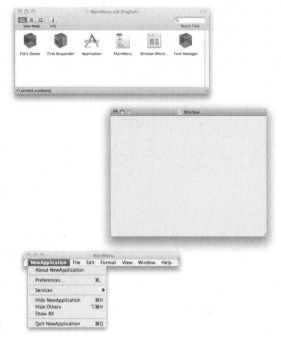

**Figure 2-6:**
Interface
Builder is
where you
design and
create your
application's
interface.

**Figure 2-7:**
The
Inspector
window lets
you change
many
aspects of
a window,
including
its title.

**3. (Optional) Change the size of the window.**

To change the size of the window, simply click and drag the resize widget at the bottom-right corner of your window, as you would resize a window in Finder.

4. **To prevent users from resizing the window while they use your application, deselect the Resize option in the Controls section of the Inspector window (refer to Figure 2-7).**

5. **Open the Library window by choosing Tools⇨Library if it is not showing by default.**

   To continue constructing the interface, you must drag controls from the Library window, which displays a variety of controls for you to use in your Cocoa interfaces.

   The Library window has two tabs: Objects and Media. Click Objects to see the available controls, as shown in Figure 2-8.

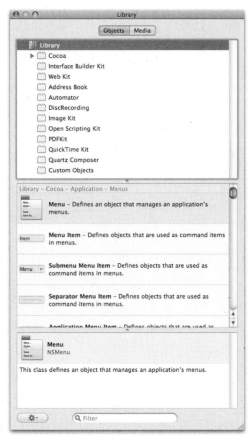

**Figure 2-8:**
The Library window has all the controls you need for creating attractive Cocoa interfaces.

# Adding controls to the interface

Controls are the interactive elements that make up an application's interface. You're probably already familiar with many different types of controls because you use them every time you use your computer. Some common interface controls include buttons, check boxes, radio buttons, scroll bars, and text fields.

For your first project, you'll use a handful of controls in your interface. Perform the following steps to add the controls you'll need for this project:

1. **Drag a Push Button control from the Library window to your application's interface window.**

   To locate the Push Button control quickly, enter **Push Button** in the search field at the bottom of the Library window.

2. **Change the button's label.**

   To change the button's label, double-click it and begin typing the text. For example, you can type **Calculate**, as shown in Figure 2-9.

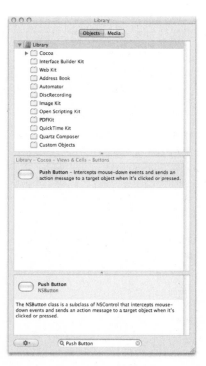

**Figure 2-9:**
Double-click a button to edit its text.

3. **Drag three large text field controls to the window.**

   The user will enter numbers (the operands) in the first two text fields that you add to the window. The result of the mathematical operation is displayed in the third text field. You need not change the properties for the first two text fields, but the third one needs a minor adjustment. The answer to the calculation will appear in the third text field, so you need to make its contents unalterable by the user.

4. **Select the third text field and then choose Tools⇨Inspector to display the Inspector window. From the list of properties, deselect the Editable option (see Figure 2-10).**

   The text field is now uneditable, as you might have guessed.

5. **Add two Label controls to serve as visual cues in the interface.**

   The Label controls have a cosmetic function. They make the interface look nice and help the user know how the interface works. Type **Label** in the Library's search field to locate the Label control easily. Because you're laying out this interface to look like a traditional math problem, change the title of one text field to + and the other to =. Figure 2-11 shows the completed interface with the new text field controls. In this chapter and Chapter 3, you worry only about addition. In Chapter 4, you add subtraction, multiplication, and division to the project.

**Figure 2-10:**
Deselect the Editable property of a text field so your users can't change its contents.

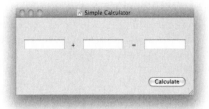

**Figure 2-11:**
The
completed
interface.

Table 2-1 lists the controls that make up your interface. Before you go on, now is a good time to double-check that everything is arranged like you want it.

| Table 2-1 | | Controls in a Calculator Interface | |
|---|---|---|---|
| *Control Type* | *Quantity* | *Identifying It in the Library Window* | *Other Info* |
| Button | 1 | Search for *Button* | Title is *Simple Calculator* |
| Text Field | 2 | Search for *Text Field* | |
| Text Field | 1 | Search for *Text Field* | Deselect the Editable option |
| Label | 1 | Search for *Label* | Title is + |
| Label | 1 | Search for *Label* | Title is = |

# *Wiring the interface*

Now that you've constructed your interface, it's time to wire it. After all, a light switch in your house can't turn on a lamp without a wire that connects the two; your interface is no different. At the center of a typical home's electrical system is a fuse box, or a circuit breaker box. All wires in the home lead back to the centrally located fuse box. Cocoa interfaces follow a similar pattern. Instead of a fuse box, however, you use a *class*. A class is an abstract representation of something that you want to model from the real world in your program — for now, you can think of it as a *virtual fusebox.* Chapter 6 has more information about classes in Objective-C programs. You then add outlets to connect the main Fusebox class to the elements of your interface.

## *Creating classes*

To create a class in Xcode:

1. **Return to your project in Xcode and choose File⇨New File.**

   A New File Wizard opens, displaying possible file templates.

2. **Select Cocoa in the left column.**

   The wizard displays Cocoa file templates.

3. **Select Objective-C Class from the section on the right side of the screen.**

   The Objective-C class is the appropriate type of class for this Cocoa project because you're using the Objective-C language to write this program.

4. **Click Next.**

5. **Name the new file Fusebox.m and make sure that the Also Create "Fusebox.h" check box is selected, as shown in Figure 2-12.**

   An Objective-C class has two parts — an implementation file with a .m file extension and an interface file with a .h file extension.

6. **Click Finish.**

   Xcode creates and adds Fusebox.m and Fusebox.h files to the project. You may discover that the Fusebox.m and Fusebox.h files aren't in the correct folder of your project. It's perfectly fine for you to drag the new files to the desired folder. In fact, they can reside anywhere in the project — in any folder or even outside the folders. Xcode is smart enough to find them for you come build-time.

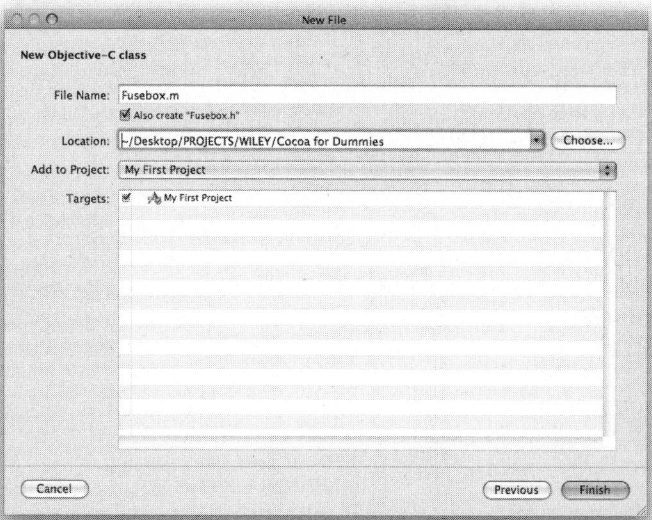

**Figure 2-12:**
The Fusebox
class
connects
the interface
elements
to your
application.

### Adding outlets

Next, add outlets to this new class. *Outlets* are references that connect your source code to elements in the interface.

In the Simple Calculator project, users will enter numbers for a calculation in two text fields. The third text field displays the result of the calculation. Therefore, you need to make three outlets — one for each text field.

To add outlets to a class in Xcode, add them to the Fusebox.h file.

```
IBOutlet id answerField;
IBOutlet id numberField1;
IBOutlet id numberField2;
```

These three outlets must appear between the `Fusebox` interface brackets, like this:

```
#import <Cocoa/Cocoa.h>

@interface Fusebox : NSObject {
    IBOutlet id answerField;
    IBOutlet id numberField1;
    IBOutlet id numberField2;
}
@end
```

### Adding an action

In addition to three outlets, add an action to the class. An *action* is a function that executes when based on some event that you assign in Interface Builder. The new action in this class calculates the answer to the math problem posed by the interface. You can name the new action `calculateAnswer` and define it this way:

```
- (IBAction)calculateAnswer:(id)sender;
```

This definition also appears in Fusebox.h after the closing bracket, but before the @end statement. The completed Fusebox.h file looks like this:

```
#import <Cocoa/Cocoa.h>

@interface Fusebox : NSObject
{
    IBOutlet id answerField;
    IBOutlet id numberField1;
    IBOutlet id numberField2;
}
- (IBAction)calculateAnswer:(id)sender;
@end
```

### Adding the class to the interface

With the class definition complete, switch to Interface Builder.

1. **In Interface Builder, choose File⇔Read Class Files.**

   An Open dialog appears, as shown in Figure 2-13.

2. **Select Fusebox.h and click the Open button.**

   You won't see much happen yet, but you have just informed your interface about the new `Fusebox` class.

**Figure 2-13:**
Read the
Fusebox.h
class.

3. **Add a new object to the project in Interface Builder.**

   In the Library window, search for **object** and drag an instance of Object into the project window, as shown in Figure 2-14.

4. **Open the Identity Inspector by choosing Tools⇨Identity Inspector.**

5. **In the Identity Inspector, choose Fusebox from the Class drop-down list.**

   You can either select Fusebox from the drop-down list or simply type **Fusebox** in the drop-down's field, as shown in Figure 2-15. After you've changed the class to Fusebox, the outlets and action appear in the Identity Inspector.

**Figure 2-14:**
Add a new Object instance to the project.

**Figure 2-15:**
Change the
class of the
object to
Fusebox.

## Making connections

Now that you've created a `Fusebox` class and added three outlets and an
action, it's time to make connections between `Fusebox` and your interface.

You've just created a new `Fusebox` object based on the `Fusebox` class.
You'll make connections between this new instance and your interface with
the outlets and action you added earlier. For starters, connect the three
outlets to the three corresponding text fields in the interface. To get you
started, here's how to connect the `numberField1` outlet to the interface:

1. **Select the `Fusebox` instance in MainMenu.xib.**

2. **Control+drag from the `Fusebox` instance to the leftmost text field in
   the interface.**

   Figure 2-16 shows what the Control+drag operation looks like.

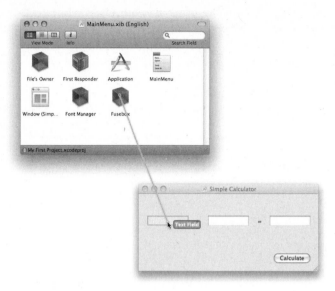

**Figure 2-16:**
To make a
connection
to an outlet,
Control+
drag from
an instance
to an
interface
element.

When you Control+drag to the text field and let go of the mouse, a black connections list overlay appears with the list of outlets available in your instance.

3. **Select the instance you want.**

To follow along with the example, select numberField1, as shown in Figure 2-17.

**Figure 2-17:**
Select an
outlet.

4. **Repeat Steps 2–3 for the other two outlets,** `numberField2` **and** `answerField`.

   Make sure to Control+drag from the instance to the appropriate control in the interface before selecting the outlet to connect.

The process for wiring your action works in a similar fashion, except for one important point: It proceeds in reverse! Instead of Control+dragging from the instance to the interface, you drag from the interface to the instance. To connect your action to the interface, follow these steps:

1. **Control+drag from the button in your interface to the** `Fusebox` **instance in MainMenu.xib.**

2. **Select an action from the list.**

   To follow along with the example, select the `calculateAnswer` action from the black overlay, as shown in Figure 2-18. It will be the only action available in the `Fusebox` class.

You've now finished creating and wiring your interface! To wrap up this part of the project, save your MainMenu.xib file:

1. **Save the interface by pressing ⌘+S.**

2. **Quit Interface Builder.**

   You have completed the interface. It's safe to quit Interface Builder now and return to the project in Xcode.

In the next section, you add code to your application.

**Figure 2-18:**
Select the
action from
the black
overlay that
appears.

# Adding Code to Make Your App Work

Back in Xcode, click the Fusebox.m file to reveal its contents. This is your main source code file and the place where you add functions to make this application do something. The file isn't empty. Interface Builder was kind enough to add some code to get you started:

```
#import "Fusebox.h"

@implementation Fusebox

@end
```

Cocoa programmers are a special breed. Instead of using the term *header files,* they speak of *interface files.* Likewise, *source code files* are called *implementation files.*

Don't worry if you don't understand everything just yet. This code is a shell for you to use when you begin coding the project. This code uses the header file with this line:

```
#import "Fusebox.h"
```

If you're a seasoned C programmer, remember that #import in Cocoa is like #include in standard C. The directive lets your code know where the definition of your class is.

After the header, the source code lists the implementation of the Fusebox class:

```
@implementation Fusebox
```

One part of that Fusebox class is a calculateAnswer action. By adding the calculateAnswer action, you can make your application functional. All code that appears between the two empty braces of the calculateAnswer method executes whenever a user clicks the button in your interface. The user clicks the button, which in turn fires the calculateAnswer action, which then executes your code.

Add the following action to the Fusebox.m file:

```
#import "Fusebox.h"

@implementation Fusebox

- (IBAction)calculateAnswer:(id)sender
{
    int num1, num2, answer;
```

```
    num1 = [numberField1 intValue];
    num2 = [numberField2 intValue];
    answer = num1 + num2;

    [answerField setIntValue:answer];
}

@end
```

Here's what the code does:

1. **Add a line to create three integer variables for temporarily storing three integer numbers in memory:**

   ```
   int num1, num2, answer;
   ```

   The code then assigns values to the num1 and num2 variables. The values it uses are ones that it pulls from the corresponding interface elements numberField1 and numberField2. These two elements are text fields. To get the integer value from a text field, send the intValue message to a corresponding outlet, which returns the integer value of the text in that field.

2. **To send a message to an object, such as an interface element, enclose the object name and message name in square brackets:**

   ```
   num1 = [numberField1 intValue];
   num2 = [numberField2 intValue];
   ```

   The code adds the two numbers and puts the result in the answer variable.

   The answer is displayed by sending answerField a setIntValue message. This particular message requires a parameter: an integer value.

3. **Add the answer variable to display the answer:**

   ```
   answer = num1 + num2;
   [answerField setIntValue:answer];
   ```

4. **Save the Fusebox.m file with its new source code by choosing File⇨Save.**

# Debugging and Building the Application

You've constructed an interface, wired it to your Fusebox instance, and added the code. Now it's time to see the results of your hard work. To test the project, choose Build⇨Build and Go (Run) or click the Build and Go button in Xcode, as displayed in Figure 2-19.

**Figure 2-19:**
Click the
Build and
Go button
to see the
fruit of your
efforts.

As Xcode builds your application, the debugger window appears with lots of text flying by at a rapid rate. This process is normal. If anything goes wrong during the build (such as an error in your code), the debugger is the first place you'll want to look for clues as to what exactly did go wrong. When the build is finished, the debugger tells you so (see Figure 2-20).

After your build succeeds, Xcode launches the completed application, as shown in Figure 2-21. Your next step in the programming process is to test the functionality of the application. Enter numbers in the first two text fields and then click the Calculate button. Does it display the answer you expect?

**Figure 2-20:**
If a build
goes off
without a
hitch, the
debugger
displays
Succeeded
in the
bottom-right
corner.

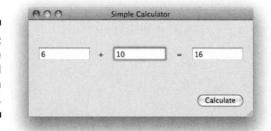

**Figure 2-21:**
The
completed
application
in action.

Keep in mind that because you're working with only integers; you won't get correct results if you enter numbers with fractional values (see Figure 2-22). If you use a number with a decimal in it, you'll get a result without the fractional part. Clearly, the calculator isn't as robust as you might need.

In Chapter 3, you expand on this project to account for decimal numbers. For now, bask in the glory of having built your first Cocoa application. The resulting executable file resides in your project's folder in Finder. Open the MyFirstProject folder and locate the Build folder within it. Open the Build folder to reveal your MyFirstProject application. You built that application, and it can run on any Mac OS X computer.

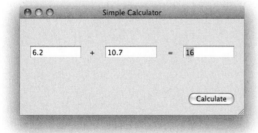

**Figure 2-22:**
Oops! The
calculator
only adds
integers
so far.

# Chapter 3

# Xcode

- - - - - - - - - - - - - - - - - - - - - - - - - - - - - - - - - - - - - - - - - - - - - - - - -

## In This Chapter

▶ Jumping headfirst into Xcode

▶ Customizing the Xcode window

▶ Adjusting the settings for your project

▶ Editing source code with Xcode

▶ Debugging your Cocoa projects to remove errors

▶ Using the built-in Help features of Xcode

▶ Building an application from your project

- - - - - - - - - - - - - - - - - - - - - - - - - - - - - - - - - - - - - - - - - - - - - - - - -

**C**ocoa programming requires the use of some sophisticated development tools. Chief among these is Xcode. With Xcode, you can manage your Cocoa projects: write code, assemble, organize, and test your project, and finally build an application that you can run on any Mac OS X computer.

Xcode is the main component of Apple's *integrated development environment (IDE)*. Xcode has everything you need for managing Cocoa projects, editing and debugging source code, and building applications. As you discover the different features of Xcode, you'll continue to improve on the calculator project you created in Chapter 2. By the end of this chapter, you'll have a calculator application that has improved functionality and is free of bugs. These two goals are what all professional programmers want from their software, and Xcode can help you achieve them.

If you didn't build the simple calculator in Chapter 2, you can find the project files for this chapter on the *For Dummies* Web site at www.dummies.com/go/ cocoafd. The chapter starts with the My First Project file.

# Xcode: The Core of Apple's Development Tools

Because Xcode is a first-class development tool, its collection of windows, menus, and settings can look daunting to a budding Cocoa programmer. Xcode is professional software, so don't be surprised if you have a bit of a learning curve. Apple created Mac OS X for use by the average Joe (and Jane), but it made Xcode for developers. Xcode has a classic Macintosh interface with windows and menus like other software, but the subject matter is technical, so don't feel too intimidated if you don't understand everything at once.

With Xcode, you can do many types of programming. Because of this fact, Xcode offers tools, documentation, and settings for doing all these different kinds of programming.

As a Cocoa programmer, you're focusing on only one aspect of Xcode's total capabilities. Thus, you'll need to use only the tools, documentation, and settings that pertain to Cocoa programming. Some features in Xcode you may use only occasionally, rarely, or never at all.

Think of Xcode as a hardware store. You might customarily go to the hardware store to buy nails, screws, or wood glue. Once in a while, you pick up a hammer, a screwdriver, or even a tape measure. Every so many years, you even buy paint for the exterior of your house. You dare not go into the roofing aisle, though. You're afraid of heights and always leave that work to the professionals.

You use Xcode in the same way you use the local hardware store. You perform some kinds of tasks all the time (writing code for your application), some tasks less frequently (assigning an icon to your application), and some rarely (adjusting the preferences for an Xcode setting). Others you may never approach at all (creating drivers for a CD burner). This isn't to say that adjusting preferences in Xcode is a task you'll seldom perform and that CD drivers are only for professionals. It's that Xcode is a tool for many kinds of development. Like a hardware store, everyone uses Xcode for specific needs. Maybe your neighbor likes to do plumbing and CD driver development. You, on the other hand, stick to furniture repair and Cocoa application development. The hardware store and Xcode can assist both you and your neighbor in your endeavors even if neither of you understands what the other does.

# *Customizing Xcode Preferences*

Open the project file by double-clicking its icon in Finder. Xcode launches, displaying the project and its components. The default Xcode settings appear in Figure 3-1. If you've read Chapter 2, this window should look familiar because you used it to create your first project.

Xcode displays the code and other components of your project in its main window. It displays a single project window by default, but you aren't limited to this setup. Follow these steps to change your layout:

1. **Close any open projects.**

   Xcode demands that all project windows be closed before it lets you change the Layout setting.

2. **Open the Xcode Preferences window by choosing Xcode⇨Preferences.**

   Across the top of this window is a row of buttons.

3. **Click the General button.**

   The Xcode settings appear, as shown in Figure 3-2.

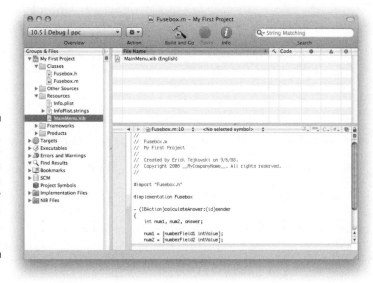

**Figure 3-1:**
Xcode displays the main window when you first open a project.

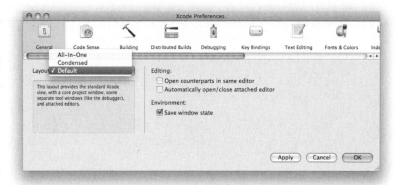

**Figure 3-2:**
You can
choose how
many
windows
Xcode
displays
during
develoment.

Xcode has three choices for the Layout setting that affect the main project window:

- *All-in-One:* All tasks appear within one window: code, build results, build log, and debugging. If you have very limited space (like on a small laptop), perhaps All-in-One is best for you.

- *Condensed:* Tasks appear in separate windows: code, build results, build log, and debugging. If you have a large monitor or a multiple-monitor configuration, you may prefer the Condensed approach to spread out your work.

- *Default:* The Default layout uses some elements from All-in-One and some from Condensed. The main project window contains most views, but displays additional windows in some cases, most notably for the debugger and console. Neat freaks love this setting, and it's the one I use in this book.

4. **Choose the setting you want from the Layout pop-up menu.**

5. **Click OK to apply the setting and dismiss the Preferences window.**

6. **Reopen your project and choose Build⇨Build and Go.**

   Your application runs as usual.

7. **Quit the application to return to Xcode.**

8. **Choose Run⇨Console to see the status of the last run.**

   If your project executed without a hitch, the Console window displays a message like this:

```
My First Project has exited with status 0.
```

The status 0 message indicates that Xcode encountered no errors during execution of the application. This is a good thing and means that your project is free from certain kinds of errors.

If you're using the Default layout, the Console window appears as a separate window, as shown in Figure 3-3.

**Figure 3-3:**
The Console
window
provides
additional
information
about the
progress of
a build.

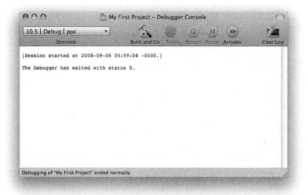

# Working with Project Files

In Chapter 2, you discovered how to make a simple calculator that could add integers but not numbers with decimals. To change the way the application operates, you'll need to alter the code in the project:

1. **In your main project window of Xcode, click to expand the Classes group.**

   The Classes group opens and displays the class files in your project. What you probably recognize as a folder, Xcode calls a *group*. The small folder icons that appear to the left side of the project window are groups. Clicking the disclosure triangle located on the left side of each group displays the files in that group.

2. **Click the Fusebox.m file.**

   The code for the Fusebox.m file displays, as shown in Figure 3-4.

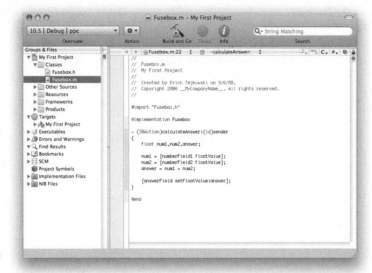

**Figure 3-4:**
The Classes
group
organizes
the source
code files in
your project.

### 3. Change the code in the Fusebox.m file to read like this:

```
#import "Fusebox.h"

@implementation Fusebox

- (IBAction)calculateAnswer:(id)sender
{
    float num1,num2,answer;

    num1 = [numberField1 floatValue];
    num2 = [numberField2 floatValue];
    answer = num1 + num2;

    [answerField setFloatValue:answer];
}

@end
```

This code has three important changes:

- You're changing the three variables from an `int` type to a `float` type. The `float` data type supports numbers with decimals.

```
float num1,num2,answer;
```

- Because you're working with `float` data types now, use the `floatValue` function to retrieve decimal data from the two number fields.

```
num1 = [numberField1 floatValue];
num2 = [numberField2 floatValue];
```

• Use the `setFloatvalue` function instead of the `setIntValue` function to display the float result in `answerField`.

```
[answerField setFloatValue:answer];
```

4. **Now that you've edited the source code in Fusebox.m, select the Fusebox.h file to view its contents.**

Fusebox.h holds the definitions for your interface.

5. **In the Groups & Files list, open the Other Sources group folder and select the main.m file.**

In this file, you see code that looks like this:

```
#import <Cocoa/Cocoa.h>

int main(int argc, const char *argv[])
{
    return NSApplicationMain(argc, argv);
}
```

This code appears in every Cocoa application project that you create. It's responsible for making your application go, much like a set of keys makes an automobile run. The nice part is that Xcode automatically adds it to the project for you, and you usually don't need to make any changes to this file.

6. **Choose Build⟹Build and Go or press ⌘+R to see your code changes in action.**

7. **After Xcode compiles and launches the project, test the Simple Calculator application, with decimal numbers.**

The calculator now adds decimals properly (see Figure 3-5).

**Figure 3-5:**
The calculator supports decimals!

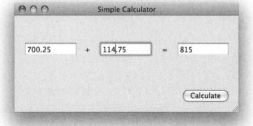

## Class models

Class models are your next stop on the Xcode tour (see Chapter 2 for more about classes). Xcode can provide you with a visual representation of the classes in your project. This can be helpful for design and debugging purposes. To view a class model, select the desired class and choose Design⇨Class Model⇨Quick Model. Xcode displays a graphical model of your class.

The calculator has only one class: the Fusebox class. Select the Fusebox class and choose Design⇨Class Model⇨Quick Model to view the Fusebox model. In this class, you implemented one function (calculateAnswer) and three outlets for the three text fields, as shown in Figure 3-6. NSObject also appears in the Quick Model because it's the superclass of the Fusebox class. All classes, except NSObject, are based on some other class in a class hierarchy. The Fusebox class is based on the NSObject class, so NSObject is said to be its *superclass*.

As your project grows, the class models help you with the big picture. The graphs show you how items in the project interconnect.

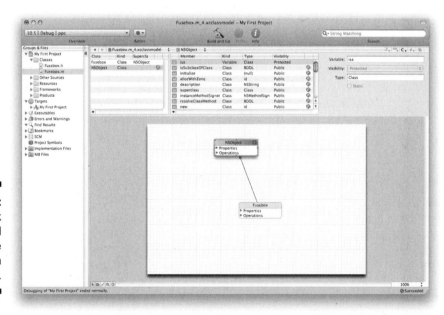

**Figure 3-6:**
The Quick Model displays the classes in your project.

## File comments

You can assign comments to any project items in Xcode. These kinds of comments differ from source comments in that you can assign them to any element in your project, not just source code files. This is a handy feature when you're working with very large projects or with other people because you can use the comments to document changes or keep other notes. Follow these steps to add comments to your project:

1. **Select Fusebox.m in the Classes group.**

   Fusebox.m holds the declarations for your implementation.

2. **Click the Info button in the project toolbar or press ⌘+I.**

   The File Info window opens, as shown in Figure 3-7.

3. **Click the Comments button at the top of the File Info window.**

   The Comments field appears where you can enter information about the file for later retrieval while keeping the information out of your source code.

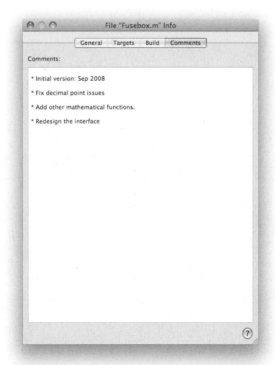

**Figure 3-7:**
The File Info window can help you document project elements.

# Using favorites to speed up development

As your projects grow, you'll find that locating code can sometimes become problematic. For large projects, jumping among dozens of source code files isn't uncommon. To help you, Xcode has a Favorites Bar, similar to a Web browser. Instead of pointing to URLs on the Web, though, the Xcode *Favorites Bar* points to specific places in your source code. It's useful when you want to quickly jump to certain spots in your code without the hassle of surfing through the numerous files that might make up your project.

To begin working with favorites in Xcode, follow these steps:

1. **Choose View⟹Layout⟹Show Favorites Bar.**

   The list of favorites for your project appears at the top of the project window, as shown in Figure 3-8.

2. **Drag any file from your project to the Favorites Bar.**

   Choose a file that you want to return to quickly. Favorites appear in the Favorites Bar at the top of the window, as shown in Figure 3-8.

3. **To delete a favorite from your project, drag it off the Favorites Bar.**

   The favorite instantly vanishes in a puff of smoke.

Favorites bar

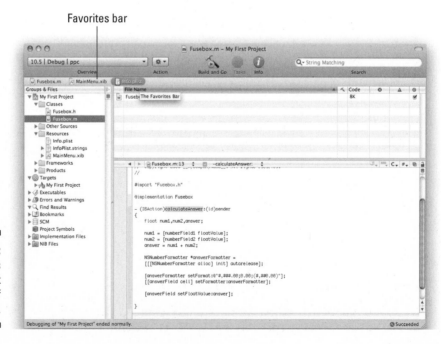

**Figure 3-8:**
Favorites
appear at
the top of
the window.

# Debugging Your Project

Because computer programming can be a complex process, it's easy to make mistakes. You can introduce errors to your code in a number of ways. Here are two:

✔ **Syntax errors** are errors in the grammar of your code that make Xcode unable to interpret the code. Typographical mistakes in your code may lead to syntax errors in your project.

✔ **Runtime errors** have nothing to do with the syntax of your code. Rather, the logic of your code contains errors that produce an application that doesn't function properly. These mistakes might be syntactically correct and still allow Xcode to compile and link your code into an application, yet produce unexpected or incorrect results. The application may run and even work as expected sometimes, but at some point, your application will do something wrong. A purple apple might be displayed instead of a red one in your graphics application, an enemy invader won't die when shot in your video game, or a miscalculation yields an incorrect numerical result in your spreadsheet application.

The only way to know if you have any bugs in your code is to thoroughly test your projects. When you debug a project, you build, run, and test your application until you're convinced that it's bug free.

To begin debugging, follow these steps:

1. **Build and run the project you've been working with throughout this chapter.**

2. **Type values in the two number fields and then click the Calculate button.**

3. **Change the numbers and click the Calculate button again.**

4. **Repeat Step 3 until you're convinced that the project operates as it should.**

For example, three consecutive tests of the project yield the following results:

1 + 2 = 3

3.25 + 4.75 = 8

3.2 + 4.75 = 7.949999809265137

Uh oh! That last test didn't produce results that you might expect. What's going on here? There seem to be three problems:

✔ The code is calculating the sum of the two numbers incorrectly in some situations.

✔ The problem seems to occur only when using decimal numbers.

✔ The error happens only when some decimal numbers are used, but not others. For example, 0.25 + 0.75 works as expected, but 4.2 + 4.2 does not. The reason that this happens is because the computer can't display *fractional* values (the numbers after the decimal point) if the values can't be represented as a non-repeating sequence in binary. If you want to know more about this topic (a word of warning; it can get very *mathy*), search for IEEE 794 on Google.com.

To help you figure out where things are going wrong, Xcode includes a powerful debugger. With the debugger, you can follow along as your project's code executes and watch for any indication of a problem.

## Adding breakpoints

To begin debugging this code, first set some breakpoints. *Breakpoints* are small markers that appear in the column to the left of the code. To insert a breakpoint, simply click in that leftmost column next to the line of code that you want to check with the debugger, as shown in Figure 3-9.

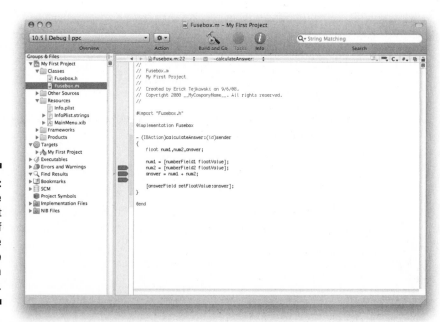

**Figure 3-9:**
Click in the leftmost column of the code editor to set a breakpoint.

For this example, it's a good idea to set three breakpoints: one for each time you assign a value to a variable (that is, num1, num2, and answer).

Notice that the breakpoints in Figure 3-9 appear after the line of code in question. The line of code that sets a variable has to execute before you can check the variable's value to see its result.

## *Stepping through the debugger*

Now that you've set some breakpoints, it's time to debug the project:

1. **Choose Build⇨Build and Debug.**

   Xcode begins building your project just as it always has, but then something happens. Xcode opens the Debug tab.

   For now, you won't see any information in the debugger. Rather, your project's main window comes to the foreground and looks like it always has.

2. **Enter numbers in your application's interface (for example, 3.2 and 4.2) and click the Calculate button.**

   The debugger comes to the foreground and displays all sorts of data in the Debug tab. In the left side of the debugger, you see the name of the class and the method that the code is currently executing. In this case, it's the Fusebox class and the calculateAnswer method. The bottom section of the debugger displays the code for the calculateAnswer method.

   Because you set breakpoints, the debugger stops at the first one it encounters. This indicates the *next* line of code that the debugger will execute.

3. **In the upper-right section of the debugger, view the current state of all variables in your code.**

   So far, only this code has executed:

   ```
   float num1,num2,answer;
   num1 = [numberField1 floatValue];
   ```

   Therefore, you might expect that the debugger displays only a value for the num1 variable. Figure 3-10 shows the debugging process thus far.

   If you don't see the debugger window when your application stops at the first breakpoint, choose Run⇨Debugger.

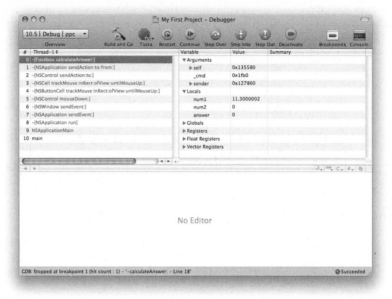

**Figure 3-10:**
As the
debugger
executes
code, it
displays the
values of
variables.

The debugger already found a problem (refer to Figure 3-10). The value of num1 isn't 3.2 as you might expect. Instead, it has a value of 3.20000005.

4. **Click the Continue button in the project toolbar to continue executing the code.**

   The debugger then displays the value of num2, 4.19999981, not the expected value of 4.2.

5. **Click the Continue button again to make the debugger jump to the third breakpoint.**

   The debugger now displays the answer value, 7.39999962, not 7.4 as you might expect.

6. **Click Continue again.**

   The debugger disappears, and the application reappears and waits for you to press the Calculate button again.

7. **Bring the project window to the foreground and click the Stop button in the project window toolbar to halt the debugging process.**

8. **Choose Run➪Deactivate Breakpoints to prevent the debugger from stopping on the next run.**

Although the numbers that your code displays are very close to the actual values entered in the interface at runtime, they aren't the exact values. Clearly, you need a solution that formats numbers according to some guidelines. For example, you may only care about two decimal points of precision.

## Fixing the code

Without getting into a bunch of technicalities, a `float` variable can have many digits in the decimal portion of its value. When `num1`, `num2`, or their sum has decimal digits that can't be represented by a non-repeating sequence in binary, rounding and truncation problems exist. These problems are an inherent fact of life based on how your computer works with floating point numbers.

To get around this problem, one solution is to format the `answer` variable before displaying it. A few lines of code and Cocoa's `NSNumberFormatter` class take care of the problem:

```
NSNumberFormatter *answerFormatter =
        [[[NSNumberFormatter alloc] init] autorelease];

    [answerFormatter
            setFormat:@"#,###.00;0.00;(#,##0.00)"];
    [[answerField cell] setFormatter:answerFormatter];
```

Don't be frightened if you don't understand this intimidating blurb of code. This chapter is about Xcode, not Objective-C code like Chapter 6.

The first two lines of code (which incidentally are just one function that appears on two lines) create an `NSNumberFormatter` object. The purpose behind an `NSNumberFormatter` object is to regulate the format of numbers.

Next, the code sends the `setFormat` message to the `answerFormatter` object, passing it a string of text. This string designates what formats are allowed for this `NSNumberFormatter` object. The string is a series of three formats, each separated by a semicolon. You don't have to worry about the precise format of these three strings, but, to give you a hint, the first one defines the format of positive numbers, the second one accounts for cases when the number is 0, and the last bit formats negative numbers.

Finally, the code applies the `NSNumberFormatter` object to `answerField` in the interface. To help you understand where this bit of code fits into the big picture, here's the listing of the completed source code for Fusebox.m (the `NSNumberFormatter` object is in bold). Note that when you add the code, the last breakpoint moves accordingly.

```
#import "Fusebox.h"

@implementation Fusebox

- (IBAction)calculateAnswer:(id)sender
{
    float num1,num2,answer;

    num1 = [numberField1 floatValue];
    num2 = [numberField2 floatValue];
    answer = num1 + num2;

    NSNumberFormatter *answerFormatter =
        [[[NSNumberFormatter alloc] init] autorelease];

    [answerFormatter
        setFormat:@"#,###.00;0.00;(#,##0.00)"];
    [[answerField cell] setFormatter:answerFormatter];

    [answerField setFloatValue:answer];
}

@end
```

Now that you've formatted `answerField` properly, choose Build⇨Build and Go to see your changes in action. You see results, as shown in Figure 3-11.

**Figure 3-11:**
With the NSNumber Formatter object, you can dictate how your application displays floating-point numbers.

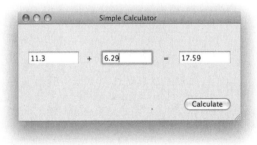

Before you leave the debugging section of this chapter, you may come across one more kind of error when using Xcode to program Cocoa applications. Change the last line of your code in Fusebox.m to this:

```
[answerField setFloatValue:answer]
```

This time you're intentionally leaving off the trailing semicolon (a common mistake that even pros make). Choose Build➪Build and Go to see what happens. The result is that the application doesn't run as expected, and an error overlay appears beneath the code in question, as shown in Figure 3-12. A circle with a white X also appears in the gutter to the left of the code showing where the error occurred.

The error shows you exactly where the problem is. In this case, the error is `syntax error before } token`. Just before the `}` token is where the semi-colon should be. Fix the code and save it.

The point behind this demonstration is to show you that you may encounter different kinds of errors when programming with Xcode. Some errors, like this last one, occur during the build and debug process, and Xcode shows you where they occur. Other bugs are trickier to track down, such as the earlier example, because the application is otherwise functional. For those, it never hurts to use the built-in debugger to solve the problem.

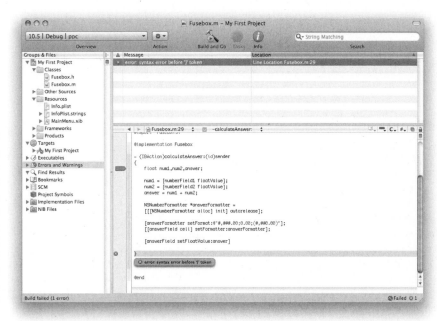

**Figure 3-12:** Xcode displays errors in the code editor when you click Errors and Warnings on the left.

## Removing breakpoints

Now that you're finished debugging your project, you may want to remove the breakpoints that you added. In Xcode, click the Fusebox.m file and look for the breakpoints on the left side of the code editor. Control+click a breakpoint and choose Remove Breakpoint from the contextual menu that appears. Do the same for the remaining breakpoints. Figure 3-13 shows the contextual menu prior to deletion of a breakpoint.

Nothing prevents you from keeping the breakpoints set in the project. You can safely leave them in place without causing any problems for yourself, so long as you deactivate them when you don't need them.

**Figure 3-13:**
Control+
click a
breakpoint
to remove it.

# Where to Go for Help

At some point, you'll want more information about how Xcode operates. Fortunately, Apple has you covered with its built-in documentation. Choose Help⇨Xcode Workspace Guide to view the built-in documentation about Xcode.

The built-in Help offers documentation on each aspect of Mac OS X development. It also includes a few helpful tutorials for getting started with programming Cocoa in Xcode.

Besides the standard Help, Xcode offers one-click access to information about Cocoa classes and frameworks in the code editor. To test this feature, do the following:

1. **Select the Fusebox.m source code file.**

   Xcode displays the file in the code editor.

2. **Locate a keyword in the source code that you want to investigate.**

   For example, you may want to find out more about the `setFloatValue` method.

3. **While holding down the Option key, double-click `setFormatter` in the Fusebox.m file.**

   A reference window opens, listing the various `setFloatValue` methods in Cocoa (see Figure 3-14).

4. **Choose a keyword from the menu.**

   Select the appropriate `setFloatValue` method to view the corresponding documentation.

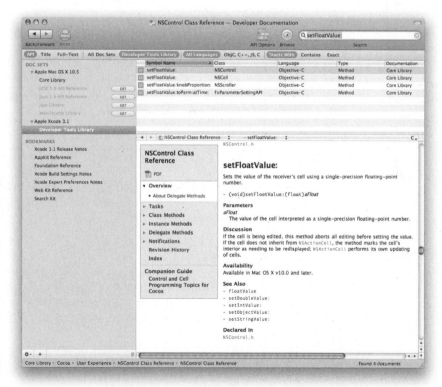

**Figure 3-14:**
Option-double-click any valid keyword in the code editor to view its documentation.

# Building an Application

Now that you've set up your project, altered its source code, and browsed the classes in it, you're ready to build the final application. Choose Build⇨ Build and Go. Xcode then compiles, links, and executes the resulting application.

You don't always have to build and run, although it's probably the most common method of working in Xcode. You can build your project without running it by choosing Build⇨Build. This compiles, links, and creates the target application but doesn't execute it. If you'd prefer to use the debugger, choose Build⇨Build and Debug. Table 3-1 lists the keyboard shortcuts for the various Build commands.

| Table 3-1 | Keyboard Shortcuts for the Build Menu | |
|---|---|---|
| *Function(s)* | *Keyboard Shortcut* | *What It Does* |
| Build | ⌘+B | Builds an application from the current project |
| Build and Run | ⌘+R | Builds an application and then executes it |
| Build and Debug | ⌘+Y | Builds and launches an application from the current project and then starts the debugger |
| Clean | ⌘+Shift+K | Cleans the current project by removing all object code from it |

In addition to the standard menu items and corresponding keyboard shortcuts, Xcode gives you easy access to the Build and Run function by means of a button in the toolbar project window. Figure 3-15 shows the location and function of this button.

Whenever you click the Build and Go toolbar button, it turns into a stop sign. While the build or debugging proceeds, you can halt the process. Sometimes it takes a while to complete a build. If you forget to do something before building, it's handy to be able to stop the build operation. That way, you can avoid the wait of completing the build and get back to work.

After you complete a successful build, your new application appears in the Build folder of your project's main folder in Finder. You can then distribute and run this application on any other computer that uses Mac OS X, which is the main goal of programming in Cocoa.

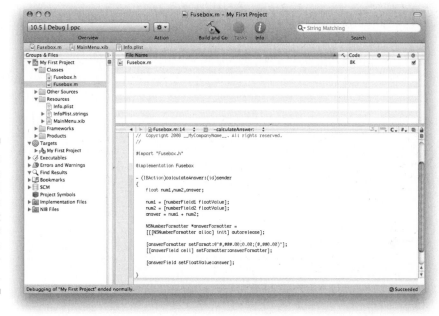

**Figure 3-15:**
Click the
Build and
Go button
in project
window
toolbar to
run your
project.

# Chapter 4

# Interface Builder

. . . . . . . . . . . . . . . . . . . . . . . . . . . . . . . . . . . . . .

## In This Chapter

▶ Finding your way around Interface Builder

▶ Adding controls to an interface

▶ Editing attributes of a control

▶ Editing and creating new menus

▶ Wiring an interface

▶ Implementing code to use an interface

. . . . . . . . . . . . . . . . . . . . . . . . . . . . . . . . . . . . . .

The second most important component of Cocoa development (Xcode is the first; see Chapter 3) is the eponymous Interface Builder application, which you use to build interfaces for your Cocoa projects. Interface Builder gives you the ability to construct beautiful interfaces for your software with drag-and-drop ease — without a lick of code. More importantly, the interfaces you create in Interface Builder follow Apple's stringent Human Interface Guidelines, so you have a good chance of producing applications that Mac users (they can be a finicky bunch) like to look at and ultimately use.

In this chapter, you take a tour of Interface Builder, examining its functionality as you go. To help you acclimate to Interface Builder, you improve the calculator application that you created in Chapter 3. By the end of this chapter, your calculator will have a new menu, additional interface elements, and added functionality.

You can find the project files for this chapter on the *For Dummies* Web site at www.dummies.com/go/cocoafd.

# A Tour of Interface Builder

To begin working with Interface Builder, make a copy of the finished Chapter 3 project folder. Always make sure that your Cocoa projects and associated files reside on write-enabled media, which is most likely your hard drive.

After you have the code copied to your hard drive, do the following to begin working on the project in Interface Builder:

1. **Open the My First Project.xcodeproj file.**

   Xcode launches, and the project opens.

2. **Expand the project's Resources folder in Xcode to reveal the MainMenu.xib file.**

   MainMenu.xib is the interface file for your calculator project. Figure 4-1 shows the location of the MainMenu.xib file in Xcode.

3. **In Xcode, double-click the MainMenu.xib file to open it in Interface Builder.**

   Although Xcode and Interface Builder are two different applications, they work together to provide you with an integrated Cocoa experience.

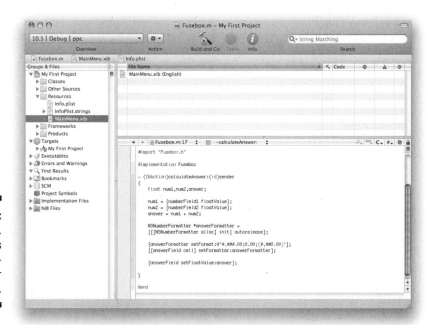

**Figure 4-1:** MainMenu. xib contains the inter- face for your project.

Incidentally, the *XIB* file extension in MainMenu.xib indicates that it's a newer Interface Builder project file format, introduced in Xcode 3. Previously, the file format had a *NIB* extension, which is short for NeXT Interface Builder. Why NeXT? *NeXT* is the name of the company that Steve Jobs headed before his return to Apple. Apple purchased the NeXT operating system, which became the core of Mac OS X. The XIB file is a carryover from those days. Cocoa geeks still call these *NIB files* — old habits die hard. Besides that, have you ever tried to pronounce "XIB?" Furthermore, the *NS* that appears at the beginning of class names in Cocoa stands for NextStep, another historical tidbit in Cocoa left over from NeXT.

When you first launch Interface Builder, you may see as many as five different windows. Figure 4-2 shows the various windows as they appear in Interface Builder. Although it isn't one of the five main windows, the Strings window might make an appearance, too. The Strings window is less likely to be present than the others but if you see it, feel free to close it. You don't use it in this chapter.

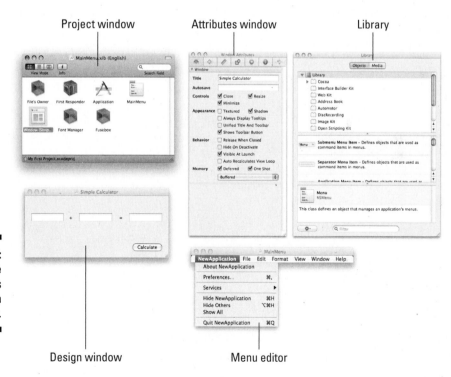

Project window     Attributes window     Library

**Figure 4-2:**
Interface Builder has five main windows.

Design window     Menu editor

Table 4-1 describes why you need each window and how to display one if it isn't currently visible.

| Table 4-1 | Main Windows of Interface Builder | |
| --- | --- | --- |
| *Window* | *How to Display It* | *What You Do With It* |
| Project window | Double-click the XIB file in Xcode | Store the components of your interface file. |
| Design window | Double-click the Window icon in the XIB project window | Use the window as part of your application's interface. |
| Inspector window | Choose Tools⇨Inspector | View and edit attributes of your interface and other classes in the project. |
| Library | Choose Tools⇨Library | Drag controls from the Library window to a design window to create an interface. |
| Menu editor | Double-click the MainMenu icon in the XIB project window | Create, delete, or edit menus for your application. |

Together these five windows form the main tools of Interface Builder. Using these tools in concert, you can build a complete interface for use in a Cocoa application. That's not all Interface Builder can do, though. You can

✔ Create and add classes to your project.

✔ Connect classes to the elements of your interface by clicking and dragging. These connections serve as a bridge between an interface and your Xcode project.

✔ Allow Interface Builder to do the dirty work of writing some of the code for your interface. With one click, it produces the necessary interface and implementation files in Xcode, where you add code later.

## The interface builder project window

The *NIB project window* is the heart of your project's interface. This is where you store the components of your project's interface. The NIB project window has three different views much like the Finder:

✔ **Icon:** List the objects in your XIB file as a grid of large icons. Figure 4-3 shows the Icon view format of the Interface Builder project window.

**Figure 4-3:**
Use the Icon view to get a quick glimpse of the items in an XIB document.

✔ **List:** Lists the objects in your XIB file as a vertical hierarchy. The List view is useful for quickly locating controls within a window. It comes in handy when you want to select a control that's embedded within other controls (see Figure 4-4). It's also useful when you want to move or copy an embedded control to another object or control or when you want to view embedded controls in context.

✔ **Column:** Lists the objects in your XIB file as a horizontal hierarchy (see Figure 4-5). The Column view is similar to List view, except that it displays the hierarchical arrangement of project items horizontally.

**Figure 4-4:**
Use the List view to see the class hierarchy of your XIB project.

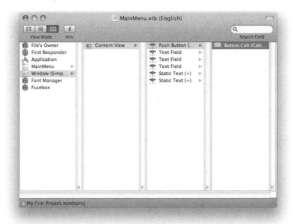

**Figure 4-5:**
The Column
view
displays
hierarchical
information
horizontally.

Each new NIB file that Xcode creates for you as part of a new project has six items by default:

✔ File's Owner

✔ First Responder

✔ Font Manager

✔ Application

✔ MainMenu

✔ Window

MainMenu and Window are what you need to concern yourself with for now. As you can probably guess, the *MainMenu* is where you edit the menus for your interface. The Window is a window object that you can use in your interface.

## Design window

The Design window represents a window in your interface and is where you add controls. Your user then uses these controls to operate your application. To view a Design window:

1. **In the NIB project window, double-click Window.**

   The contents of the Window object are displayed, as shown in Figure 4-6.

2. **With the window opened, select a control.**

   For example, select the Calculate button.

**Figure 4-6:**
The Design
window is
where you
lay out the
controls for
your inter-
face.

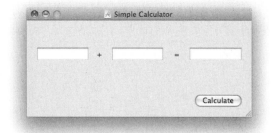

**Figure 4-6:**
The Design
window is
where you
lay out the
controls for
your inter-
face.

**3. Press and hold the Option key and move your cursor around the window.**

As you pass over each control, Interface Builder displays guidelines and numbers informing you of the distance between the selected control and the one with the cursor over it. Figure 4-7 illustrates the distance between the button and the answer field.

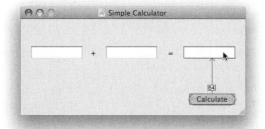

**Figure 4-7:**
Select a
control and
hold the
Option key
to display
guidelines.

**4. With the button still selected, press and hold the Option key and move your cursor into a section of the window where no control resides.**

You see guidelines that define the location of the selected button. Figure 4-8 shows the position of the button in the Calculator interface.

You can move the controls in a Design window by dragging them with the mouse. You can also select a control and move it with the arrow keys. As you move a control around a window, Interface Builder displays guides to help you accurately position the control.

**Figure 4-8:**
Hold the
Option key
and move
the cursor
outside the
selected
element to
see its
coordinates.

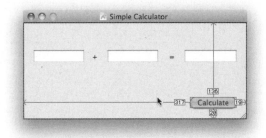

## Library window

To create an interface, you need an assortment of buttons, sliders, and other controls. The Library window provides these controls for you to use in your interface. To view the controls that are available to you, follow these steps:

1. **Choose Tools⇨Library.**

   The Library window appears, with a row tabs across the top, as shown in Figure 4-9.

2. **Click the Objects tab to see the controls and other objects that are available to you.**

3. **Select Cocoa from the frameworks listed at the top of the Library.**

   The Library window is organized by framework. Selecting Cocoa displays the controls that are available to you via the Cocoa framework.

4. **Search for a control.**

   You can search for specific class names, such as `NSButton`. Or, you can search for controls using descriptive terms like `button`.

Table 4-2 describes the sets of controls available in the Library window.

| Table 4-2 | Objects in the Library Window |
|---|---|
| *Frameworks* | *Reveals These Types of Controls and Objects* |
| Cocoa | Windows, menus, toolbars, controllers, buttons, views, radio groups, image well, sliders, progress indicators, and others |
| Interface Builder Kit | Library template (for advanced users) |
| Web Kit | Web view |

| Frameworks | Reveals These Types of Controls and Objects |
| --- | --- |
| Address Book | Address Book People Picker view |
| Automator | Objects for integrating applications with Automator |
| DiscRecording | `MSFormatter`, an object for use with disc burning |
| Image Kit | Image Kit browser and image views |
| Open Scripting Kit | Objects used in making applications scriptable |
| PDFKit | PDFView and PDFThumbnailView for displaying PDF documents |
| QuickTime Kit | QuickTime Movie view for playing movies and QuickTime Capture view for displaying video previews while capturing video |
| Quartz Composer | Objects for displaying and manipulating Quartz Composer compositions |
| Custom Objects | Third-party controls or your own custom controls and objects |

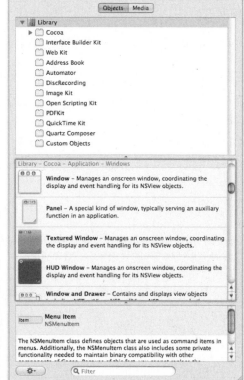

**Figure 4-9:**
The Library window contains a variety of objects and controls that you can use in your interface.

Chapter 9 goes into greater detail about the controls in the Library window. Most chapters throughout this book also deal with some aspect of the Library window because it's an important window! In particular, you'll use controls and objects in the Cocoa section of the Library window most often because that collection has all the most common interface controls.

The Library window is the starting point and main toolbox for creating attractive interfaces. You'll use it frequently.

## Inspector window

The Inspector window is another important window that you'll use frequently when building an interface. The Inspector window displays important contextual information about whatever element you're working with in Interface Builder. To see how the Inspector window works, perform these steps:

1. **Choose Tools⇨Inspector.**

   The Inspector window appears. The purpose of the Inspector window is to give you the opportunity to view and edit the attributes of the controls and objects in your NIB file.

2. **Open a window from your XIB file.**

   The Inspector window displays the attributes for that window (see Figure 4-10).

   The Inspector window is a bit of a chameleon, altering to match its surroundings. Figure 4-10 shows the properties of a window. If you have a window open and its properties don't appear in the Inspector window, click the window's title bar.

3. **Click the Calculate button in the Design window to select it.**

   The Inspector window immediately changes to display the attributes of that button.

4. **Alter the window properties as you need.**

   For example, to add a key assignment in the Inspector window, click the Key Equiv. field to select it and then press Return. An icon appears in the Key Equiv. field, representing the Return key (see Figure 4-11).

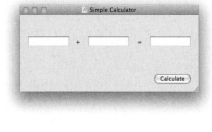

**Figure 4-10:**
For win-
dows, the
Inspector
window
gives you
access to
a variety
of window
attributes.

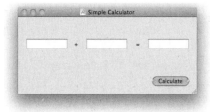

**Figure 4-11:**
Choose
Return to
give users
one-key
access to
calculations.

This assignment has two effects:

- It changes the Calculate button to a blue pulsating color in Interface Builder, indicating that it's the default button in that window. The purpose is to draw a user's attention to the button because the button triggers the functionality that the user most likely wants to perform in that window.

- The Key Equiv. assignment causes that button to respond to the Return or Enter key on the keyboard. Now, instead of forcing users to click the button with a mouse, they can simply press Return or Enter to make a calculation. And, you gained all that functionality with only one click. Fantastic!

## Menu editor window

The last window to discuss is the Menu editor. The Menu editor window displays a miniature version of your application's menu bar. You can click a menu to display its menu items. It's also easy to change the text or keyboard shortcut for a menu item or to add a new menu item altogether.

To prepare the menu for your application, follow these steps:

1. **In the XIB project window, double-click the MainMenu icon.**

   The Menu editor appears.

2. **Open the New Application menu.**

3. **Double-click the About MyFirstProject menu item and rename it.**

   For example, rename it to About SimpleCalculator.

   You can also rename the About menu (or any other menu, for that matter) by single-clicking it and making the change in the Info window.

4. **Change the Hide NewApplication and Quit NewApplication menus.**

   For example, change them to Hide SimpleCalculator and Quit SimpleCalculator, respectively. Figure 4-12 shows all three menus; About, Hide, and Quit changed in the Menu editor.

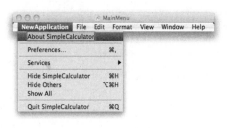

**Figure 4-12:**
Change the text of menu items with the Menu editor.

**5. Edit the text of the top Application menu item.**

Figure 4-13 shows I've changed the menu to Simple Calculator.

**6. Choose File⇨Save to save the interface changes.**

**7. Press ⌘+R to test the interface.**

Interface Builder hides your XIB project window and displays your interface as it would appear in a running application.

**8. Select menu items, move the calculator window, and type numbers in the fields of the window.**

When you click the Calculate button, though, nothing happens. That's because you aren't using the actual application. This is just an interface test.

Although the About SimpleCalculator menu item looks just fine, the Application menu isn't displaying its name properly. Rather, it displays Cocoa Simulator to let you know that you're viewing an Interface Builder preview of your application and not your actual application.

**9. Choose Cocoa Simulator⇨Quit Cocoa Simulator to return to Interface Builder.**

If you check your application by running it in Xcode, you'll see the changes that you made to the interface in Interface Builder.

**Figure 4-13:**
Change the name of the Application menu.

10. **Bring Xcode to the foreground and press ⌘+R to run your application.**

    Something isn't quite right, as shown in Figure 4-14. The Application menu is still stuck with MyFirstProject.

    What's going on here? Your application supplies the text for your Application menu item by using a string in its Info.plist file, not from the text you entered in Interface Builder. Go figure!

    The Info.plist file is a text file that contains information about your application. You can find the version number for your application, assign an icon to the application, and set the default language for the application, among other tasks.

**Figure 4-14:**
Despite changes to the menu in Interface Builder, the project is still displaying the wrong name in the Application menu.

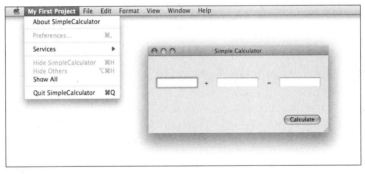

11. **Change the Info.plist file as follows:**

    *a. In Xcode, expand the Resources group.*

    *b. Select the InfoPlist.strings.*

    The Code editor displays the contents of this file, which you can edit.

    *c. Change the first line of code to read*

    ```
    CFBundleName = "SimpleCalculator";
    ```

12. **In Xcode, press ⌘+R.**

    The Application menu appears with the corrected name. Figure 4-15 shows the results of the InfoPlist change.

13. **Click the Interface Builder icon on the Dock to return to it.**

**Figure 4-15:**
Make adjustments to the InfoPlist. strings file in Xcode to cause the name of your application to appear in the Application menu.

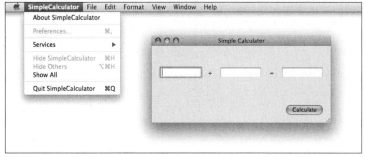

# The Interface Building Process

Now that you've surveyed the basics of Interface Builder, it's time to put it to use. If you built the interface in Chapter 2, you have a Simple Calculator that adds two numbers together. That limited functionality doesn't make for a very useful calculator.

If you haven't built the Simple Calculator in Chapter 2, you can use the My First Project.xcodeproj file.

To give users a choice of mathematical operations, you can add a pop-up menu. Instead of being limited to addition, a user can also, subtract, multiply, or divide. This additional functionality clearly makes for a more useful calculator.

If you simply drag a new pop-up button into your application's interface and connect it to a new outlet in the Controller class (Fusebox), your source and header files in Xcode have no way of knowing about the change. Either you have to alter the source code files by hand or merge new files with the ones you already created. When doing so, you run the risk of deleting all your existing work. Interface Builder offers a solution to this dilemma. When you attempt to create header and implementation files that already exist, Interface Builder asks (see Figure 4-16) whether you'd prefer to overwrite existing files (thus deleting your previous work) or merge the new files with the existing ones (thus retaining your previous work).

**Figure 4-16:**
To retain
previous
work, merge
your new
header and
implemen-
tation
files with
existing
files.

Because of this special consideration, you need to create the files and add them to Xcode. If files already exist in your Xcode project, you can edit them by hand or merge them with the new files:

✔ **If your project doesn't have header (.h) or implementation (.m) files,** create them by choosing File➪Write Class Files.

✔ **If the files already exist in your project in Xcode,** choose File➪Write Class Files and click Merge when queried in the dialog that appears. When you choose to merge files, Interface Builder launches the FileMerge application, which handles the sometimes complex task of merging source code and header files.

If you're making small changes to your interface, sometimes it's just as easy to edit the header and source code files in Xcode by hand rather than to go through the merge process.

Improving your existing project to include addition, subtraction, multiplication, and division is simple. I show you how in the next sections.

## Adding a pop-up menu

One way to give readers a choice of functions is through a pop-up menu. Follow these steps:

1. **Open an XIB file in Interface Builder.**

   If you don't have your calculator's MainMenu.xib open in Interface Builder, double-click it from your project in Xcode.

2. **Open the window for your interface by double-clicking Window in the XIB file window.**

   Your interface currently displays a plus sign text field between numField1 and numField2 to indicate that the calculator performs addition only.

3. **Click the plus sign text field to select it and then press Delete to remove it.**

4. **Open the Library window and search for** popup, **drag a pop-up button from the Library window to the calculator interface, and click the pop-up button again to reveal its contents.**

   By default, a popup has three menu items — Item 1, Item 2, and Item 3.

5. **Select the last menu item in the pop-up button and choose Edit⇨Duplicate to add a new item to the pop-up button.**

6. **Edit the title of each menu item by double-clicking the item and changing the text to mathematical symbols for addition, subtraction, multiplication, and division.**

   See Figure 4-17.

7. **Change the Tag property of each menu item. Starting with 0 (zero), assign 0, 1, 2, and 3 to addition, subtraction, multiplication, and division, respectively.**

   When a user uses the calculator, you can identify which pop-up item is selected based on its Tag value.

8. **Resize the pop-up button to its smallest width and place it between the two number fields. Because the pop-up button won't quite fit between the two fields as is, resize the window and move the controls around until the button fits properly.**

**Figure 4-17:**
Change
the items
in the pop-
up button
to math-
ematical
symbols that
represent
addition,
subtraction,
multiplica-
tion, and
division.

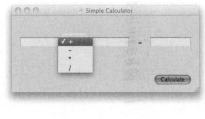

## Adding a menu

In addition to the pop-up button, giving a user menu access to the different mathematical computations would be handy. It's a cinch to add keyboard shortcuts to menus, which in turn can give your users keyboard access to the mathematical choices in the pop-up button. To create a new menu item, follow these steps:

1. **Open the Menu editor for MainMenu from the project window.**

2. **Drag a menu item from the Library window and drop it onto the menu bar.**

3. **Rename the new menu Calculate and press Return to accept the new name.**

4. **Drag a menu from the Library window to the new Calculate menu item.**

   A new menu appears with three items by default.

5. **Select the last of the three menu items, Item 3, and press ⌘+D to duplicate the item and add it to the menu.**

6. **Select the first menu item, Item 1, and press ⌘+1 to open the Inspector window.**

7. **Alter the attributes of the menu item to match Figure 4-18. Change the Title attribute to** Add, **click the Key Equiv. field, and press + on your keyboard to assign + as the keyboard shortcut for that menu item.**

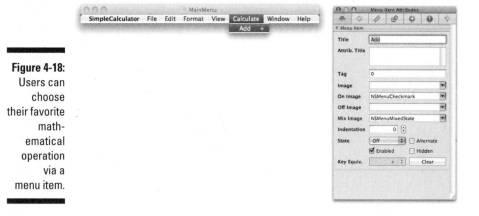

**Figure 4-18:**
Users can choose their favorite mathematical operation via a menu item.

8. **Alter the new menu items to look like Figure 4-19 by following a similar procedure as in Steps 6 and 7.**

9. **Change the Key Equiv. attribute for each item to the appropriate symbol: +, -, *, and /. Assign a unique Tag value to each menu item, starting with 0 (zero).**

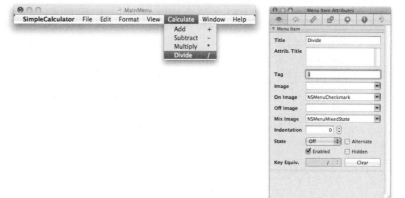

**Figure 4-19:**
Users can now choose from all four mathematical operations.

## Creating a Controller class

Because you're updating an existing project, this one already has a Controller class (Fusebox). Therefore, you can skip this step. Normally this step would be required but not this time. If you weren't updating an existing project, create a Controller class by dragging an NSObject from the Library window to the project window and change its type in the Inspector window.

## Connecting the interface

When you have your interface done, you must connect it to the actions and outlets. Follow these steps:

1. **In the XIB project window, select the Fusebox object and press ⌘+6.**

   The Inspector window appears, displaying the outlets and actions for Fusebox.

2. **Add an operationPopup outlet, which corresponds to the pop-up button in your project's window.**

3. **In the Inspector window, create one new action:** `changeOperation:`, **making sure to include the trailing colon.**

   Figure 4-20 shows the new outlet and two actions for the `Fusebox` class.

4. **To connect your interface, Control+drag from the** `Fusebox` **object in the XIB file window to the new** `popupButton` **in the interface. In the black connections list overlay that appears, select the** `operation Popup` **outlet.**

5. **Open the Menu editor by double-clicking the MainMenu item in the project window.**

6. **Select the Add menu item from the Calculate menu and Control+drag from it to the** `Fusebox` **class. From the black connections list overlay, select the** `changeOperation` **action.**

7. **For each menu item in the Calculate menu, Control+drag from the menu item to** `Fusebox` **and connect it to the same** `changeOperation` **action.**

   When you're finished, the Inspector window looks like Figure 4-21.

**Figure 4-20:**
Add an action to Fusebox to cover the operations in the Calculate menu.

**Figure 4-21:**
Connect the individual menu items in the Calculate menu to the new action.

8. **Create files and add them to Xcode. If the files already exist, edit them by hand or merge them with the new files.**

   Because your project files already exist in Xcode, you have to tread carefully here. You've added only one new action and one new outlet to your `Fusebox` controller, so it won't be difficult to add them by hand to the existing files, which you will do in the next section.

9. **Choose File⇨Save to save the XIB file.**

   You're finished with Interface Builder.

# Using an Interface in Xcode

Now that you have the interface improvements completed, you need to return to Xcode and add some code. For starters, you need to define a few items in the Fusebox.h file. Because you added an outlet and an action to the controller, you do the same in Fusebox.h:

**1. Change Fusebox.h to read as follows:**

```
/* Fusebox */

#import <Cocoa/Cocoa.h>

@interface Fusebox : NSObject
{
    IBOutlet id answerField;
    IBOutlet id numberField1;
    IBOutlet id numberField2;
    IBOutlet id operationPopup;
}
- (IBAction)calculateAnswer:(id)sender;
- (IBAction)changeOperation:(id)sender;
@end
```

**2. Choose File⇨Save to save the header file.**

**3. Select Fusebox.m to edit its code.**

**4. Modify the** `calculateAnswer` **function by adding an integer that keeps track of the currently selected item in the pop-up button:**

```
int operation;
```

**5. Find out which item the user has selected from the pop-up button by sending it the** `selectedTag` **message.**

When you do, the pop-up button returns the tag of its currently selected menu item, which you then store in the `operation` variable. The first menu item in a pop-up button has a tag of 0 (zero), so all items in the `operationPopup` control are covered by the indices 0 through 3:

```
operation = [operationPopup selectedTag];
```

**6. After you know which item the user selected from** `operationPopup`, **do the math based on that index:**

```
switch (operation) {
    case 0://addition
                        answer = num1 + num2;
                            break;
    case 1://subtraction
                        answer = num1 - num2;
                            break;
    case 2://multiplication

                        answer = num1 * num2;
                            break;
    case 3://division
                        answer = num1 / num2;
                            break;
}
```

The completed `calculateAnswer` action looks like this.

```
- (IBAction)calculateAnswer:(id)sender
{
        float num1,num2,answer;
    int operation;

    num1 = [numberField1 floatValue];
    num2 = [numberField2 floatValue];

    operation = [operationPopup selectedTag];
    switch (operation) {
                        case 0://addition
            answer = num1 + num2;
                        break;
            case 1://subtraction
            answer = num1 - num2;
                        break;
            case 2://multiplication
            answer = num1 * num2;
                        break;
            case 3://division
            answer = num1 / num2;
                        break;
    }

    NSNumberFormatter *answerFormatter =
        [[[NSNumberFormatter alloc] init]
        autorelease];

    [answerFormatter
        setFormat:@"#,###.00;0.00;(#,##0.00)"];
    [[answerField cell] setFormatter:answerFormatter];
        [answerField setFloatValue:answer];
}
```

7. **To account for the Calculate menu that appears in your menu bar, add a new action to Fusebox.m:** `changeOperation`.

When a user selects a particular menu item, the code changes the `operationPopup` control to match the operation in that menu item. For example, if a user selects the Add menu item, the code sets the index of the `operationPopup` control to 0 (zero). The Subtract menu item sets the index of the `operationPopup` control to 1, and so on. The code looks like this:

```
- (IBAction)changeOperation:(id)sender
{
    [operationPopup selectItemAtIndex:[sender tag]];
}
```

The completed Fusebox.m source code file combines the `calculate` `Answer` action and the new menu item action into one file. To keep your bearings straight, here's the completed Fusebox.m file:

```objc
#import "Fusebox.h"

@implementation Fusebox

- (IBAction)calculateAnswer:(id)sender
{
        float num1,num2,answer;
    int operation;

    num1 = [numberField1 floatValue];
    num2 = [numberField2 floatValue];

    operation = [operationPopup selectedTag];
    switch (operation) {
        case 0://addition
                                answer = num1 + num2;
                                    break;
        case 1://subtraction
                                answer = num1 - num2;
                                    break;
        case 2://multiplication
                                answer = num1 * num2;
                                    break;
        case 3://division
                                answer = num1 / num2;
                                    break;
    }

    NSNumberFormatter *answerFormatter =
        [[[NSNumberFormatter alloc] init]
        autorelease];

    [answerFormatter
        setFormat:@"#,###.00;0.00;(#,##0.00)"];
    [[answerField cell] setFormatter:answerFormatter];
        [answerField setFloatValue:answer];
}

- (IBAction)changeOperation:(id)sender
{
    [operationPopup selectItemAtIndex:[sender tag]];
}
@end
```

8. **Choose File⇨Save to save the Fusebox.m file.**

9. **Choose Build⇨Build and Go to see your work in action.**

   The result is an application that performs addition, subtraction, multiplication, and division. You can choose a mathematical operation by selecting it from the popupButton in the interface, choosing it from the Calculate menu in the menu bar, or using the keyboard shortcuts listed in the Calculate menu. Figure 4-22 shows the completed calculator application.

**Figure 4-22:**
The completed calculator can add, subtract, multiply, and divide.

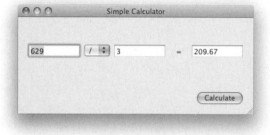

 If you get lost somewhere during the interface-building process or the code additions, you can get the completed project from www.dummies.com/go/ cocoafd. The finished project is in the following directory:

```
Chapter 4/End Code/Calculator
```

# Chapter 5

# Putting Polishing Touches on Your Application

*A*fter you finish building an interface, writing code, and debugging your application, you'll want to prepare it and build it for use as a stand-alone executable file to distribute. You may think that after you design and write an application, it's ready for the world to see, but you still have a few more steps to complete before it passes muster with Mac users (they can be a demanding bunch!) and before it's truly ready for public consumption.

Mac users expect particular things to be present in a "good" Mac application. In this chapter, I show you some of the most common features that you can add to an application and settings that you need to tweak before releasing it to friends, family, co-workers, or the public.

The bulk of your development tasks take place in Xcode and Interface Builder. Some of the items in this chapter can be completed using features found in Xcode and Interface Builder. However, these aren't the only tools Apple gives you for creating Cocoa applications. Nestled in the Applications folder of your Developer folder, you'll find more than a dozen additional tools and utilities that can help you create great Cocoa software. I show you how to use a couple of them in this chapter: Icon Composer to create icons and icns Browser to manage the icons in your project. Disk Utility, which comes stock with all Macs, also makes an appearance in this chapter.

# Adding an About Panel

Within every application menu is a menu item titled *About My Application,* where *My Application* is the name of your application. This is commonly known as the *About Menu,* and clicking it opens an About Panel. The *About Panel* typically conveys important information about the application (imagine that!). For many years, developers created their own About Panel (sometimes also called an *About Box* or *About Window*), but Apple has standardized this use. Following Apple's guidelines, an About Panel can display the following information about an application:

✔ **Name or title:** The name of the application

✔ **Icon:** The application's icon

✔ **Version number:** A number, such as 1.0, indicating which version this is

✔ **Copyright date:** A copyright note stating the year that the application copyrighted

✔ **Credits:** Other pertinent information about the application, which usually includes names of the team that built the application and other acknowledgements

An application doesn't have all these elements in the About Panel by default. You must either add them to the project or alter the project settings for them to appear in the About Panel. Figure 5-1 shows the default About Panel, with the name of the application and the version number, when you create a Cocoa Application (in this case, the application is named *Utility*).

**Figure 5-1:**
The default About Panel of a Cocoa application is pretty bland.

After you alter the appropriate settings and add a couple items to your project, the resulting About Panel is far more interesting to look at and is much more useful to users. Figure 5-2 shows an About Panel that includes the basic elements of an About Panel.

Surely an improvement as big as that requires some code, right? Nope! By setting a few parameters and adding the necessary files, Cocoa takes care of the rest!

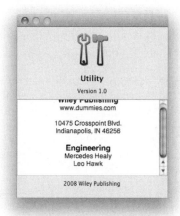

**Figure 5-2:**
The enhanced About Panel looks a lot better and is helpful to users.

Most of the settings you need to address to customize an About Panel are in the Info.plist file of your project. The Info.plist file resides within the Resource folder of your project. Figure 5-3 shows its location in the project window.

The Info.plist file is somewhat unique. At its heart, it's nothing more than a text file. But, that text file consists of XML (eXtensible Markup Language), which is parsable by special applications, such as the Property List Editor, one of the tools that resides in the Applications folder within your Developer folder. (Property List Editor resides within the Utilities folder there.)

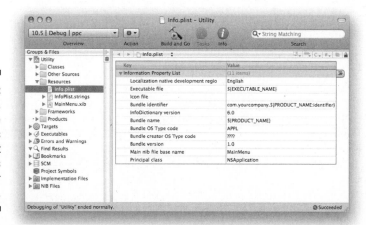

**Figure 5-3:**
The Info. plist file contains important settings for your applcation.

There's no need to pull out the big guns though because Xcode can also parse the data in Info.plist. Instead of displaying the file as plain old text, Xcode parses the data and displays it as a hierarchical tree (the way XML is formed structurally). Each element in the hierarchy consists of a key/value combo. You can double-click any value and alter it from within Xcode.

## Setting an icon

Toward the top of the About Panel stands the application's icon, which identifies your application at a glance but is present mostly for cosmetic reasons. Set the icon for an application, and as a result, you set the icon in the About Panel. You need to do two things to set the icon:

1. **Add an icon file (with an** `.icns` **file extension) to the project window by dragging and dropping it from Finder.**

   It's customary for the icon file to reside in the Resources folder of a project. Later in this chapter, I show you how to build an icon with Icon Composer.

2. **In Info.plist, enter the name of the icon in the Icon File field.**

   Type the name of the icon file exactly as you see it in Finder. The file extension (`.icns`), however, is optional.

   Figure 5-4 shows that an icon file UtilityIcon.icns has been added to the project.

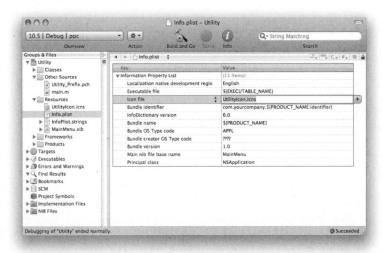

**Figure 5-4:**
Set the Icon File field in Info.plist to establish the icon for your application and the About Panel.

# Setting the name or title

Next, you need to change the Bundle Name to affect the application name that appears in the About Panel. This is probably the single-most important element in the About Panel because it's the panel that appears when you click the About This Application menu. The title simply identifies that application.

You might be tempted to change the data next to the Bundle Name key in Info.plist, but don't. Instead, you set the application's name in the Info window for your project's target. By default, projects assign the value $\texttt{\$\{PRODUCT\_NAME\}}$ to the Bundle Name key in Info.plist. Thismeans that the product name comes from elsewhere in your project because $\texttt{\$\{PRODUCT\_NAME\}}$ is a variable. When you change the value in the Info window for your project's target, the Info.plist automatically reflects those changes at runtime.

The default name of the product usually matches the name of your project, but it doesn't have to. To change the product name, and in turn, the application name that appears in the About Panel, follow these steps:

1. **Locate and expand the Targets folder in the project.**

   The Targets folder has a red bull's-eye icon, so it should be easy to spot.

2. **Select the application target within the Targets folder.**

   The target will have a name that you recognize; probably the same name as the project itself. Figure 5-5 shows the Utility target selected.

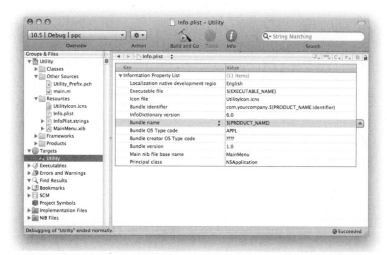

**Figure 5-5:** Select the appropriate target.

3. **Click the Info button in the project's toolbar to open the Info window.**

4. **In the Info window, click the Build tab.**

5. **Locate and change the Product Name key value.**

   The Product Name resides within the Packaging section of the Info Window, as shown in Figure 5-6. Changing the Product Name here causes your built application to have a new name, and that new name is reflected in the About Panel.

**Figure 5-6:** Change the Product Name in the Build tab of the target's Info window to change the application name that appears in the About Panel.

# Displaying a version number, a copyright date, and credits

Besides using a title to identify your application, it's also a good idea to provide a version number, a copyright, and credits in the About Panel:

✔ The version number helps users know at a quick glance what version of the application they're using, in case they want to know when it comes time to download a newer version of the application.

✔ The copyright date is useful for reminding users that your work is copy-righted, and it also provides a convenient time stamp.

✔ The credits in the About Panel permit you to credit the various team members that helped create the application. This element isn't strictly necessary, but sometimes it feels good to brag about your application.

To include the version number of your application in the About Bundle, change the Bundle Version key value in the Info.plist. Figure 5-7 shows version 1.5.

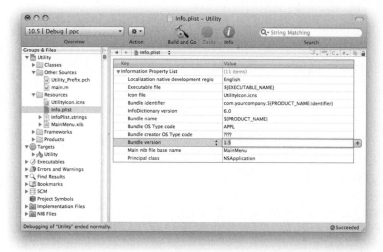

**Figure 5-7:** Change the Bundle Version key to affect the version number that appears in the About Panel.

You can display a copyright date at the bottom of the About Panel with the Copyright key in Info.plist. By default, the Copyright key doesn't exist, so you must add it. Follow these steps:

1. **In Info.plist, select the top item in the hierarchy, Information Property List, as shown in Figure 5-8.**

2. **Click the button to the right of the Value column to add a new key to the Info.plist. Select Copyright (Human-Readable) from the list of possible key names.**

3. **Change the Value of the Copyright (Human-Readable) key to whatever you desire at the bottom of your About Panel.**

   Figure 5-9 shows a completed Copyright (Human-Readable) key.

**Figure 5-8:**
Select
Information
Property List
in Info.plist.

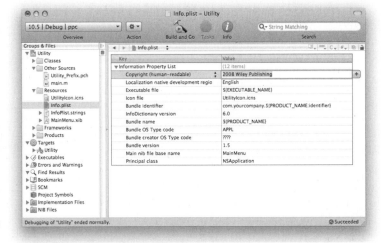

**Figure 5-9:**
Add the
Copyright
(Human-
Readable)
key to Info.
plist to
display the
copyright at
the bottom
of the About
Panel.

You can display all sorts of interesting and useful credits in a scrolling text field in the middle of the About Panel. All you have to do is add a Credits file to your project's Resource folder. The Credits file can be either a rich text file (`.rtf` or `.rtfd`) or an HTML (HyperText Markup Language) file. Both formats can display stylized text and images. HTML has the added benefit that it can display clickable links, which can be useful for adding your company's URL or an e-mail address for support. Be forewarned, though, HTML files don't contain images; instead they reference separate image files. So, if you plan on using HTML, more files are involved than just the HTML if you want to display graphics. Figure 5-10 shows a rich text Credits file in the project.

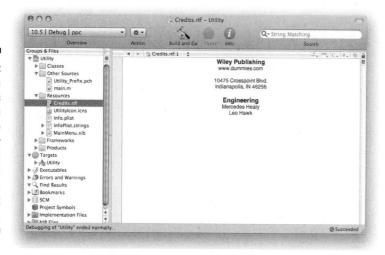

**Figure 5-10:**
Add a
Credits
file to the
project to
display
stylized
text and
graphics in
the About
Panel.

# Assigning an Icon to Your Project

One of the first things that users notice about your application is its
icon. When you first build an application with Xcode, it assigns a Generic
Application icon, as shown in Figure 5-11.

**Figure 5-11:**
Xcode
assigns a
generic
icon to all
applications
that
it builds.

You can assign a different icon to your application by adding an icon (ICNS)
file to your project and setting the Icon key in Info.plist. Before you do that,
though, you need an icon file in the first place. Apple gives you two utilities
to help you work with icon files: Icon Composer and icns Browser.

# Icon Composer

Icon Composer is a tool for constructing ICNS icon files. You can use it to gather, in one ICNS file, all the possible sizes for a particular icon. You can find Icon Composer here:

```
/Developer/Applications/Icon Composer
```

To create your own ICNS file, you need an image-editing application, such as Adobe Photoshop, Photoshop Elements, Pixelmator, GIMP, or Graphic Converter. Then follow these steps:

1. **In your image-editing application, create a new RGB (red, green, blue) document with dimensions of 512 x 512 pixels.**

   This is the document you'll use to create an icon image.

2. **With the various graphics tools in the application, create the image that you want to use as your icon.**

3. **If the image doesn't consume the entire 512 x 512 pixels, delete the unused portions.**

   Leave unused portions of the image blank because icons can be transparent. Also, deactivate any background layer to maintain transparency.

4. **Save the result as a PNG document.**

   The PNG format supports transparency. Figure 5-12 shows a sample Photoshop image for use in an icon. Note the checkerboard pattern that appears in the background. It represents the transparent portion of the image. It will also be transparent when added to an icon in Icon Composer.

After you complete the design and creation of your icon artwork, you can use Icon Composer to build an icon file:

1. **Launch Icon Composer by double-clicking its icon in Finder.**

   An empty icon template opens, as shown in Figure 5-13.

2. **Drag the PNG image from Finder to the 512 x 512 square in Icon Composer.**

   Icon Composer displays a sheet asking if you want to use this PNG image for all the other image components in the icon, as shown in Figure 5-14.

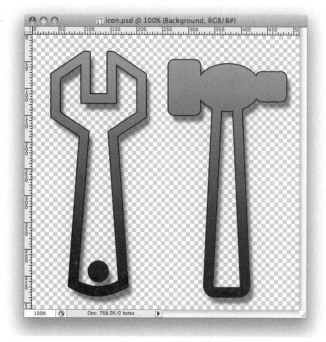

**Figure 5-12:**
Don't forget to remove the unused portions from the background.

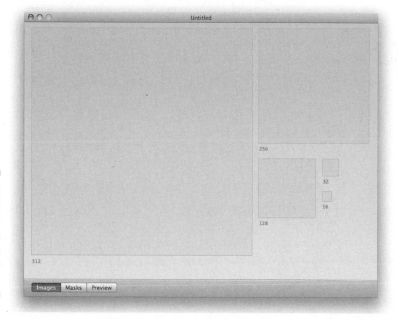

**Figure 5-13:**
Icon Composer presents you with a blank icon template.

**3. Select Copy to All Smaller Sizes and click the Import button.**

Icon Composer imports the image and adds it to all image sizes, as shown in Figure 5-15.

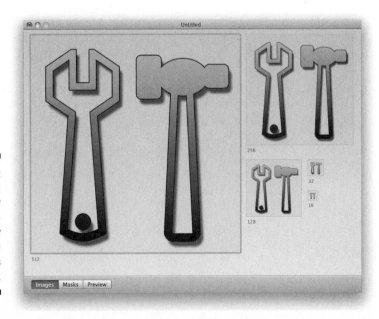

4. **Choose File⇨Save to save the icon template and then give it a name.**

5. **Choose File⇨Export to export the icon as an ICNS file.**

   Be sure to use the ICNS file format for Xcode.

6. **To use the ICNS file, drag it into the Resources folder of your Xcode project folder.**

7. **Change the Bundle Icon entry in the Info.plist file.**

   I describe how in the "Setting an icon" section earlier in this chapter.

The next time you build this project, the resulting application uses the newly added ICNS file as its icon. Double-click the application to launch it, and you'll see the new icon in the Dock as well.

## Managing your icons

Unlike the Icon Composer application, which lets you create icon files, the icns Browser application is strictly an icon viewer. With icns Browser, you can view the contents of any ICNS file, but you can't change those contents.

The icons Browser utility is handy for finding out why a particular application isn't displaying an icon properly. For example, your application might display a nice-looking icon when viewed at 128 x 128, but display nothing at the 32 x 32 size. The icns Browser can help you discover which icon elements are missing so you can correct the situation.

icns Browser resides here:

```
/Developer/Applications/icns Browser
```

To see how icns Browser works, launch it and choose File⇨Open to open the ICNS file you created with Icon Composer. You see something that looks like Figure 5-16. Notice that several elements of the icon file are missing.

This ICNS file doesn't contain all the elements possible in an ICNS file because you made it for Mac OS X only. The blank elements in this ICNS file are for maintaining compatibility with earlier versions of the Mac OS. As a Cocoa programmer, you can't target earlier versions of the Mac OS anyway, so forget about that old technology! The Mac OS is smart enough that it can scale down larger icons for use at smaller sizes. You'll notice the icns Browser application is getting a little dated because it doesn't yet support 512 x 512 or 256 x 256 icons. It's still a useful tool for sanity checks, though.

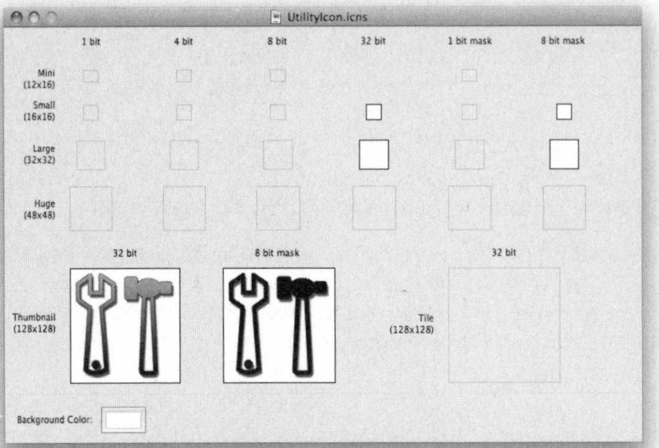

**Figure 5-16:**
Viewing the
contents of
an ICNS file.

# Creating a Disk Image for Distribution

After you build a finished application with Cocoa, you'll no doubt want to distribute it to friends, co-workers, or maybe even the world via the Internet. The easiest way to provide your users with an application is to put it on a disk image. Disk Utility is a tool that accompanies the Mac OS, and if you aren't familiar with it already, it's located here:

```
/Applications/Utilities/Disk Utility
```

To create a new disk image for your application, perform these steps:

1. **Launch Disk Utility.**

2. **Choose File⇨New⇨Blank Disk Image.**

   A window opens asking you to name the new disk image, as shown in Figure 5-17.

3. **Name the file and volume name and assign a volume size, volume format, and image format:**

   - *Save As*: The name of your disk image.

   - *Volume Name:* The name that appears on the mounted volume when a user double-clicks the disk image.

   - *Volume Format:* You can create disk images in a variety of formats, but generally speaking, you want to use Mac OS Extended format for distributing your application to others.

- *Volume Size:* Make sure that the volume size is large enough to hold your application and any auxiliary files you wish to include. Don't worry if the volume size is too large; you can compress it later. In fact, make sure that the volume size is larger than the size of the application and auxiliary files in case you want to add something else to the image later. You can find the combined size of your application and its auxiliary files by selecting the parent folder of the application in Finder and choosing Files➪Get Info.

- *Encryption:* You can encrypt disk images, but for most purposes, you don't need this feature and you can safely set it to None. If you need your disk image secure from other eyes, encrypting the disk image lets you password-protect the image. Only those who know the password can open the disk image.

- *Partitions:* The Partitions setting lets you split a disk image into multiple sections. In general, this isn't a setting you need to adjust if you want to make your software available on a disk image. Unless you're creating a disk-image master for burning CDs, usually select Single Partition — Apple Partition Map in the Partitions popup.

- *Image Format:* Set as read/write. This permits you to read from and write to the disk image and is handy when you want to add more files to the disk image later.

**Figure 5-17:**
Name the disk image and set its properties.

4. **Click Create.**

   Disk Utility churns for a second and produces the desired disk image at the location you specified.

5. **Locate the disk image in the location that you specified in Step 4 and double-click it.**

   The disk image mounts a new volume if it hasn't done so automatically already.

6. **Copy your application and any extra files to the new volume.**

7. **With the disk image in the foreground and eject the volume by pressing ⌘+E.**

8. **Return to Disk Utility and open the disk image via File⇨Open Disk Image.**

   Disk Utility opens and mounts the image, as shown in Figure 5-18.

9. **Choose Images⇨Convert to convert the disk image to a compressed format. Name the new disk image and select Compressed from the Image Format drop-down list, as shown in Figure 5-19.**

10. **Click Save to create the new compressed disk image.**

    When Disk Utility is finished, you can upload the resulting disk image to a Web server or send it to others via e-mail.

**Figure 5-18:** Disk Utility opens the disk image and mounts its volume when opened.

**Figure 5-19:**
Create
a new
compressed
disk image
to eliminate
the extra
space from
the original
disk image.

# Part II

# Instant Cocoa and the Objective-C Language

The 5th Wave                    By Rich Tennant

"You know kids — you can't buy them just any Web authoring software."

## In this part . . .

Cocoa programmers use their own language, a big brother to the popular C language, called Objective-C. Part II starts by giving you the information you need to make sense of this funny-looking language. You see how the Objective-C language works, how it handles object-oriented programming, and what it shares with its kid sister, C.

Throughout the remainder of Part II, you continue to expand your Cocoa interface knowledge by working with classes, windows, and the huge collection of controls that the Cocoa frameworks have to offer.

# Chapter 6

# The Basics of Objective-C

*In This Chapter*

▶ Using object-oriented programming

▶ Knowing the differences among classes, variables, and methods

▶ Understanding and coding in Objective-C

▶ Using your own classes

*O*bjective-C is the language that most developers use to program Cocoa applications. Although it's not the only language that you can use for Cocoa development, it's by far the most popular. Objective-C is a superset of the popular C programming language that bears an uncanny resemblance to SmallTalk (which is no accident). If you're an experienced C programmer already, you'll find that Objective-C makes you feel like you're in familiar surroundings, with a few language oddities thrown in. If you aren't well versed in C but know another programming language, you can probably figure out what's going on anyway.

This chapter examines the basics of object-oriented programming and the Objective-C language. After you get the hang of how Objective-C works, the chapter helps solidify your skills by building a project and using Objective-C. In the process, you find out how to create objects in code. Next, the chapter runs you through another important topic in Objective-C: class methods. The chapter concludes with a look at the way you should name things in Objective-C. Naming schemes plays an important role in Objective-C. As you can see, this chapter is a collection of several small facts. These bits of knowledge form a larger body of information that you'll use every time you program with Cocoa using the Objective-C language.

# Why Use Object-Oriented Programming?

Objective-C, as you may have already guessed, extends C by adding object-oriented features to it. Object-oriented programming is a paradigm whereby you group related data and functionality into a construct called an *object*.

Because an object bundles together data and functionality into one "package," your programming efforts gain several benefits:

- ✔ It's easier to design and write software that's object-oriented. Objects in object-oriented computer programming (*OOP,* not to be confused with an *OOPS!*) are analogous to objects in the real world. Consider an everyday object like a kitchen window, which has properties like height, width, glass color, thickness, and so on. Likewise, an OOP object like a computer window has properties like height, width, color, and transparency.

  You can do several things to an object like a kitchen window. You can open it, close it, wash it, and even break it. Again, the analogy follows with an OOP window. You can open it, close it, and can change its size. But, I hope you don't try to break one.

- ✔ You classify various elements of your application as objects in a sort of modular relationship to one another, making the process of programming applications proceed much quicker. The structure that OOP enforces helps you to build very sophisticated software, but still be able to keep track of things.

- ✔ Because OOP makes your software modular, your software is much easier to maintain, to repair if it's broken, or to modify later when you want to upgrade it.

# *Class Is No Object!*

Objects in OOP, like objects in the real world, have properties and functions. Objective-C calls these *instance variables* and *methods,* respectively. The methods determine what functionality an object has, and they operate on the instance variables, or the properties of the object.

For instance, every GUI (Graphical User Interface) application uses windows. A window object might have instance variables that describe its height, width, and color. Its methods would then do something with those instance variables. One method might change the width of the window. Another method might change its height. Yet another method might change the color.

Methods of an object are like gatekeepers for the instance variables. In Objective-C, other objects and their methods can't access instance variables directly. Instead, they must access instance variables via methods.

# Declaring instance variables

*Instance variables,* as the name implies, are variables that belong to an instance of a class. *Instance* is another name for *object.* Objective-C variables, like variables in many other programming languages, are references to data about a particular state of the object. For example, to declare an instance variable that references a button control, called aButton, your class interface would look like this:

```
@interface MyClass : NSObject
{
  NSButton *aButton;
}

@end
```

Here's how this code works:

✔ The @interface line begins the class declaration and @end denotes the end of the class declaration.

✔ MyClass is the name of the class, and NSObject is the superclass from which MyClass inherits. NSObject is a generic class type, and it is ultimately the superclass of all classes.

✔ Within the class declaration are two curly brackets. You must declare instance variables within those brackets of the interface file.

The *interface file* is the file in your project with an .h file extension, and in C you'd call it a *header file.* Interface files usually begin with an import statement to load appropriate frameworks. C programmers would load libraries (and in fact, libraries are allowed in Objective-C too!):

```
#import <Cocoa/Cocoa.h>
```

Pointers to objects aren't the only type that can be declared as instance variables. All the usual C variable types are fair game too in a class interface:

```
@interface MyClass : NSObject
{
  NSButton *aButton;
  int      age;
  float    percent;
}

@end
```

Objective-C also has new and improved versions of data types that you might recognize from C. For example, bool in C is BOOL in Objective-C, and it too can be used to declare an instance variable:

```
@interface MyClass : NSObject
{
   NSButton *aButton;
   int      age;
   float    percent;
   BOOL     collapsed;
}

@end
```

## Declaring methods

Besides instance variables, you find method declarations in the interface. Unlike the instance variables, however, method declarations appear after the curly braces (but before the @end). Here's a declaration for a doSomething method:

```
@interface MyClass : NSObject
{
   NSButton *aButton;
   int      age;
   float    percent;
   BOOL     collapsed;
}
-(void)doSomething;
@end
```

If you're coming to Objective-C from C, you notice something different right away. All method declarations in Objective-C begin with a dash (-). Thereafter, you assign a return type (in this case void) with parentheses. A return type works just like those found in C. A method can return a value, or not, in which case you assign void, just like in C. Following the return type is the method name. It's customary to name methods beginning with a lower-case letter in Objective-C. Notice too, that the doSomething method has no parameters. In the following example, doSomethingElse is declared with a single parameter, an NSString:

```
@interface MyClass : NSObject
{
   NSButton *aButton;
   int      age;
   float    percent;
   BOOL     collapsed;
}
```

```
-(void)doSomething;
-(void)doSomethingElse:(NSString *)aString;
@end
```

The method name is followed by a colon and then the parameter's data type in parentheses. The parameter's name appears in the declaration, as it's used in the method itself. This is slightly different than what you might be accustomed to in C function declarations, but so far it's not too strange.

When you begin adding additional parameters to a method, however, things start looking really weird to a C programmer. Besides having a name, every parameter after the first one also has a label. In the following example, drawAString has two parameters: aString and an int. The second parameter has the label atThisXPosition.

```
@interface MyClass : NSObject
{
  NSButton *aButton;
  int      age;
  float    percent;
  BOOL     collapsed;
}
-(void)doSomething;
-(void)doSomethingElse:(NSString *)aString;
-(void)drawAString:(NSString *)aString
        atThisXPosition:(int)xPos;
@end
```

This can look very peculiar to seasoned C developers, but you'll quickly adjust to it. In fact, you may find that you prefer it because each parameter is documented in the declaration itself. As you add additional parameters, simply append a label, a colon, a data type in parentheses, and the parameter name. For example, here's the drawAString method with three parameters instead of two:

```
@interface MyClass : NSObject
{
  NSButton *aButton;
  int      age;
  float    percent;
  BOOL     collapsed;
}
-(void)doSomething;
-(void)doSomethingElse:(NSString *)aString;
-(void)drawAString:(NSString *)aString
        atThisXPosition:(int)xPos atThisYPosition(int)
        yPos;
@end
```

## Defining methods in an interface file

After you define a class in the interface file, you can move on to the implementation file. The implementation file has a filename extension of .m as in MyClass.m. It's where you define the various methods for your class. The implementation file usually begins with an import statement to load the interface file:

```
#import "MyClass.h"
```

The implementation and end lines come after the import statement, within which you define the methods for the class:

```
#import "MyClass.h"


@implementation MyClass
@end
```

So far, this is all done for you by Xcode when you create a new class. You then define the various methods that appear in the interface file. Following the previous example interface file, the implementation file looks like this:

```
#import "MyClass.h"


@implementation MyClass
-(void)doSomething {

}

-(void)doSomethingElse:(NSString *)aString {

}

-(void)drawAString:(NSString *)aString
        atThisXPosition:(int)xPos atThisYPosition(int)
        yPos {

}
@end
```

Each of the class methods are defined here. They look just like their declaration counterparts in the interface file, but instead of each ending with a semi-colon, curly braces begin and end the method. You put the code for each method between those braces. Again, C programmers should feel more or less at home here because C does the same thing (as does C++, Java, and even JavaScript).

# Coding in Objective-C

After you declare a class, add instance variables and methods to its declaration, and set up the shell of the implementation file, it's time to write some code!

## Sending messages to objects

One of the most basic ideas in Objective-C is the capability to send messages from one object to another. To do this in Objective-C, you typically send a message to an object telling it to perform that method. Objective-C uses square brackets to denote that you're sending a message to an object.

Sending messages is similar to calling functions in other programming languages.

For a generic object (named `object`), you'd send a message (named `message`) like this:

```
[object message];
```

Note two things:

✔ The syntax of this statement makes it behave much like a command in English. For example, you might say this to a taxicab driver:

```
Driver, go!
```

In Objective-C, the same command looks like this:

```
[driver go];
```

✔ Each line of code ends with a semicolon. Except for the usual places where you might leave one out in C (for example, an `if` statement), Objective-C also requires a semicolon at the end of each line of code. Objective-C is C, after all!

## Passing parameters

Like traditional C functions, Objective-C lets you pass parameters (also known as *arguments*) to methods. Going back to the taxi analogy, you might want to tell the driver where to go:

```
Driver, go left!
```

In Objective-C, the command might look like this:

```
[driver go:left];
```

For C programmers, the `go` method should seem roughly analogous to a standard C function. If you add another parameter, though, the analogy breaks down. Suppose, for example, that you want to pass two parameters (`direction` and `distance`) to the `go` method:

```
[driver go:left distance:10];
```

In Objective-C, the first parameter follows the colon after the name of the method (in this case `go:left`). Each subsequent parameter has a name, followed by a parameter (in this instance, `distance:10`). In contrast, a parallel C function might be

```
go(left,10);
```

In Objective-C, the meaning of the first parameter is usually obvious based on the name of the method. Additional parameters have names to help you identify their purpose.

## *Returning values*

Like C functions, an Objective-C method can also return a value. If you tell a taxicab driver to go a particular direction and distance, the next you're likely to hear is the price of the fare. You tell the driver to do something. The driver replies with a price. In Objective-C, this works much like it does in C.

```
price = [driver go:left distance:10];
```

Because some methods can return values, Cocoa programmers are fond of nesting them within other methods. Suppose that you based your directions to the cabbie on a map. You know that the driver should go left, but not necessarily how far. In this situation, you might use a map object to find the distance to the desired location, embedding it in the `go` method.

```
[driver go:left
    distance:[map startAt:location1
            destination:location2]];
```

Returning to the class that you defined earlier in this chapter, you'll want to write code in each of those methods that sends messages to other methods in the same class. To call other methods within the same class, use `self` like this:

```
-(void)doSomething {
    [self drawAString:@"hello" atThisXPosition:10
            atThisYPosition:6];
}
```

# Instantiating an object

After you create a class, you'll want to use it as an object. When you want to create an Objective-C object, you send the `alloc` message to the class, like so:

```
MyClass* anInstance = [MyClass alloc];
```

The `alloc` message allocates memory and creates the class. An instantiated object must also be initialized. You do so by sending the `init` method to the instance, like this:

```
[anInstance init];
```

Because `alloc` and `init` are both required for a generic instantiation, it's customary to embed them in one statement:

```
MyClass * anInstance = [[MyClass alloc] init];
```

Then, you're free to work with the object (`anInstance`) as you need. You could send the `drawAString` message to the instance:

```
[anInstance drawAString:@"hello" atThisXPosition:10
        atThisYPosition:6];
```

Because you used `alloc` to create the instance, you must free up that memory using `release`.

```
[anInstance release];
```

# Managing memory

Recent versions of Cocoa provide support for garbage collection, but historically Cocoa hasn't had garbage collection. *Garbage collection* is the process whereby Cocoa dynamically frees memory that you've allocated for various objects. Because this is a newer feature and because so many sources of sample code do things the old way, it's best that you understand memory management in Cocoa without garbage collection.

Cocoa keeps track of memory by way of *reference counting.* This is a simple counter that runs behind the scenes, keeping track of how many objects have allocated memory and how many objects have released that memory. When you create an object with `alloc`, you increase the reference count by one. When you send a `release` message to the object, you decrease the count by one. The name of the game here is that your reference count should end up being zero after you're finished using an object. If the count is greater than zero, you're leaking memory. And if the reference count is less than zero, you've freed an object in memory that you still need. Your code will crash when you try to access this freed object.

As you saw in the previous section, an object is allocated with the `alloc` method. The `alloc` method increases the reference count by one, so it needs a corresponding `release`.

```
SomeClass *someObject = [[SomeClass alloc] init];
… do stuff with someObject here…
[someObject release];
```

So far, this is pretty simple because the allocation and release of the object are all within the same block of code. Where things get a little mind-bending is in the case of instance variables. Although it's legal to access instance variables by name in your methods, it's far wiser to access them *only* via accessor methods.

Because of memory management issues, things can get ugly quickly if you don't use accessor methods to access instance variables. If you don't use accessor methods, there's a very real possibility that your application will leak memory or that it will crash when you try to release an object that's already been released.

For example, suppose that you have a class that has an `NSString` instance variable called `name`. Declare two methods for accessing the instance variable. A *getter* (`name`) and a *setter* (`setName`):

```
@interface MyClass : NSObject {
  NSString *name;
}
-(NSString *)name;
-(void)setName:(NSString *)aName;
@end
```

Then, in your implementation file, define the methods like this:

```
@implementation MyClass
-(NSString *)name {
  return name;
}
-(void)setName:(NSString *)aName{
  [aName retain];
  [name release];
  name = aName;
}
@end
```

The setName method sends the retain message to aName. The retain method, just like alloc, increases the reference count by one. (It might help to think of retain as the opposite of release.) So, the code keeps aName around in memory for use elsewhere in the class. And because you're done with whatever object name is pointing to, you then release name. The method assigns aName to name. Following this simple plan prevents you from leaking memory because each time name is used, whatever it was pointing to previously is released and the new thing it's pointing to is retained.

If you're following along so far, you might be wondering what happens when the object is finally destroyed. Won't you still have a reference count of one for the name instance variable? The answer is yes! You must release the last lingering name object in the dealloc method of the class.

```
-(void)dealloc {
  [name release];
}
```

Here are some special cases where you don't have to worry about retaining and releasing objects:

✔ **When you create an object with one of the built-in convenience methods of a class:** That object is said to be *autoreleased,* which means you don't have to release it. Cocoa does the releasing for you. For example, the NSString class has a stringWithString convenience method. You can use it instead of alloc to create an NSString object:

```
+ (id)stringWithString:(NSString *)aString
```

Note that the definition of stringWithString begins with a + character. This means that it's a *class method,* and instead of sending the message to an object, you send it to the class itself. For example, to create an NSString with this method, you'd do something like this:

```
*aString = [NSString stringWithString:@"Hello,
    World!"];
```

You don't have to use alloc to create the object. And, because you use a convenience method, stringWithString, it's autoreleased, so no need to release it yourself.

✔ **When objects are autoreleased in code:** For example, if you see an object that has autorelease, there's no need to release that object either:

```
SomeClass *someObject = [[[SomeClass alloc] init]
    autorelease];
```

The autorelease method decreases the reference count by one, which negates the increase by one of the reference count by alloc.

# Working with Your Own Classes

Because classes form the basis of your Cocoa projects, you use them frequently. Most often, you create a class to store and manipulate the data for your application. Cocoa geeks call this type of class a *Model*. The class that takes care of displaying your data is the *View*. A third class — a *Controller* — mediates between the Model and the View.

Here's how you create and use your own class in broad terms:

1. Create a class.

2. Build an interface.

3. Add a Controller class and connect it to the interface.

4. Define the methods for the class.

5. Define an action for the class.

To try your hand at working with classes in Objective-C, follow these steps:

1. **Create a Cocoa project.**

   Launch Xcode and choose File⇨New Project. In the dialog that appears, choose Cocoa Application from the list of choices, name the project, and create it.

2. **Create a class.**

   You can create classes in Xcode or Interface Builder. For this class, use Xcode:

   *a. Choose File⇨New File.*

   *b. In the window that appears, choose Objective-C Class and click Next.*

   *c. In the next pane that appears, name the implementation file of the new class. Name it Driver.m, as shown in Figure 6-1.*

   This is the class you'll use to create a taxi driver object. When you create the `Driver` class, the header and implementation files — Driver.h and Driver.m, respectively — appear in your project.

3. **Create a new Controller class:**

   *a. Double-click the MainMenu.xib file in Xcode to switch to Interface Builder.*

   *b. In the Library window, search for **object** and drag an `NSObject` item to the project window.*

   *c. Press ⌘+D and name the new class `MyController` in the Identity Inspector, as shown in Figure 6-2.*

   This class will communicate with your interface.

### 4. Create an interface:

*a. In Interface Builder, open the default window in your NIB file.*

*b. From the Library window, drag a push button (an* `NSButton`*), a check box, and four* `Label` *controls to your window.*

You use two of the `Label` controls to display the name of your cab driver and the fare for your trip. The other two `Label` controls are simply labels for the interface (Fare: and Driver:).

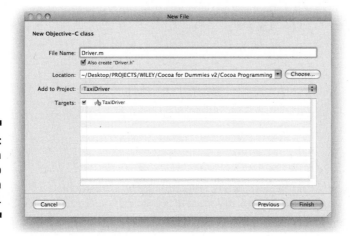

**Figure 6-1:**
Create a
class to
represent a
taxi driver.

**Figure 6-2:**
Name the
class My
Controller in
the Identity
Inspector
window.

Figure 6-3 shows the interface with the two empty `Label` controls selected.

**Figure 6-3:**
Add four
Label
controls, a
push button,
and a check
box to the
interface.

**5. Add outlets to the** `MyController` **class.**

For this project, you need to define three outlets as part of the `MyController` class:

 a. *In the XIB project window, select the* `MyController` *class (see Figure 6-2).*

 b. *Press ⌘+6 to open the Identity Inspector window and add three outlets (*`distanceCheckbox`*,* `driverDisplay`*, and* `fareDisplay`*) to the class.*

 The `driverDisplay` and `fareDisplay` outlets give you access to the two `Label` controls in the interface, so you can display the fare and the name of the driver there. The third outlet (`distanceCheckbox`) permits you to find out whether the Distance > 10 miles check box is selected.

Figure 6-4 shows the new outlets.

**6. Add an action to the** `MyController` **class.**

Add one action to `MyController` and name it `calculateFare:` (note the required trailing colon), as shown in Figure 6-5. This is the action that the Calculate Fare button triggers. When a user clicks this button, the application displays the name of the cabbie and calculates the fare based on one parameter: `distance`. If the trip is longer than ten miles, the program returns a fare. If the trip is less than ten miles, the program returns a different fare.

**Figure 6-4:**
Add three
outlets to
the My
Controller
class.

**Figure 6-5:**
Add a
calculate
Fare: action
to the My
Controller
class.

7. **Wire the interface to the** `MyController` **instance.**

You can't do anything with the three outlets and one action in your code until you connect them to the interface.

a. *Control+drag from the* `MyController` *instance in the NIB file window to the* `Label` *control that's adjacent to the Fare label.*

b. *In the small black connections list overlay that appears when you let go of the mouse, choose* `fareDisplay`.

With `MyController` selected in the project window, press ⌘+5 to see the connections while you make them.

c. *Repeat the same process for the other* `Label` *controls and the* `NSButton` *that looks like a check box by connecting them to their respective outlets (*`driverDisplay` *and* `fareCheckbox`*).*

Figure 6-6 shows the completed connections.

8. **Create the files for** `MyController`.

Select the `MyController` class in the project window and then choose File➪Write Class Files. The MyController.h and MyController.m files are added to your project in Xcode.

**Figure 6-6:**
The My Controller outlets and actions.

9. **After you complete your work in Interface Builder, choose File⇨Save to save the NIB file.**

10. **Return to Xcode to add code that makes your project work.**

    You find the following four files: Driver.h, Driver.m, MyController.h, and MyController.m. See Figure 6-7. If the Driver and MyController header and implementation files aren't in the Classes folder already, move them there. When you create them, they appear in whatever folder was last selected in the project. It helps you keep things organized.

Continue with the following sections to finish your project.

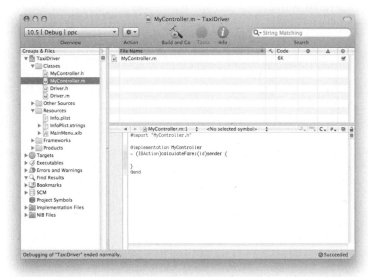

**Figure 6-7:** Move the Driver and My Controller header and implementation files to the Classes folder in Xcode.

# Defining the class

Click the Driver.h file to view its contents. The `Driver` class serves as the *model*. To this file, add the following code to define the class interface:

```
#import <Cocoa/Cocoa.h>

@interface Driver : NSObject {
    NSString *firstName;
}
```

```
-  (int)go:(int)direction theDistance:(BOOL)distance;
-  (NSString *)firstName;
-  (void)setFirstName:(NSString *)name;

@end
```

The code begins by including the appropriate header files:

```
#import <Cocoa/Cocoa.h>
```

The Cocoa framework provides basic functionality for your Cocoa applications.

The code then defines a `Driver` class, which inherits functionality from `NSObject`:

```
@interface Driver : NSObject {
    NSString *firstName;
}
```

Almost all classes that you use in Cocoa inherit from `NSObject`. In fact, *all* classes in this book inherit from the `NSObject` superclass. `NSObject` is the primary base class for programming in Cocoa. You can think of `NSObject` as a kind of generic class that contains methods and variables for creating objects. When you aren't creating a class based on a window, a button, or some other existing class, use an `NSObject`. In this example, you're defining a class (`Driver`), which is an `NSObject`. The `Driver` class has one `firstName` instance variable that stores the taxi driver name.

The rest of the code defines the three methods for the `Driver` class:

```
-  (int)go:(BOOL)distance;
```

The first method, `go`, is what your code executes when a user wants the driver to take him somewhere. `go` has one parameter: a Boolean that represents the distance. For this example, imagine that the cab driver charges one rate for short trips (less than ten miles) and another rate for longer trips. Because this rate scheme includes only two prices, you can use a Boolean variable to determine which rate to charge. A Boolean can have one of two possible values: `YES` or `NO`.

The remaining two methods set and get the name of the cab driver. Later, you assign the name of the cab driver with `setFirstName` when you create an instance from this class:

```
-  (void)setFirstName:(NSString *)name;
```

Then when you want to display the name, you ask the `Driver` instance for it with the `firstName` method:

```
- (NSString *)firstName;
```

The `@end` marks the end of the `Driver` class declaration.

## Implementing the class

Click the Driver.m file to reveal its code. To this file, add the following code:

```
@implementation Driver

- (int)go:(BOOL)distance {
    if (distance)
        return 10;
    else
        return 5;
}

- (NSString *)firstName {
    return firstName;
}

- (void)setFirstName:(NSString *)name {
    [name retain];
    [firstName release];
    firstName = name;
}

- (void)dealloc {
    [firstName release];
    [super dealloc];
}

@end
```

Here's how the code works:

✔ This code begins by importing the Driver.h interface, where the declaration of your `Driver` class resides.

✔ The code then defines the methods for that class. All methods appear within the `@implementation` and `@end` lines.

As you know from the header file, this class has three methods. The `go` method returns a value of 5 or 10 based on the `distance` parameter.

The firstName method returns the value of the firstName variable that belongs to the instance.

It's perfectly valid to give the same name to a variable and a method of the same class.

✔ The Driver.m file defines the setFirstName method.

This is where things can get a bit strange. A newcomer to Cocoa might assume that you could assign a value to firstName like this:

```
firstName = name;
```

Unfortunately, it's not as simple as that. Because the name parameter (which is part of the setFirstName method) is a pointer to an NSString object, you must be careful to clean house. ("Out with the old and in with the new.") If the name value is different than the firstName value, you must release the firstName pointer and retain the name pointer. This has to do with memory management in Objective-C, as I describe earlier in this chapter.

Because the firstName and setFirstName methods give you access to the firstName variable of the Driver class, programmers call these *accessor* methods. It's best to provide accessor methods when you want to access variables that are internal to a class, rather than have a user poke around in the guts of your class.

✔ The final method in the Driver.m file is the dealloc method, which takes care of releasing the firstName pointer and de-allocating the superclass.

```
[firstName release];
[super dealloc];
```

## *Using the class*

Now that you've defined a Driver class, you may be wondering how you go about using it.

```
Click the MyController.m file in Xcode and change the
         code to look like the following listing:#import
         "MyController.h"
#import "Driver.h"

@implementation MyController

- (IBAction)calculateFare:(id)sender
{

    NSString *name = @"Frederick";
    Driver *driver = [[Driver alloc] init];
```

```
    int fare;

    [driver setFirstName:name];
    [driverDisplay setStringValue:[driver firstName]];

    fare = [driver go:[distanceCheckbox state]];
    [fareDisplay setIntValue:fare];

    [driver release];
}

@end
```

Here's how the code works:

- It declares and assigns a value to an NSString. Your taxicab company is a small one; it has only one driver, Frederick:

  ```
  NSString *name = @"Frederick";
  ```

  Working with strings in C can be a nuisance. To get around this problem, Objective-C gives you a convenient method for assigning string literals. Simply place the @ character before the string. The @ character signifies the beginning of a string literal in Objective-C.

- The code uses the alloc and init methods to create a driver object:

  ```
  Driver *driver = [[Driver alloc] init];

  // code here

  [driver release];
  ```

  When you create objects using the alloc and init method, it's crucial that you also release them after you've finished using them. If you don't, you'll leak memory.

  Notice that the object name (driver) has a lowercase spelling, but its class (Driver) has an uppercase spelling. See the "Naming things in Objective-C" sidebar to see why.

- After you create a driver object, you can begin using its various methods. The code assigns a name to the driver object:

  ```
      [driver setFirstName:name];
  ```

- You calculate the cab fare with the go method:

  ```
  fare = [driver go:[distanceCheckbox state]];
  [fareDisplay setIntValue:fare];
  ```

- The code passes a second parameter based on the current state of distanceCheckbox. The go method returns a value for the parameters you pass to it, which you can then display in the interface with the fareDisplay outlet.

## *Testing*

Press ⌘+R to test your handiwork. You see something that looks like Figure 6-8.

Figure 6-8:
The
completed
project
assigns
Frederick
a fare.

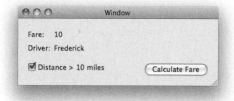

When the user clicks the button in the interface, the calculateFare method of the MyController class creates the driver object, uses its methods, and releases it. Therefore, each time the user clicks the button, the code creates a new object, works with it, and releases it.

---

# Naming things in Objective-C

Most programming languages have naming conventions, and Objective-C is no exception. Although these so-called rules aren't mandatory, they have the following benefits:

✔ Improve the legibility of your code.

✔ Give you hints about code functionality.

✔ Make your code work with Key-Value Coding (KVC) and bindings (Chapter 18).

✔ Make it easier for others to interpret your code.

**Class names:** Class names in Objective-C begin with an uppercase letter. Using the class presented earlier in this chapter, Driver is the (capitalized) name of the class. This

convention doesn't pertain to only the classes that you create. It applies also to the classes that Apple provides in the Cocoa framework. For example, look at the following built-in class names:

✔ NSString

✔ NSNumber

✔ NSArray

✔ NSImage

Each of these classes begins with a capital letter. Further, they begin with the same two capital letters, *N* and *S*. The classes have this naming system because they're refugees of the NeXT STEP operating system, upon which Apple based Mac OS X. With this little naming convention, you can instantly tell which classes in your code are your own and which ones come from the Cocoa framework.

Xcode and Interface Builder try to help you remember to capitalize class names. Each time you create a new class with either application, it provides you with a default class name that's capitalized.

**Instance names:** In contrast to class names, instances begin with a lowercase letter. For example, earlier in this chapter, you created an instance of the `Driver` class like this:

```
Driver *driver = [[Driver
    alloc] init];
```

The name of the instance is `driver`. You created an instance of `NSString` similarly:

```
NSString *name =
    @"Frederick";
```

When you use the lowercase names for your instances, it's easy to discern between instances and classes. This is especially handy when the class and instance names are the same.

**Filenames:** Cocoa source code files must follow the prescribed naming scheme. You've already witnessed that Objective-C classes consist of a header file and an implementation file. For example, the Driver class has the following two files.

✔ Driver.m: The implementation file

✔ Driver.h: The interface (or header) file

# Chapter 7

# MVC Design

• • • • • • • • • • • • • • • • • • • • • • • • • • • • • • • • • • • • • • • • • • •

## In This Chapter

▶ Getting familiar with the Model-View-Controller (MVC) design pattern

▶ Building a project with MVC

▶ Adding a View and a Controller

• • • • • • • • • • • • • • • • • • • • • • • • • • • • • • • • • • • • • • • • • • •

*I*f you read Chapter 6, you looked at some of the basics of object-oriented programming with Cocoa. You examined how to define a class and how to create an object with that class. Along the way, I promised that this would make programming simpler and, more importantly, reusable.

Sure, you can make classes and objects all day long, but how do they actually fit together to make an application? This chapter takes object-oriented programming to the next level and shows you at a more abstract level how to design an application with all these classes. A thoughtful Cocoa programmer doesn't just throw a bunch of classes together and come out on the other side with a masterpiece. Instead, a Cocoa programmer thinks about how the various parts of an application work together and then designs the application using the famous Model-View-Controller (MVC) design pattern.

By following this design pattern, you can build applications that are modular, easier to read, and consist of components that you can reuse in other applications. One of the great benefits of object-oriented programming is the ability to reuse code. By reusing code, you can reduce the amount of time you need to spend programming, reduce the number of bugs you have in your code, and ultimately create better software. All is not necessarily smiles and sunshine when it comes to code reuse, however. You must rigorously debug your code and maintain a single version. If you don't, you might inject a bug that propagates across all applications where you use the code.

# Taking a Look at MVC Design

MVC stands for the Model-View-Controller design pattern. Don't let the words scare you, though. What it really means is that you can *design* your software according to a specific *pattern* that gives you the most bang for your buck. In case you haven't guessed already, an application that follows the MVC design pattern has three different objects (at a minimum):

- **Model:** An object that provides data to your application.

- **View:** An object that displays data in your application.

- **Controller:** An intermediary object that obtains data from the Model and passes it to the View for display. Alternatively, the Controller might take data that's changed in a View and inform the Model that it has changed, so the Model too can change.

For a real-world example analogy, suppose you're a student sitting in a classroom with a chalkboard and a dictionary:

- The dictionary is a storage of information, or in MVC terms, the *Model*.

- The chalkboard is the *View,* a place to display information.

- You, the student, are the *Controller*.

Someone asks for a definition of a word. You (the Controller) consult the dictionary (the Model), and report the definition to the chalkboard (the View).

What makes the MVC pattern so great is that at any time, you could replace any of the objects:

- You could replace the Model (the dictionary), with a different Model (a dictionary from a different publisher). The Controller and the View stay the same, but the Model changes. You (the Controller) and the chalkboard (the View) keep doing the same tasks that you always do. The Controller looks up a new word, and the View displays it.

- You could replace the chalkboard with a dry-erase board. This time, the View changes, but the Controller (you) and the Model (the dictionary) remain the same. You look up a word in the dictionary (the Model) and display it on the dry-erase board (the View) instead.

- Someone else could take your place as the Controller. A new student could step in as your replacement. The Model (the dictionary) and the View (the chalkboard) don't change, but a new Controller (another student) takes your place. He can look up the word in the same dictionary (the Model) and display the definition on the same old chalkboard (the View).

With MVC, the Dictionary-Chalkboard-Person pattern can also work in reverse. For example, suppose that a new definition appears on the chalkboard (the View). The Controller would see the new definition and, knowing that the definition isn't already in the dictionary (the Model), could tell the Model that it needs to be updated with the new definition. The analogy starts to break down a little here, but hopefully you get the gist.

By separating the tasks that your Cocoa objects perform, you can make your software much more modular. This permits you to reuse classes quite easily. You can always move the chalkboard into a different classroom completely and use it there. Similarly, you can move dictionary, or even the student, into a different classroom, and they'll function in much the same way as they did in the original classroom.

By following the MVC design pattern, your Cocoa objects can gain the same benefits. If you have an interesting or useful Model in one application, you can easily move it for use in another application. Similarly, if you have a really nice-looking View in one application, you can use it in other applications as well.

Another great benefit of using MVC design patterns in your applications is that several Cocoa technologies rely on MVC. By using MVC in your applications, you can take advantage of these other Cocoa technologies. For example, Cocoa's bindings technology requires the use of MVC design. By incorporating MVC into your own application, you can then take advantage of all the goodies that bindings provide. Check out Chapter 18 for more on bindings.

# Building a Project with an MVC Design

To design an application that follows the MVC design pattern, you differentiate the classes in your application based on the functions they perform. For example, suppose that you want to create a banking application to track the money in your bank account. Your design works like this:

- ✔ A Model class stores the balance in the account. The View class, the interface of the application, displays information to the user and accepts data input from that user. The Controller sits between the Model and the View.

- ✔ When the application wants to display the current balance, the Controller gathers the information from the Model and passes it to the View for display.

- ✔ When a user changes something in the View (for example, via a deposit or a withdrawal), the Controller gathers the information from the interface and passes it to the Model, so the Model can update the information. And in a round-trip fashion, the Controller can then ask the Model what the new account balance is and pass it to the View for display.

To see how the MVC design works in a Cocoa application, follow these steps to build a project:

1. **Launch Xcode and choose File⇨New Project.**

   The New Project window opens (see Figure 7-1).

2. **Select Application from the left column and then Cocoa Application from the list of project templates and click the Choose button.**

**Figure 7-1:**
Select
Cocoa
Application
from the
templates
listed.

3. **Name the project and click the Save button.**

   For example, you can name your project Bank Account, as shown in Figure 7-2.

4. **Select the Classes folder in the Groups and Files list of the Xcode project window.**

   When you create a new class, it appears in this folder because you selected it before creating the new class.

5. **Choose File⇨New File.**

   The New File window opens, as shown in Figure 7-3.

6. **Select Objective-C Class from the Cocoa option and then click the Next button.**

**Figure 7-2:**
Name the
new project.

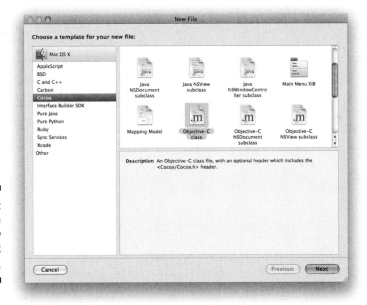

**Figure 7-3:**
Create
a new
Objective-C
class.

**7. Name the new class and then click the Finish button.**

For example, you can name your class filename Account.m, as shown in Figure 7-4.

**8. Open the BankAccount.h file and add this code:**

```
#import <Cocoa/Cocoa.h>

@interface Account : NSObject {
  float balance;
}

-(float)balance;
-(void)setBalance:(float)aBalance;

-(void)deposit:(float)anAmount;
-(void)withdraw:(float)withdrawAmount;

@end
```

This code defines a balance as an instance variable, adds accessor methods for the balance so the Controller object can retrieve and set the balance, and includes a couple methods for depositing and withdrawing money from the account.

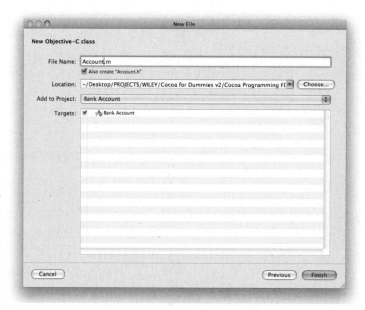

**Figure 7-4:**
Name the
new class
filename
Account.m.

**9. Open the Account.m implementation file and add the following code:**

```
#import "Account.h"


@implementation Account

-(float)balance {
  return balance;
}

-(void)setBalance:(float)aBalance {
  balance = aBalance;
}

-(void)deposit:(float)depositAmount {
  balance += depositAmount;
}

-(void)withdraw:(float)withdrawAmount {
  balance -= balance withdrawAmount;
}

- (id) init
{
  //initialize the superclass and assign it to self
  if (self = [super init]) {
    //now that you know self has been inited,
    //you can work with its instance variables
    balance = 100.0f;
  }
  return self;
}

@end
```

This code implements the two accessor methods and the `deposit`
and `withdraw` methods, as well as initializes the balance by giving the
account $100 to start.

# Adding a View

You could build and run the project as it stands now, but it won't do anything
particularly interesting because it consists of only a Model and no interface.
You still need the interface, which serves as the View in the Model-View-
Controller paradigm.

1. **Double-click MainMain.xib to open Interface Builder.**

2. **In Interface Builder, open the Library window and drag two Label controls and two push buttons to the window of your interface.**

   Change the text in one of the Label controls to `Balance:` and leave the other Label blank. Figure 7-5 shows the blank Label selected. Change the text of the two buttons to Withdraw and Deposit, respectively.

**Figure 7-5:**
Add two labels and two buttons to the interface.

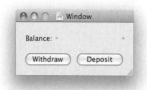

3. **Select the window's title bar and press ⌘+1 (or choose Tools⇨Window Attributes) and change the window's title.**

   Figure 7-6 shows the Attributes Inspector with the window's title changed to Bank Account.

4. **Choose File⇨Save to save the interface and press ⌘+R to test the interface.**

**Figure 7-6:**
Change the window's title in the Attributes Inspector.

# Adding a Controller

You have now created a Model (Account) and a View (the interface). To get these two objects to talk to each other, you need a Controller class that sits in between them. You could return to Xcode and implement a Controller, but for now it's easier to just do it in Interface Builder.

1. **In Interface Builder, open the Library window and search for** object. **Drag a new** NSObject **to the project window.**

   Figure 7-7 shows the newly added object.

2. **With the new object selected in the project window, press ⌘+6 and change the class name to** AccountController.

   This is the Controller class that stands between the Model and the View in this project. Figure 7-8 shows the new Controller class.

3. **Add an outlet and two actions to the** AccountController **in the same Attributes Inspector window.**

   The display outlet points to the Label field where you want to display the current balance. The withdraw: and deposit: actions correspond to the same functionality in the Model. Figure 7-9 shows the newly defined outlet and actions.

**Figure 7-7:**
Add a new object to the project.

**Figure 7-8:**
Name the
new class
Account
Controller.

**Figure 7-9:**
Add an out-
let and two
actions to
Account
Controller.

4. **Connect the interface by Control+dragging from the Withdraw button to the** AccountController **in the project window. Select** withdraw: **in the small black connections list overlay that appears.**

Figure 7-10 shows the connection being made.

5. **Connect the interface by Control+dragging from the Deposit button to the** AccountController **in the project window. Select** deposit: **in the small black connections list overlay that appears.**

Figure 7-11 shows the connection.

6. **Control+drag from the** AccountController **to the empty Label field in your interface. Select** display **in the small black connections list overlay that appears.**

Figure 7-12 shows the process.

**Figure 7-10:**
Connect the
Withdraw
button to the
withdraw:
action in the
Account
Controller.

**Figure 7-11:**
Connect
the Deposit
button to
the deposit:
action in the
Account
Controller.

**Figure 7-12:**
Connect the
Account
Controller to
the empty
Label field
and select
display from
the list of
choices.

7. **To create files for the Controller, select the** `AccountController` **in the project window and choose File⇨Write Class Files, save the file as AccountController, and click the Save button, as shown in Figure 7-13.**

**Figure 7-13:**
Write the files, saving as Account Controller.

8. **Click the Add button to add the files to the Xcode project (see Figure 7-14).**

9. **Quit Interface Builder by pressing ⌘+Q and return to Xcode.**

10. **In Xcode, click the AccountController.h file to view its contents and find the line that says:**

```
@interface AccountController : /* Specify a superclass
            (eg: NSObject or NSView) */ {
```

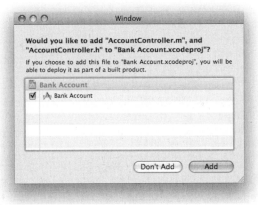

**Figure 7-14:**
Add Account Controller to the Bank Account project.

11. **Specify a superclass for the** `AccountController` **class by changing it to this:**

```
@interface AccountController : NSObject {
```

12. **Add an Account instance variable (**`account`**) to the interface file:**

```
@interface AccountController : NSObject {
  IBOutlet id display;
  Account *account;
}
- (IBAction)deposit:(id)sender;
- (IBAction)withdraw:(id)sender;
@end
```

13. **Open the AccountController.m file, where two actions are in place:**

```
#import "AccountController.h"

@implementation AccountController
- (IBAction)deposit:(id)sender {

}

- (IBAction)withdraw:(id)sender {

}
@end
```

14. **Implement the two actions by adding the code for deposit and withdraw. Also add an** `awakeFromNib` **and a** `dealloc` **method to the file.**

In `awakeFromNib`, you can create an `account` object and assign it to the Account instance variable (`account`). Then, update the display in the interface by setting its value to the account balance.

For this example, the deposit will always be $20 (or whatever denomination you wish), and the withdraw will always be $5.

```
#import "AccountController.h"

@implementation AccountController

-(void)awakeFromNib {
  account = [[Account alloc] init];
  [display setFloatValue:[account balance]];
}

- (IBAction)deposit:(id)sender {
  [account deposit:20.00f];
  [display setFloatValue:[account balance]];
}
```

```
- (IBAction)withdraw:(id)sender {
    [account withdraw:5.00f];
    [display setFloatValue:[account balance]];
}

-(void)dealloc {
    [account release];
    [super dealloc];
}

@end
```

15. **In Xcode, choose Run⇨Go to test your work.**

   Figure 7-15 shows the completed application.

**Figure 7-15:**
The com-
pleted Bank
Account
applica-
tion after
a couple
deposits.

When you run the application, the AccountController creates a new object based on the Account class and displays the current balance in the View, which the Account has initialized to 100. When you click the Deposit button, you send a deposit message to the account object and update the interface. Likewise, when you click the Withdraw button, the code sends a withdraw message to the account object and updates the interface.

Hopefully you're beginning to appreciate the merits of this sort of application design pattern. With the Model, View, and Controller all separated, you can reuse these classes in other projects. Suppose that you need to create a new application for tracking another kind of account. You wouldn't need to re-create an Account class. You could just use the existing Account class.

If at some point in the future, you must change your accounting model radi-cally, you can pull out the Account class and replace it with a new one. The rest of the code and interface could remain the same. All these benefits stem from using the Model-View-Controller design pattern.

# Chapter 8

# A Window with a View

*P*erhaps the most important element of any GUI-based application is the window. In fact, the window is so important that those guys from Redmond used it to name their operating system. The windows in an application are like pieces of paper that you use to collect ideas, display information, and record input.

Windows in Cocoa are equally important. Mac OS X continues using the fine window traditions that made the Mac OS famous, but Cocoa builds on and improves those ideas from the past with exciting new features. In this chapter, you examine some of the most common window features of Cocoa applications. In the process, you create two projects that demonstrate these features.

## Working with Windows

Because windows form the basis for nearly all interfaces, you'll use them often as part of your projects. Some of the most common functions that you'll perform include

✔ Opening and closing windows

✔ Moving windows

✔ Adding windows to the Windows menu

In the following sections, you discover how to accomplish all these tasks and more.

## Opening and closing a window

When you work with windows in your Cocoa projects, you'll often use Interface Builder to design them. Further, if you leave a window open in Interface Builder when you're designing an interface for an application, that window opens automatically when the application runs. Thus, if you're building a one-window application, you may not even have to issue a command to open a window.

Assume that `theWindow` is an outlet in your project. Closing the window in code is as simple as

```
[theWindow close];
```

The `close` method hides the window from view. If you want the window to also be released from memory when you close it, also use the `set ReleasedWhenClosed` method:

```
[theWindow setReleasedWhenClosed:YES];
[theWindow close];
```

When you close a window in this fashion, the window is gone. Its contents are gone from memory. It is no more. That means to see the window again, you have to create a new window object altogether. If the window has been released from memory, you have to create a new window like so:

```
theWindow = [[NSWindow alloc] init];
```

Then, to show the window, send it the `makeKeyAndOrderFront` message like this:

```
[theWindow makeKeyAndOrderFront:self];
```

## Hiding and showing a window

If you'd prefer to keep a window around instead of deleting it from memory, you can hide it instead of closing it. Hiding a window is also an easy task to perform. Suppose you have an outlet (named `theWindow`) as part of your object class. The outlet represents a window in your interface. To hide that window, a `hideWindow` action might look like this:

```
- (IBAction)hideWindow:(id)sender
{
```

```
        [theWindow orderOut:sender];
    }
```

The `orderOut` method of the `NSWindow` class hides a window from view.
The window still exists in memory; it just isn't visible anymore. To find
out whether a window is visible, you can check the return value of the
`isVisible` method:

```
- (IBAction)hideWindow:(id)sender
{
    if ([theWindow isVisible])
        [theWindow orderOut:sender];
}
```

To make the window reappear, use the `orderFront` method, but first check
to see if the window is already visible:

```
- (IBAction)showWindow:(id)sender
{
    if (![theWindow isVisible])
        [theWindow orderFront:sender];
}
```

If you want a specific window to appear on the screen and act as the main
window, thus intercepting keystrokes, use the `makeKeyAndOrderFront`
method. You might use this method in the `awakeFromNib` method to force a
main window to the foreground:

```
- (void)awakeFromNib {
    [theWindow makeKeyAndOrderFront:nil];
}
```

## Positioning windows

Positioning windows is another important task that you'll need to perform.
Before you go bossing around a window, you first need to find out its current
position on the screen. Use the `frame` method of the `NSWindow` class to discover the origin and size of a window. The `frame` method returns an `NSRect`
structure, which contains `NSPoint` and `NSSize` elements that describe the
window's origin and size, respectively:

```
typedef struct _NSRect {
    NSPoint origin;
    NSSize size;
} NSRect;
```

When you know the origin of a window, it's a trivial matter to reposition
it. First, define an origin to your liking and then call the `setFrameOrigin`

method to apply the new origin. This code moves a window 20 pixels to the right of its current position:

```
- (IBAction)moveRight:(id)sender
{
    NSRect theFrame = [theWindow frame];
    NSPoint theOrigin = theFrame.origin;
    theOrigin.x = theOrigin.x + 20;
    [theWindow setFrameOrigin:theOrigin];
}
```

To position a window in the middle of the screen, use the handy center method. This code centers a window on the screen:

```
- (IBAction)centerWindow:(id)sender
{
    [theWindow center];
}
```

## Keeping track of windows

Most Cocoa applications have a Window menu to help users keep track of open windows. Normally, this menu lists the open document windows. (You probably wouldn't display, say, a toolbar window in the Window menu.) The great thing about the Window menu is that Cocoa takes care of it for you automatically. If your window has the following properties, Cocoa automatically adds it to the Window menu:

  ✔ Has a title bar
  ✔ Is resizable
  ✔ Can become the main window

You can exclude a window from the Window menu by altering any one of these properties.

If you have a window that obeys each of these rules but you still want it left out of the Window menu, use the setExcludedFromWindowsMenu method. The awakeFromNib method is a good place to use this call because the method takes effect when your application launches and the window resources is loaded from the NIB file.

```
- (void)awakeFromNib {
    [theWindow setExcludedFromWindowsMenu:nil];
}
```

## Putting windows to work for you

To see how these window features work, do the following:

1. **Launch Xcode and create a new Cocoa application project:**

    a. *Double-click the Xcode icon in the Finder to launch it.*

    b. *Choose File⇨New Project.*

    c. *In the window that appears, select Cocoa Application and click OK.*

2. **Create a new window in the MainMenu.xib file.**

    a. *Double-click the MainMenu.xib file in the Resources Group of your project to open the file in Interface Builder.*

    b. *In the XIB project window, double-click to open the default window if it's not open already.*

    c. *Press ⌘+1 to open the Attributes window and name the window* MenuWindow.

3. **Add three buttons to** MenuWindow, **as shown in Figure 8-1, and label them Hide Window, Move Left, and Center Window, respectively.**

    For more information on adding buttons, see Chapter 2.

**Figure 8-1:**
The Menu Window has three buttons.

4. **Add an object to the project:**

    a. *Drag an Object item from the Library window to the project window.*

    b. *Name the object* MyWindowController.

5. **Double-click the new** MyWindowController **instance and add outlets and actions to the instance in the Inspector window.**

    a. *Add these outlets:* theMenuWindow, theShowButton, *and* theWindow.

    b. *Add these actions:* centerWindow, moveRight, *and* showWindow.

    For details on adding outlets and actions, see Chapter 2.

     c. *Connect the three new actions to the buttons in* MenuWindow *by Control-dragging from each button to the* MyWindowController *instance and then click Connect in the Inspector window to connect each action.*

     d. *Connect the two window-related outlets to their corresponding windows: Control-drag from the* MyWindowController *instance to each window in the MainMenu.xib file window and then click Connect in the Inspector window to connect to the appropriate outlet.*

     e. *Connect the* theShowButton *outlet to the top button in the* MenuWindow.

6. **Double-click the** MyWindowController **instance, choose Classes⇨Create Files for MyWindowController, and add the header and implementation files for the instance.**

7. **Return to Xcode and add this code to the MyWindowController.m file to implement the functionality of the three buttons:**

```
#import "MyWindowController.h"

@implementation MyWindowController

- (IBAction)centerWindow:(id)sender
{
    [theWindow center];
}


- (IBAction)moveRight:(id)sender
{
    NSRect theFrame = [theWindow frame];
    NSPoint theOrigin = theFrame.origin;
    theOrigin.x = theOrigin.x + 20;
    [theWindow setFrameOrigin:theOrigin];
}


- (IBAction)showWindow:(id)sender
{
    if ([theWindow isVisible])
        {
            [theWindow orderOut:sender];
            [theShowButton setTitle:@"Show Window"];
        }
    else
        {
            [theWindow orderFront:sender];
            [theShowButton setTitle:@"Hide Window"];
        }
}
```

```
- (void)awakeFromNib {
    [theWindow makeKeyAndOrderFront:nil];
    [theMenuWindow makeKeyAndOrderFront:nil];
}

@end
```

8. **Choose Build⇨Build and Go to test the project.**

# Changing the Appearance of Windows

Beauty may be only skin deep, but when it comes to using your application, an attractive interface is mandatory. In this section, you explore some of the possible window settings for nice-looking interfaces. These features also enhance the functionality of your applications, so you have some brawn to go with that beauty.

## Using different windows for different tasks

The standard Mac window style has a gray background, as shown in Figure 8-2. However, this isn't the only appearance a window can have. Apple has strict guidelines about how windows should look, which are outlined in the famous Human Interface Guidelines document available online at developer.apple.com. The basic gist of the Apple guidelines is that windows should look the same for the same tasks. A document window looks one way. A toolbar window looks a different way. A window in a one-window application should look yet another way. Always follow Apple's guidelines when designing interface windows because your users expect windows to look and behave identically across applications.

Open the default XIB file from a Cocoa application in Interface Builder. You can change the appearance of a window by following these steps:

1. **Open the default window in Interface Builder.**

   Double-click it in the XIB project window.

2. **Press ⌘+1 to open the Inspector window.**

   In the Attributes section of the Inspector window, you find the Textured check box for the window.

**Figure 8-2:**
A standard
Mac
window is
light gray.

3. **Toggle the Textured check box to change the appearance of the
   window.**

   If the Inspector doesn't display the textured attribute, click the window's
   toolbar to display the Inspector appropriate to the window.

   The window now has a textured appearance (see Figure 8-3).

**Figure 8-3:**
The textured
appear-
ance gives
windows a
metallic look
by drawing
a gradient
in the
background.

In addition to the new look, the textured property also changes the behavior of windows that have the property set. Whereas a non-textured window permits dragging from its title bar, you can drag textured windows by clicking and dragging anywhere in the window that isn't within the bounds of a control.

The first time you see the cool metallic look of the textured window, you'll be tempted to make the windows in every application with this style. After all, Apple does with many of its applications (such as iTunes and iPhoto).

Before you start giving every window in sight a textured look, keep in mind that the Apple guidelines recommend that you use a textured window only when hardware is involved. This explains why you see it in many Apple applications, such as iMovie and iPhoto, which use hardware in one way or another. Although textured windows look tempting, try to use them only when necessary. Your users will thank you.

## Sizing up your windows

When you want to know the size of a window in code, use the `frame` method in the same way that you did earlier in this chapter. It gives you access to the window's position and size. To alter the size of a window in code, use the `setFrame` method. You can use the following code to resize a window to half its current width:

```
- (IBAction)halfAsWide:(id)sender
{
    NSRect theFrame = [theWindow frame];
    theFrame.size.width = theFrame.size.width/2;
    [theWindow setFrame:theFrame display:YES];
}
```

If you want to zoom a window without forcing the user to click the zoom button on that window, all you have to do is call the window's `zoom` method.

```
[theWindow zoom];
```

## Setting a window's title

Sometimes you'll want to change the title that appears in the title bar of a window. This is an easy task to perform with the `setTitle` method:

```
[theWindow setTitle:@"My New Window Title"];
```

Of course, you can also set the title of the window in the Inspector window of Interface Builder.

If the window title is the name of a document, use the `setTitleWith RepresentedFilename` method instead of `setTitle`. This method converts from a file path to a window title suitable for viewing:

```
[theWindow setTitleWithRepresentedFilename:theFileName];
```

## *Windows that you can see through*

Cocoa windows have an alpha setting that enables you to set the translucency of a window. To see this magic in action, use the `setAlpha` method of `NSWindow`, passing it a value between 0.0 and 1.0. A value of 1.0 means that a window is fully visible; a value of 0.0 displays a window that's completely transparent. This line of code makes a window 50-percent transparent:

```
[theWindow setAlphaValue:0.5];
```

Figure 8-4 shows the difference between a window with `setAlpha` values of 0.5 and 1.0.

**Figure 8-4:**
Use the setAlpha method to make windows transparent.

# *Beneath the Sheets*

Besides the run-of-the-mill windows that you've used so far, Cocoa offers a special animated window — a *sheet.* A sheet is sort of a parasitic window, in that it needs a host, or a *parent,* from which to spring. Because its functionality is directly connected to another window, it appears from out of the blue at the top of its parent window, as shown in Figure 8-5. You're probably already familiar with sheets because many common applications use them — often when working with files.

Besides looking neat when they open, sheets also serve a useful purpose. Because they're attached to a parent window, they indicate a specific scope for a task: that of the parent window. In other words, if a sheet appears, you can be certain that any actions you perform in that sheet are pertinent to the parent window when the sheet closes. This is a subtle, but important, distinction.

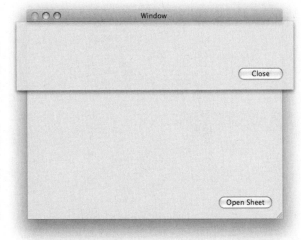

**Figure 8-5:**
When the functional-
ity of your
window is
directly tied
to another
window,
display it as
a sheet.

A sheet behaves in a particular manner — modally; it takes over a window and doesn't let the user perform any other action in the parent window until you dismiss it. Usually the user has to make some kind of decision before the sheet can be dismissed.

Implementing sheets takes some special preparation. To see how they work, launch Xcode and create a new Cocoa application. In the project window, double-click MainMenu.xib to open the interface in Interface Builder and then perform the following steps to add a sheet to your project:

1. **Drag a panel from the Library (as shown in Figure 8-6) to your MainMenu.xib file window.**

2. **Change the panel settings.**

   Open the Inspector window by choosing Tools⇨Inspector and deselect all the Style and Controls settings for the new panel, as shown in Figure 8-7. Also change the new Panel's title to Sheet.

3. **Open the default window in the project (named `Window`) and add a push button to the window; then, open the new panel from Step 1 and add a push button to it too.**

   At runtime, the button in the default window causes the panel to open as a sheet. The button in the sheet causes the sheet to close. Figure 8-8 shows the buttons as they appear in their respective windows.

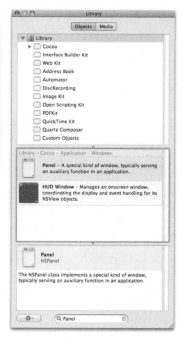

**Figure 8-6:**
Add a Panel
to your
project.

**Figure 8-7:**
Adjust the
attributes of
the panel.

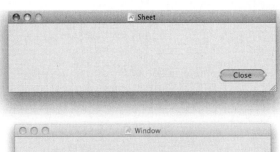

**Figure 8-8:**
Add one
button to
the project's
default
window and
one to the
sheet.

**4. Add a new object to the project.**

Drag an object class from the Library to the XIB window (as shown in Figure 8-9) and name it `MySheetController`. If you have problems locating the object class in the Library, search for it via the search field at the bottom of the Library window.

**5. Add outlets and actions to the object.**

Press ⌘+6 to open the Identity Inspector and add two outlets `MySheet Controller` class to the Class Outlets section of the Identity Inspector. To follow along with the example, name the two outlets `theWindow` and `theSheet`, respectively. Likewise, add two actions to the `MySheet Controller` class and rename the actions as `openSheet` and `close Sheet`. Figure 8-10 demonstrates what the Inspector window looks like.

**6. Connect the outlets and actions:**

a. *Control-drag from the* `MySheetController` *instance to the main window and connect it to the* `theWindow` *outlet.*

b. *Control-drag from the* `MySheetController` *instance to the panel in MainMenu.xib and connect it to the* `theSheet` *outlet.*

c. *Control-drag from the button in the main window to the* `MySheet Controller` *instance and connect it to the* `openSheet` *action.*

d. *Control-drag from the button in the Sheet panel to the* `MySheet Controller` *instance and connect it to the* `closeSheet` *action.*

**Figure 8-9:**
Drag an object from the Library to the project window.

**Figure 8-10:**
Add outlets
and actions
to the
controller.

**7. Create the class files.**

*a. Click* MySheetController *in the project window, choose Classes⇨ Write Files, and save as* MySheetController.

*b. Make sure that the Create '.h' file check box is selected, as shown in Figure 8-11.*

*c. Click the Save button.*

**Figure 8-11:**
Writing
class files.

**8. Add the new files to the Xcode project.**

When you write the files for MySheetController, Interface Builder asks whether you want to add the files to the current Xcode project (see

Figure 8-12). Toggle the check box for the desired project and click the Add button.

9. **Exit Interface Builder and return to Xcode where you find the new files.**

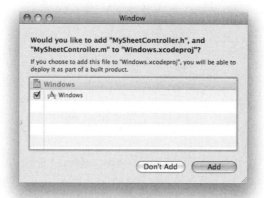

**Figure 8-12:**
Add the new
class files to
the Xcode
project.

10. **Tweak the header.**

Change the interface definition by adding NSObject in the MySheet Controller.h file like this (the changed line is shown in boldface):

```
#import <Cocoa/Cocoa.h>

@interface MySheetController : NSObject {
    IBOutlet id theSheet;
    IBOutlet id theWindow;
}
- (IBAction)closeSheet:(id)sender;
- (IBAction)openSheet:(id)sender;
@end
```

11. **Change the MySheetController.m file.**

The file looks like this (changed lines are shown in boldface):

```
#import "MySheetController.h"

@implementation MySheetController

- (IBAction)closeSheet:(id)sender
{
    [theSheet orderOut:nil];
    [NSApp endSheet:theSheet];
}

- (IBAction)openSheet:(id)sender
```

```
{

    [NSApp beginSheet:theSheet
    modalForWindow:theWindow
    modalDelegate:self
    didEndSelector:NULL
    contextInfo:nil];

}

@end
```

The `openSheet` method displays the sheet with the `beginSheet` class method of `NSApp`. The `closeSheet` method hides the sheet with the `orderOut` method and disposes of the sheet with `endSheet`.

**12. Choose Build⊏⟩Build and Go to see the project in action.**

This sheet demonstration is purposely simple, so you can see how to display a sheet in your own projects. You can enhance the sheet by adding controls to the sheet and wiring them to outlets and actions depending on the desired effect.

# Responding to Window Events by Delegating Authority

Cocoa has an interesting construct — *delegates* — which lets a class take over the task of handling certain events for you. Much like you might delegate authority to another person in the workplace, you can delegate the authority of a class to handle things when a particular event(s) occurs.

For example, you can tell a class to be a delegate for window events like *miniaturizing* (also known as *minimizing*). Therefore, every time a window miniaturizes, your delegate class would do something in response.

Open MainMenu.xib in Interface Builder and perform these steps to see how delegates work:

**1. Assign delegate status to** `MySheetController`**:**

*a. Control-drag from* `Window` *to* `MySheetController` *in the project window.*

When you let go of the mouse, a black connections list overlay appears listing options (see Figure 8-13).

*b. Select Delegate from the list.*

Delegate status is assigned to the `MySheetController` class.

2. **Close Interface Builder and return to Xcode.**

3. **Add the following delegate method to the MySheetController.m file:**

```
- (void)windowDidMiniaturize:(NSNotification *)
        notification {
    NSBeep();
}
```

4. **Choose Build➪Build and Go to test the code changes.**

The `windowDidMiniaturize` method is a special delegate method that Apple has predefined for you. You can see what delegates are available by searching for a specific class in the built-in Help. For example, search for `NSWindow` to see the delegates that respond to window events.

In the previous example, the application plays a system beep whenever the user miniaturizes the window. If you prefer to do something just before the window miniaturizes instead, here's a delegate method for that:

```
- (void)windowWillMiniaturize:(NSNotification *)
        notification {
    NSBeep();
}
```

Many of the built-in classes have delegate methods like this that you can use. `NSWindow` has more than 24.

**Figure 8-13:**
Make
MySheet
Controller a
delegate.

# Chapter 9

# Working with Interface Controls

*T*he Mac OS has long been renowned for its graphical user interface, which probably stems from the fact that people like interacting with computers by using metaphors that relate to the real world. Interface Builder is your tool for creating these metaphors. With it, you build your interface by adding different elements that your users will use to control the application. Because they're controlling the application, Cocoa calls these elements *controls*.

Cocoa has a rich set of interface controls for you to use in your own applications. With drag-and-drop and a few lines of code, you can add a variety of useful controls to your projects. This chapter guides you through the basics of interface controls in Interface Builder. You'll see how to use each of these controls by adding them to small projects.

By the end of the chapter, you'll have enough experience with controls to strike out on your own. The Cocoa framework is a vast one, and nothing prepares you better for programming than practice and experimentation.

## Button Controls

Perhaps the most ubiquitous interface control is the button. From the bank's automatic teller machine to the doorbell at your front door, buttons are a nearly universal piece of hardware. Even your mouse and keyboard have button interfaces. Because so many people recognize buttons and know how to use them in the real world, it makes sense that they're popular in the virtual world as well.

Cocoa provides many kinds of useful and attractive buttons for your interfaces. All buttons in Cocoa are the NSButton type. Most NSButton controls look and act the way you'd expect, but some may alter your notion of what constitutes a button.

This section looks at the different types of buttons available to you in Cocoa. To begin working with buttons, follow these steps:

1. **Launch Project Builder and create a new Cocoa application.**

2. **Double-click the MainMenu.xib file to open it in Interface Builder.**

3. **Open the window found in the NIB file window.**

4. **Choose Tools⇨Library and enter** Button **in the Library's search field to find all the** NSButton **controls in Interface Builder.**

   Figure 9-1 shows the Library with the various buttons listed.

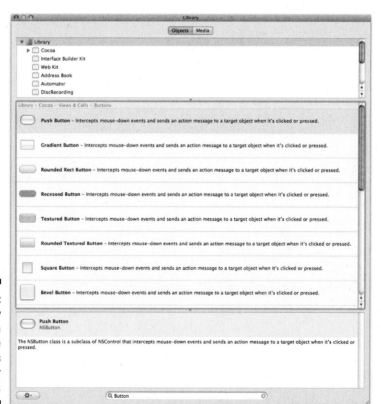

**Figure 9-1:**
The Library provides a multitude of buttons for your interfaces.

Although each button in Figure 9-1 looks and behaves differently, they're all examples of the NSButton class. This means you could drag a push button to your interface, for example, and later convert it to a square button. You'll see how the buttons differ through the remainder of this section.

## Push button

Perhaps the most recognizable form of NSButton, the push button is a staple of nearly all applications. The push button works simply: A user clicks the button, and your program does something in response. Probably the most common buttons are the OK and Cancel buttons, but you can also use buttons to perform almost any task. To add a push button to your interface, simply drag it from the Library to a window in your project. A default push button has a centered text label, as shown in Figure 9-2. You can change the text in a button by double-clicking it or by altering the Title entry in the Inspector window (also shown in Figure 9-2). (The Inspector window changes its title based on context, so its title is now Button Attributes.)

**Figure 9-2:**
Push buttons typically display only a text label.

Besides the `Title` property, `NSButton` controls have many properties that you can customize. One that you'll use frequently is Key Equiv (see Figure 9-3). Click in this box and enter a keystroke that acts as if the user clicked the button with the mouse. The symbol representing that key then appears in the Key Equiv. field. One common keyboard equivalent is Return, which means a user can trigger the push button by pressing Return (or Enter) on the keyboard. When you set it to respond to the Return key, ⤶ appears in the Key Equiv. box, and the button automatically takes on a pulsating colorized appearance at runtime (but not when you're designing in Interface Builder). The color of the button will be aqua or graphite, depending on which appearance setting the user selected in System Preferences. This colorized appearance suggests to users that this button performs the default action for the window in which it appears. For example, when a window has OK and Cancel buttons, OK is often the default button. This offers a hint to users that OK is probably the button that they want to click.

In addition to appearance, an `NSButton` can play a sound when clicked. Follow these steps to make your button play a sound when it's clicked:

1. **Find a sound to play.**

   Click the Media tab at the top of the Library window. You find all the familiar system sounds that you can use. You can also drag your favorite audio files into the Xcode project window (yes, Xcode, not Interface Builder), and then those sounds appear in the Media section of the Library window.

**Figure 9-3:**
Set the
Key Equiv
property to
Return to
make the
button
pulsate.

2. **In your application's interface window in Interface Builder, click the `NSButton` that you want to alter and open the Inspector window. In the Sound field, type the name of the sound file that you want to play or select it from the drop-down list.**

Alternatively, you can drag sound files from the Media tab of the Library window directly on top of the push button that you want to play the sound. The sound filename appears automatically in the Sound field of the Inspector window as if you typed it by hand.

Figure 9-4 shows a button that plays the frog system sound.

3. **Press ⌘+R in Interface Builder to test your work.**

A frog sound plays when you press ⌘+R.

**Figure 9-4:**
Type the name of a sound file in the Sound field. (Ribbit.)

# Round button

A close relative to the push button is the round button. As its name implies, the *round button* has a circular shape, and that's the main difference between a round button and a push button. In addition to text, a round button can display icons. For example, one common use for a round button is as an arrow button.

To set the icon displayed on a button, perform the following steps:

1. **Drag a round button from the Library to the main window of your interface.**

2. **Select an image to use as the button's icon from the Image drop-down list in the Button Attributes window.**

   Interface Builder provides you with many different default system icons that you can use. For example, Figure 9-5 shows the NSRefreshTemplate image name. *Note:* The vertical alignment of the button doesn't look so great. Step 3 fixes this.

   Conversely, you could add an image file to your project window in Xcode (again, *Xcode,* not Interface Builder). The new image automatically appears in the list of choices in Interface Builder.

**Figure 9-5:**
To assign an image to a button, select it in the Image drop-down list.

3. **Set the alignment of the button image.**

   In the Inspector window, click the second button in the Position button. The image on the button now centers vertically, as shown in Figure 9-6. The other elements of the segmented Position button vary the manner in which the button image is aligned in relation to text on the button. The segments display an icon to give you a visual indicator of how that segment aligns the button image.

**Figure 9-6:**
The button's image is centered vertically now.

# Check box

So far, you've looked at buttons that users click to perform an action. Not all buttons have to trigger an action, though. The check box button, for example, can behave more passively. Rather than firing some action, a check box button might simply indicate a binary state, such as toggling a feature on and off or for answering a Yes/No question. A check box can act like a button, however, in that it's also capable of triggering an action just like a push button. Figure 9-7 shows a check box control.

You can add a check box to your interface by dragging one from the Library window in Interface Builder. In the Inspector window, you can set the default state of the check box as well as its title and other cosmetic features.

When using check box controls, your code typically checks the state of the control and performs an appropriate operation. To demonstrate, this snippet of code checks the state of a check box control outlet, `prefsCheckbox`, and acts accordingly:

```
if ([prefsCheckbox state])
  // Save Preferences
else
  // Don't Save Preferences
```

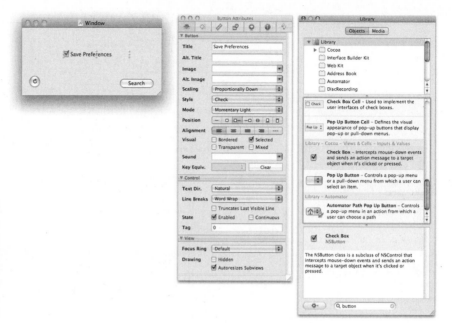

**Figure 9-7:**
A check
box button
shows the
state of a
setting.

# *Square and rounded bevel buttons*

Bevel buttons are another style of button available to you. They come in two
varieties: square and rounded. Besides the beveled appearance, they differ
from standard push buttons and round buttons in that they often are used to
display both text and icons. Further, they can perform other functions that a
push button can't.

To add a bevel button to your application, search for `Bevel Button` in the
Library window of Interface Builder and then drag one to your interface.

You can use a bevel button like a standard button to trigger an action
when a user clicks it. Beyond this simple button behavior, bevel buttons
can also mimic other controls. Like the check box, a bevel button can indicate state by displaying a depressed look. Bevel buttons can also act like a
menu by displaying a selection from a list of choices. Figure 9-8 shows the
square and rounded bevel buttons with the pre-supplied NSEveryone and
NSFolderBurnable images assigned to each button respectively.

**Figure 9-8:**
Bevel
buttons can
display text
and icons.

# Radio Control

The *radio control* is a specialized form of the button that gives a user multiple options. When the user chooses one of these options, the other radio buttons become deselected. Because you typically use more than one radio button at a time, it is customary to use an NSMatrix of radio buttons instead of several individual buttons set to the radio style. An NSMatrix is a collection of cells. A radio button resides in each cell in the NSMatrix.

Follow these steps to add radio buttons to your interface:

1. **Drag the Radio Group control from the Library window.**

   Interface Builder adds a *matrix* (or group) of radio buttons to your window.

   Figure 9-9 shows the NSMatrix that appears in your window when you drag a radio button control from the Library window.

2. **Double-click the cell and edit the Title text.**

   The Title text becomes editable until you click elsewhere in the interface or press Return.

   You can also change the Title of an NSMatrix element by using the Inspector window.

**Figure 9-9:**
Radio but-
tons usually
appear as
part of an
NSMatrix.

3. **Click the** NSMatrix **in your interface and add more radio controls to the** NSMatrix. **Open the Matrix Attributes Inspector window by choosing Tools⇨Inspector and change the Rows field of the Cells section, as shown in Figure 9-10.**

Figure 9-10 shows an NSMatrix with three rows that have edited titles.

**Figure 9-10:**
Add rows to
an NSMatrix
in the
Matrix
Attributes
Inspector
window for
that control.

4. **Connect the** NSMatrix **to an outlet of a Controller class by Control+dragging from the controller to the** NSMatrix **control.**

When connecting an outlet to an NSMatrix, make sure that you Control+drag from the Controller class to the entire matrix, not to an element of the matrix. If one element becomes highlighted when you Control+drag from the controller to the NSMatrix, move the cursor around until a dark outline appears around the entire NSMatrix (see Figure 9-11).

**Figure 9-11:**
When you connect an outlet to an NSMatrix, make certain to attach it to the entire control, not just one of its elements.

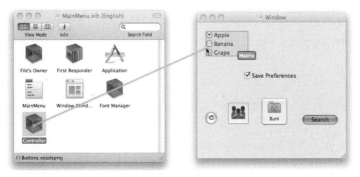

After you have an outlet to the NSMatrix, you can find out which element the user selected in code by using the selectedRow method of NSMatrix. The selectedRow method returns an integer indicating the index of the currently selected row. Row numbers start from the top, with the first row having an index of 0. To illustrate, here's a sample action that checks the selectedRow of colorRadios. Based on the index, it displays a message in the console telling you which color was chosen:

```
- (IBAction)doSomething:(id)sender
{

    switch ([colorRadios selectedRow])
    {
        case 0:
            NSLog(@"User chose red.");
                break;
        case 1:
            NSLog(@"User chose green.");
            break;
        case 2:
            NSLog(@"User chose blue.");
            break;
    };

}
```

# Slider Control

*Sliders* are the controls you use to represent a range of values. The control gives users an opportunity to select a value in that range by moving (or sliding) the knob of the slider control. NSSlider is the class behind the slider functions in Cocoa. Again, the NSSlider control appears in the Library window, as shown in Figure 9-12.

Sliders come in a variety of styles. They can span horizontally or vertically or even in a circular fashion. They can also display tick marks. Figure 9-13 illustrates the different combinations of styles that sliders can have.

Sliders have two modes of operation: continuous and not continuous. When you check the Continuous property of an NSSlider in the Inspector window, that slider fires its action any time the user moves it. Conversely, when you deselect the Continuous property, the slider triggers its action when, and only when, the user lets up on the mouse.

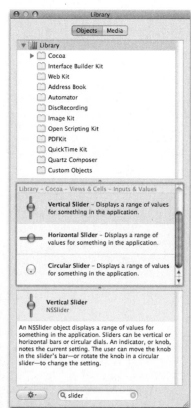

**Figure 9-12:** The sliders are located in the Library window.

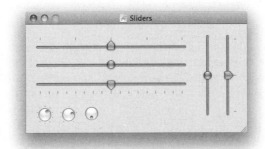

Because sliders represent a range of values, they have minimum and maximum values. They also have a current value, which represents the position of the slider button in the range of minimum and maximum values. You can set these values in the Inspector window.

If you want to find out what the current value of the slider is in code, do something like this:

```
float x = [theSlider floatValue];
```

You can also set the current position of the slider by using the setFloat Value method:

```
[theSlider setFloatValue:3.14];
```

You aren't restricted to the setFloatValue method, however. Because NSSlider inherits from NSControl, among other classes, you can use the methods of NSControl to work with the slider. The setFloatValue method is just one method of NSControl. There are others, which you can view in the built-in documentation. For example, if you don't care about slider values that contain decimal points, you can use the setIntValue method of the NSControl:

```
[theSlider setIntValue:5];
```

# Tab Views

If you need to reduce clutter or if space is at a premium, tab views are for you. The NSTabView is the class in the Application Kit that provides you with tab views for your interface. A *tab view*, as its name implies, is a view consisting of multiple tabs that when clicked display a particular pane of the view. Figure 9-14 shows a tab view with four tabs. Each pane can hold any number of other controls. When a user clicks a tab, the controls from all other tabs disappear and the controls for the selected tab come into view.

**Figure 9-14:**
The tab view controls help organize many controls into a reduced space.

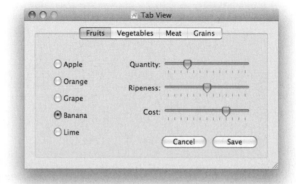

To use a tab view, follow these steps:

1. **Drag a tab view control from the Library window to your interface.**

2. **Click once on the tab view and change the number in the Tabs field in the Tab View Attributes Inspector window to add tabs to the tab view, as shown in Figure 9-15.**

**Figure 9-15:**
Add tabs to a tab view with the Tabs field.

3. **Change the label at the top of each tab by clicking the tab's text once and change the Label field in the Tab View Item Attributes Inspector window, as shown in Figure 9-16.**

4. **Add the controls to each tab.**

   Select a tab and then drag the desired controls to that tab. Repeat for the other tabs until you've populated the tab view.

**Figure 9-16:** Change the Label field to alter the text that appears at the top of each tab.

When the application is running, you may want to know which tab a user selected. An `NSTabView` control can have any number of tabs, which are instances of the `NSTabViewItem` class. Each `TabViewItem` in a `TabView` has a corresponding index, beginning with 0 (zero). To find out which tab index a user selected, you must first figure out which `NSTabViewItem` is selected. Then you pass that `TabViewItem` to the `indexOfTabViewItem` to get the index of the tab.

```
NSInteger selectedTabViewItem;
selectedTabViewItem = [theTabView
        indexOfTabViewItem:[theTabView
        selectedTabViewItem]];
NSLog(@"selectedTabViewItem = %d", selectedTabViewItem);
```

In this snippet, `NSLog` sends text output to the console. To view the Xcode's Debugger Console, choose Run➪Console. Figure 9-17 shows the open Console window.

**Figure 9-17:**
Use the
console
to display
text when
debugging.

# Making Progress at the Bar

Anyone who has ever used a computer knows that some functions —
such as creating a large movie in iMovie or ripping a bunch of MP3 files in
iTunes — require a long time to process. As lengthy operations proceed,
the thoughtful programmer displays some sort of feedback to let the user
know that the computer is working on something. To do this in Cocoa, use
the NSIndicator control. To add an NSIndicator control to your project,
search for Indicator in the Library window of Interface Builder and then
drag one to your interface.

NSIndicator can display two kinds of progress bars:

- **Indeterminate:** Display an indeterminate progress indicator when you
  don't know how long the process will take, such as when you're searching
  for files on a hard drive. The indeterminate progress indicator has two different looks — one variety looks like a barber pole and the other spins.

- **Determinate:** Use determinate progress indicators when you know how
  long a process takes to complete, such as when you repeat a task ten times.

The window in Figure 9-18 displays each type of NSIndicator.

**Figure 9-18:**
The inde-
terminate
NSIndicator
looks like a
barber pole
or spin in a
circle. The
determinate
NSIndicator
shows the
progress of
an opera-
tion, step
by step.

Indeterminate progress     Indeterminate progress

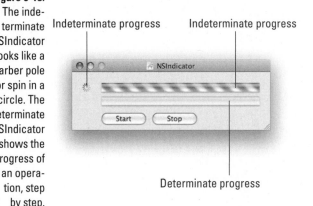

Determinate progress

To use the indeterminate NSIndicator control, call the startAnimation method. This causes the barber pole to move. The following example calls the startAnimation method using an indeterminateProgress outlet from within an action:

```
- (IBAction)startIndeterminateProgress:(id)sender {
    [theIndeterminateProgress startAnimation:sender];
}
```

When you've finished processing whatever you need to process, you can stop the animation by using the stopAnimation method:

```
- (IBAction)stopIndeterminateProgress:(id)sender {
    [theIndeterminateProgress stopAnimation:sender];
}
```

With a determinate NSIndicator, you set the value of the control with the setDoubleValue method. This code snippet sets the indicator to the middle position, assuming that the control has a minimum and maximum of 0 to 100, respectively:

```
[theDeterminateProgress setMinValue: 0.0];
[theDeterminateProgress setMaxValue: 100.0];
[theDeterminateProgress setDoubleValue: 50.0];
```

# Table Control

One of the most versatile controls that you can add to your applications is the table control. Unfortunately, it's also one of the trickiest to use. With an `NSTableView`, you can display a table or list of data with all sorts of display options. You'll find the `NSTableView` control in the Library window, as shown in Figure 9-19.

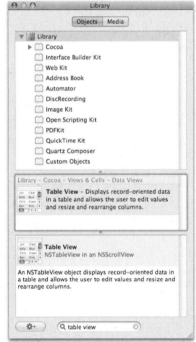

**Figure 9-19:**
The NS TableView control can display information in tabular form.

To begin using an `NSTableView` in a Cocoa project, follow these steps:

1. **Launch Xcode, choose File⇨New Project to create a new project, and name the project** `SimpleTable`.

2. **Double-click the MainMenu.xib file to open it in Interface Builder and drag an** `NSTableView` **control from the Library window to the default window of your interface.**

**3. Assign the first column identifier.**

Double-click the white space below the text at the top of the first column to select the first column. Set its identifier to `launchedApplications.NSApplicationName`, as shown in Figure 9-20.

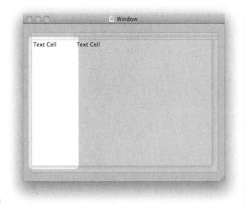

**Figure 9-20:**
Assign an
identifier
to the first
column.

The reason you're doing this is because `NSWorkSpace` has defined keys for elements in the `launchedApplications` dictionary. This key represents the name of an application. Using keys like this one can greatly simplify your code.

**4. Assign the second column identifier.**

Double-click the `NSTableView` twice until you've selected its second column. Set its identifier to `launchedApplications.NSApplicationPath`, as shown in Figure 9-21.

**5. Add a controller:**

   a. *Drag a new Object control from the Library window to the XIB project window.*

   b. *Name the new object `MyDataController`.*

   c. *To this new object, add an outlet named `tableView`, as shown in Figure 9-22.*

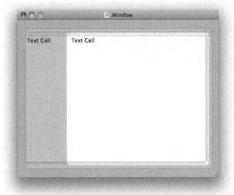

**Figure 9-21:**
Assign an
identifier to
the second
column.

**Figure 9-22:**
Add an
outlet to the
Controller
class.

6. **Connect the controller.**

   Control+drag from the MyDataController class to the center of the
   NSTableView in your interface, and then select tableView from the
   list of choices in the black connections list overlay that appears.

   Be sure to drag to the center of the control. The NSTableView lies
   within another control called the NSScrollView. As you slowly
   Control+drag to the center of the control, you see the focus ring highlight the outer NSScrollView first and then the NSTableView, which
   is what you want.

7. **Connect the data source.**

   Control+drag from the NSTableView to the MyController class.
   Select the dataSource outlet from the black connections list overlay
   that appears. A TableView control must have a data source class that
   feeds it data.

8. **Select** MyDataController **in the Interface Builder project window
   and choose File➪Write Class Files to create the class files for**
   MyDataController.

9. **Click Save in the Save dialog that appears and add the class to the
   current Xcode project in the dialog that appears after that.**

10. **Return to Xcode and select the MyDataController.h file.**

11. **Replace the code in MyDataController.h with the following:**

    ```
    #import <Cocoa/Cocoa.h>

    @interface MyDataController : NSObject
    {
        IBOutlet id tableView;
        NSArray *_launchedApps;
        NSWorkspace *_workSpace;
    }
    @end
    ```

    The code begins by declaring the tableView outlet and a pointer to an
    *_launchedApps array. The array holds the names of all currently run-
    ning applications. The *_workSpace variable assists you in retrieving
    the application names and paths later.

12. **Select the MyDataController.m file and add the following code to it:**

    ```
    #import "MyDataController.h"

    @implementation MyDataController
    ```

```
- (void)awakeFromNib {
    _workSpace = [NSWorkspace sharedWorkspace];
    _launchedApps = [_workSpace launchedApplications];
    [tableView reloadData];
}

- (int)numberOfRowsInTableView:(NSTableView *)
        tableView {
    return [_launchedApps count];
}

- (id)tableView:(NSTableView *)tableView
objectValueForTableColumn:(NSTableColumn *)tableColumn
        row:(int)row {
    return [[[_workSpace valueForKeyPath:[tableColumn
        identifier]] objectAtIndex:row];
}

- (void)dealloc {
        [super dealloc];
}

@end
```

Here's what the code does:

- ✔ The `awakeFromNib` method starts the source code off by populating the `_launchedApps` array. It does this using an `NSWorkspace` object to find the names of the currently running applications.

- ✔ Next comes the `numberOfRowsInTableView` method. Because the number of rows in the table matches the number of elements in the `_launchedApps` array, you return the size of the array.

- ✔ The `objectValueForTableColumn` method takes care of returning the data to the `NSTableView`. To distinguish between the two columns, this method passes the `valueForKeyPath` method the identifier of the requested column. Because `_launchedApps` is really an array of dictionary objects, you need to extract the information from the dictionary if you want something suitable for display. The first column displays the name of the running application, and the second column displays its path.

Without adding any other code, this table would display the running applications on your computer. The background of the table is white with black text.

To spruce up the interface a little bit, you can colorize the background of the rows in the table. Return to Interface Builder and select the `NSTableView` in the interface. Select the Alternating Rows check box, as shown in Figure 9-23.

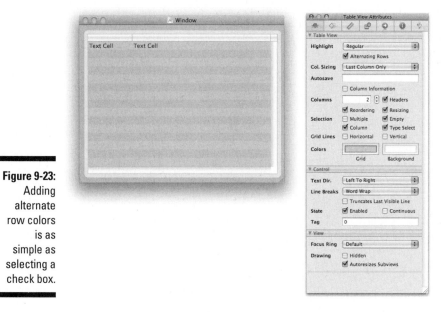

**Figure 9-23:**
Adding
alternate
row colors
is as
simple as
selecting a
check box.

Figure 9-24 shows what the table view looks like at runtime. The names of the running applications vary depending on which computer you're using and which applications are running at the time you launch this app.

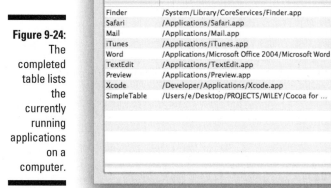

**Figure 9-24:**
The
completed
table lists
the
currently
running
applications
on a
computer.

# Chapter 10

# Cocoa Data Types

• • • • • • • • • • • • • • • • • • • • • • • • • • • • • • • • • • • • • • • • • • •

• • • • • • • • • • • • • • • • • • • • • • • • • • • • • • • • • • • • • • • • • • •

*O*ne of the main tasks that computers do well is manipulate data. Whether you need to calculate the national debt or keep track of the telephone numbers of the players in your poker club, computer programs can ease the task of handling information. Cocoa improves upon the various ways that you work with data in C.

This chapter takes you on a tour of some data types unique to Cocoa. The Foundation Framework defines these data types. You can continue to use the data types that you know from C, but after you see what Cocoa has to offer, you just might stop thinking about those old C types altogether.

# Working with Numbers

When you program in Objective-C, you can use all the usual standard C numerical data types for making calculations. If you want to use these values with Cocoa's array objects, however, you're left out in the cold. For this reason, Cocoa offers you the `NSNumber` class. One of its great uses is to wrap numbers in a Cocoa object, for use with other objects, such as `NSArray`. The `NSArray` class is an array class that comes with the Foundation Kit. You hear more about it later in this chapter.

To create an `NSNumber` object based on an integer value of 42, use code like this:

```
NSNumber *n = [NSNumber numberWithInt:42];
```

Here are methods for creating NSNumbers based on a variety of numerical types:

- ✔ numberWithDouble
- ✔ numberWithFloat
- ✔ numberWithInt
- ✔ numberWithLong
- ✔ numberWithUnsignedShort

To retrieve values from an NSNumber, use one of the many NSNumber accessor methods. Some of these include

- ✔ doubleValue
- ✔ floatValue
- ✔ intValue
- ✔ longValue
- ✔ unsignedShort

If you want to compare the values of two NSNumber instances, use the isEqualToNumber method. Because an NSNumber is an object, you can't opt for the brevity in C of "if (num1==num2)". This example shows how to compare two NSNumbers named num1 and num2:

```
if ([num1 isEqualToNumber:num2])
  NSLog(@"Numbers are equal");
else
 NSLog(@"Numbers are not equal");
```

# Working with Arrays

One of the most common programming tasks that you'll encounter is working with a list of data. To pull off this task, Cocoa programmers use NSArray and NSMutableArray, which are storage units for a list of data. You use arrays when you need to keep track of a list of information, such as the titles of books in your bookcase, the people in your family, or the number of windows that are open currently. What makes Cocoa arrays unique is the fact that, unlike traditional C arrays, they can store references to objects.

# NSArray

The NSArray class is handy for storing a group of objects in one place.

To demonstrate, here's one way you might create and populate an array with NSString objects:

```
NSArray *theArray;
NSString *name1;
NSString *name2;
NSString *name3;
NSString *name4;

//assign values to the four names
name1 = @"Maria";
name2 = @"Mercedes";
name3 = @"Leopold";
name4 = @"Frederick";

//create and populate the array
theArray = [NSArray arrayWithObjects:name1, name2,
        name3, name4, nil];
```

Note the arrayWithObjects method lets you create an NSArray by listing the objects in that array. The last object must always be nil to indicate the end of the array.

If you want to find out how many items were in that array, use the count method:

```
int i = [theArray count];
```

You can then use the size of the array to retrieve the objects within that array, based on the index. This code snippet displays each item in the array that you just created:

```
NSLog(@"object1 = %@",[theArray objectAtIndex:0]);
NSLog(@"object2 = %@",[theArray objectAtIndex:1]);
NSLog(@"object3 = %@",[theArray objectAtIndex:2]);
NSLog(@"object4 = %@",[theArray objectAtIndex:3]);
```

Don't forget that the index is always zero-based.

Put it all together, and the code looks like this:

```
int i;
NSArray *theArray;
NSString *name1;
NSString *name2;
NSString *name3;
NSString *name4;

//assign values to the four names
name1 = @"Maria";
name2 = @"Mercedes";
name3 = @"Leopold";
name4 = @"Frederick";

//create and populate the array
theArray = [NSArray arrayWithObjects:name1, name2,
        name3, name4, nil];

NSLog(@"object1 = %@",[theArray objectAtIndex:0]);
NSLog(@"object2 = %@",[theArray objectAtIndex:1]);
NSLog(@"object3 = %@",[theArray objectAtIndex:2]);
NSLog(@"object4 = %@",[theArray objectAtIndex:3]);

i = [theArray count];
NSLog(@"theArray count = %d",i);
```

The resulting output looks like this:

```
2008-07-28 04:45:54.518 CocoaData2[944] object1=Maria
2008-07-28 04:45:54.520 CocoaData2[944] object2=Mercedes
2008-07-28 04:45:54.520 CocoaData2[944] object3=Leopold
2008-07-28 04:45:54.520 CocoaData2[944] object4=Frederick
2008-07-28 04:45:54.520 CocoaData2[944] theArray count = 4
```

## *NSMutableArray*

The NSArray class's one shortcoming is that you can't alter it after you've created it. When you can't change something (such as an array), it's *immutable*. Conversely, those that you can change are *mutable* arrays. Thus, Cocoa also offers the NSMutableArray. To create an NSMutableArray, you can use its arrayWithCapacity method:

```
NSMutableArray *theArray = [NSMutableArray
        arrayWithCapacity:0];
```

Because you can grow or shrink NSMutableArrays at will, it's safe to create the array with space for zero items.

With an NSMutableArray, you can change elements in the array after you create it. This makes it more suitable for maintaining dynamic lists of information:

✔ **Add items to an NSMutableArray:** Use the addObject method:

```
[theArray addObject:name1];
[theArray addObject:name2];
[theArray addObject:name3];
```

✔ **Remove an item from the array:** Use the removeObjectAtIndex method. This method removes an object from the array and resizes the array in the process. For example, to remove the second name (which is at index 1), use code like this:

```
[theArray removeObjectAtIndex:1];
```

✔ **Insert an object:** Use the insertObject method. The method inserts an object into the array, resizing it as a result. This example reinserts the second name (name2) into the array:

```
[theArray insertObject:name2 atIndex:1];
```

✔ **Replace an element of the array with another object:** Use the replace ObjectAtIndex method. This snippet replaces the second name in the array with name3:

```
[theArray replaceObjectAtIndex:1 withObject:name3];
```

Because NSMutableArray inherits from NSArray, you can use the methods from earlier in this section to find out the size of the array and to query it for specific elements.

# Working with Boolean Data Types

A Boolean data type represents information that can occur in two, and only two, states. For example, an On/Off switch acts in a Boolean fashion because you have only two options. A Yes/No question works similarly. Objective-C has its own Boolean data type: BOOL. Instead of the usual TRUE and FALSE values, Objective-C uses YES and NO. This code snippet shows some of the ways in which you'd typically use BOOL variables:

```
BOOL answerWasFound;

answerWasFound = FindTheAnswer();

if (answerWasFound)
// OR
if (answerWasFound == YES)
```

Besides using YES or NO for the Objective-C BOOL type value, it's important for another reason: It works with other objects in Cocoa. Again, arrays and other types of collection objects expect their elements to be objects themselves. If you wanted to create an NSArray of Boolean values in Cocoa, you'd pass the BOOL type to the numberWithBool class method of NSNumber:

```
//create an NSNumber with a BOOL
n = [NSNumber numberWithBool:YES];

//add the NSNumber to an array
[theArray addObject:n];
```

# Working with Dates

The NSCalendarDate class gives you many options when it comes to working with dates and times. One of the most common tasks you perform is finding the current date or time. You can do this in one line of code with an NSCalendarDate class method:

```
NSDate *theDate = [NSCalendarDate date];
```

After you retrieve this date, you can easily convert it into an NSString, suitable for display. Simply use the description method to display the date in standard international format. In this example, NSLog displays the date in the console:

```
NSLog(@"theDate = %@",[theDate description]);
```

This yields results like this:

```
theDate = 2008-08-05 05:08:13 -0500
```

The description method is okay for quick-and-dirty date displays, but sometimes you want to display the date in a more human-friendly format. The descriptionWithCalendarFormat method can help you build an NSString that holds the date or time. The descriptionWithCalendar Format method has three parameters. The first parameter is the only one that you have to worry about for simple date work. That parameter is an NSString that represents the date in the format you desire.

Cocoa gives you lots of flexibility when it comes to formatting your date for display. For example, the following code snippet formats a date as you might expect to see it in the United States:

```
NSLog(@"theDate = %@",
  [theDate descriptionWithCalendarFormat:@"%A, %B %d, %Y
          (%I:%M)" timeZone:nil locale:nil]);
```

This results in a date formatted like so:

```
theDate = Monday, August 04, 2008 (10:15)
```

That odd-looking string that you pass to the `descriptionWithCalendar Format` method dictates which elements of the date you want to display. Apple calls those strange characters *date conversion specifiers*. Each *specifier* is a one-letter code that corresponds to some aspect of the date. In the preceding example, `%A` represents the name of the day of the week, which in this case is Monday. Next comes `%B`, which stands for the name of the month (in this case, August). You can continue to string together these specifiers until you've built a date in the format you prefer. Table 10-1 details some of the more common specifiers.

| Table 10-1 | Date Format Specifiers |
| --- | --- |
| *Code* | *What It Represents* |
| %B | Month name |
| %m | Month as an integer |
| %e | Day of the month as an integer |
| %d | Day of the month as a two-digit integer |
| %A | Weekday name |
| %I | Hours |
| %M | Minutes |
| %S | Seconds |
| %Y | Year |

# Part III

# Putting It All Together: Cocoa Programming in Depth

## In this part . . .

You know how the Developer Tools work, you have a handle on the Objective-C language, and you've even built your own applications. Now it's time to step it up a notch.

Part III elevates your Cocoa skills to new heights. You discover how to add the features found in every cool Cocoa application by creating a variety of programs with a range of functions from text and graphics to audio and video. Every Mac user expects an application to work with files, so Part III covers that, too.

# Chapter 11

# Text

- - - - - - - - - - - - - - - - - - - - - - - - - - - - - - - - - - - - - - - - - - - - - - - - - -

- - - - - - - - - - - - - - - - - - - - - - - - - - - - - - - - - - - - - - - - - - - - - - - - - -

*E*ver since the first Macintosh computer, Apple has led the consumer computer world in design, layout, and typography. Mac OS X continues this tradition by providing some of the best-looking text that you'll ever see on a computer monitor. Cocoa gives programmers instant access to these wonderful features of OS X.

This chapter shows you how to work with text for a variety of purposes. First, you display some text in a window. Then, you manipulate that text, contorting its sizes and altering its hue. Next, you discover how easy it is to add professional text-editing features to your applications with little or no code. Finally, you save the text from your interface to a file for later recall. Stylized text is a great feature for many types of applications, and Cocoa gives you a wide range of tools for manipulating that text.

# Working with Text

Cocoa has many different controls for working with text in applications. Some text controls display text as a label; other controls permit full editing like a word processor. Interface Builder offers several controls for working with text, but they generally inherit from one of two controls:

- ✔ **NSTextField:** Displays static or dynamic text. Use this control to display one line of text.

- ✔ **NSTextView:** The star of the text fields in Cocoa. This baby can work with multiple lines of text. When you think of a word processor, think of `NSTextView`.

This chapter focuses on the NSTextView control because it's the most full-featured. If you can work with it, you can easily handle the other controls for displaying text.

## Building an interface

To get started working with text, you need a project and an interface. Perform the following steps to prepare a project for the examples in this chapter:

1. **Create a project in Xcode.**

2. **Double-click the MainMenu.xib file in Xcode in the Resources folder.**

3. **In Interface Builder, open the** Window **window from the XIB project window if it isn't already open. Add an** NSTextView **to the window.**

   You can find the NSTextView in the Library window by scrolling or searching for NSTextView or simply TextView, as shown in Figure 11-1.

**Figure 11-1:**
The NSTextView control is located in the Library window.

**4. Add two** `NSButton` **check box controls to the interface.**

One check box toggles the display of a ruler in the `NSTextView`. The other check box causes text color changes to affect only that text which is selected. You can find the check box control in the Library window by searching for `Check Box`. Change the title of the check boxes by double-clicking each control and typing the new label. Figure 11-2 shows the check boxes with new titles. Select the `Selected` property for the top check box, so Apply to Selection is activated only when the application launches. Also, deselect the `Selected` property in the Button Attributes Inspector for the bottom Rulers check box because the `NSTextView` rulers aren't visible when the application launches.

**5. Drag two** `NSColorWell` **controls and two** `NSTextField` **labels from the Library to the interface.**

You can find the `NSColorWell` control in the Library window by searching for `Color Well`. To label the `NSColorWell` controls, drag two `NSTextField` controls to the window. The Library has more than one `NSTextField` control available. Search for `Label` to find the one that you want here. A `Label` control is an `NSTextField` with properties set to make the `NSTextField` display text that a user can't edit. One `NSColorWell` dictates the color of the text in the `NSTextView`. The other represents the background color of the view. Figure 11-3 shows the completed interface.

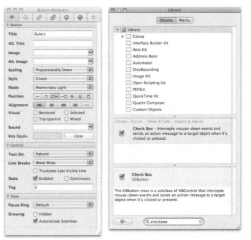

**Figure 11-2:**
Add two
NSButton
check boxes
to the
window.

**Figure 11-3:**
Add two
Color Well
controls and
two labels
to the
window.

## Adding a controller class

As you might be expecting, the next step is to create a class that controls your interface:

1.  **In the Library window of Interface Builder, search for the** `NSObject` **class and add it to the XIB project window.**

2.  **With the new object selected, press ⌘+6 to open the Identity Inspector.**

    By default, the Class is `NSObject`.

3.  **Change the class name.**

    To follow along with the example, name the class `MyTextController`. Figure 11-4 shows the result.

4.  **Add outlets to the class.**

    Define the following outlets for the new class in the same Identity Inspector:

    - `applyCheckbox`
    - `backgroundColorWell`
    - `textColorWell`
    - `textView`

    You may notice that one of the `NSButton` check boxes is missing from the list. That's because you won't need to reference it by name in code. Instead, it performs its function through an action.

5. **Add the following actions to the** MyTextController **class:**

- setBackgroundColor:
- setTextColor:
- toggleRuler:

**Figure 11-4:**
Create a
new class
to act as the
controller.

## Wiring the interface

To wire the components of your interface to the new Controller class, perform the following steps:

1. **Connect the outlets of** MyTextController **to the controls in the
interface.**

   Control+drag from the XIB window MyTextController object to each
   of the four controls in turn, selecting the corresponding outlet from
   the black connections list overlay that appears. Figure 11-5 shows the
   appleCheckbox outlet connecting to the Apply to Selection check box.

2. **Connect the actions of the** MyTextController **object to the two**
   ColorWells **and the ruler check box.**

   To connect them, Control+drag from each control to the MyText
   Controller object. Figure 11-6 shows the toggleRuler action
   connected to its switch.

3. **Select the** MyTextController **class in the project window and choose**
   **File⇨Write Class Files to create the class files and add them to your**
   **project in Xcode.**

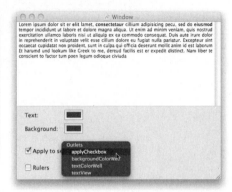

**Figure 11-5:**
Connect the
outlets
for the
interface.

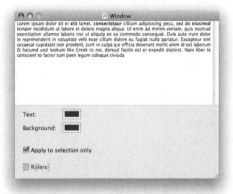

**Figure 11-6:**
Connect the
actions
for the
interface.

# Adding the code

Now that you've assembled the interface for this chapter, it's time to quit
Interface Builder and add some code in Xcode. For starters, you need to specify which superclass `MyTextController` will use. Follow these steps:

1. **In MyTextController.h, change this line:**

```
@interface MyTextController : /* Specify a superclass
     (eg: NSObject or NSView) */ {
```

**to this:**

```
@interface MyTextController : NSObject {
```

The `NSColorWell` controls in this project display the standard Color
panel when a user clicks them. Depending on which `NSColorWell` a
user clicks, it alters either the text color or the background color of the
`NSTextView` in the window respectively.

2. **Add the code to alter both Color panels in the** `setBackgroundColor`
   **and** `setTextColor` **actions in MyTextController.m:**

```
@implementation MyTextController
- (IBAction)setBackgroundColor:(id)sender {
    [textView setBackgroundColor:[backgroundColorWell
        color]];
}

- (IBAction)setTextColor:(id)sender {
    if ([applyCheckbox state]) {
        [textView setTextColor:[textColorWell color]
        range:[textView selectedRange]];
        }
    else {
        [textView setTextColor:[textColorWell color]];
        }
}
```

Setting the background and text colors is as easy as using the `set
BackgroundColor` and `setTextColor` methods of the `NSTextView`
class. If the state of `applyCheckbox` is `YES`, the `setTextColor` method
sets the color of the text of the currently selected text, passing the range
as one of its parameters. This allows you to choose which portion of the
text you want to colorize.

3. **To have the two ColorWells display particular colors by default, set
   them in Interface Builder or do so programmatically in the** `awake
   FromNib` **function.**

   For example, the following code sets the default colors for a white background and black text:

```
- (void)awakeFromNib
{
    //set the NSColorWells to preset colors
    [textColorWell setColor:[NSColor blackColor]];
    [backgroundColorWell  setColor:[NSColor
        whiteColor]];
}
```

The `NSTextView` control can perform all sorts of other fantastic text
manipulation operations besides color. One of these great features is the
ruler.

4. **In Xcode, add the following code to the** `toggleTheRuler` **action to
   add a full-fledged ruler:**

```
- (IBAction)toggleTheRuler:(id)sender
{
    [textView toggleRuler:[sender state]];
}
```

**5. Choose Build⇨Build and Go to see your handiwork.**

Figure 11-7 illustrates the use of a ruler in an `NSTextView`.

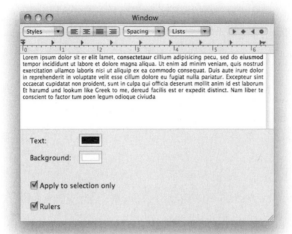

**Figure 11-7:**
With one
line of code,
you can add
a ruler!

# Doing Style the Easy Way!

You can continue to add style functions to this project by manipulating the `NSTextView` programmatically. This may work great for some projects, but for others, there's a much easier way to stylize text in an `NSTextView`. If you're looking for traditional word-processor styles in your application, Cocoa can deliver!

Follow these steps to stylize your text:

**1. In Xcode, click the Build and Go button in the toolbar to launch the application.**

**2. Choose Format⇨Font⇨Show Fonts.**

Yes, that's right . . . Cocoa has already implemented a Font menu for you. You don't need to add a single line of code nor make any changes in Interface Builder. That's all there is to it!

**3. Select a font and use it while typing in the text view.**

Figure 11-8 shows the Fonts panel after being opened by the Font menu.

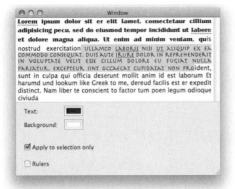 

**Figure 11-8:**
Cocoa pro-
vides fonts
for free.

You'll quickly discover that all the items in the Font menu work. No code is necessary. No connections are necessary. It doesn't get any simpler than that. Because many types of applications use a Font menu, Apple decided to include this feature for you. That way, you can add a standardized Font menu to your project without worrying about how to implement it. And don't forget about the ruler. When you show the ruler, many of the Font menu items are also displayed just above the section that the ruler occupies. Figure 11-9 shows the Styles menu above the ruler.

By now, you should begin to see the power of Cocoa. The high-level classes that Apple includes with Cocoa ensure that your projects maintain a consistent look and feel while providing the full features your users expect from an application.

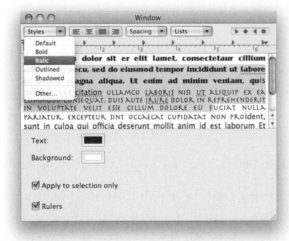

**Figure 11-9:**
Wow! The
ruler comes
equipped
with font
formatting
too.

# Manipulating Text

So far in this chapter, I've shown you how to create style over substance. Other important aspects of working with text in NSTextView are the capability to edit, copy, paste, and alter its text.

## Pasteboard manipulations

One common feature that every Mac OS X application has is access to the Pasteboard (or Clipboard). Like the Font menu, Cocoa takes care of the Edit menu too; you don't have to do anything to implement it. The Edit menu just works! The Edit menu in OS X offers the typical cut, copy, and paste features that you might expect and also implements full-blown spell check and find functions. Figure 11-10 shows the spell-checker.

**Figure 11-10:**
You don't have to do a bit of work to give your application Edit menu functions, such as spell check.

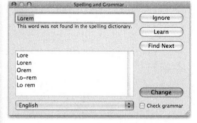

The Edit menu hasn't enabled its Undo and Redo menu items. The fix for this is simple enough:

1. **In Xcode, double-click the MainMenu.xib file to open it in Interface Builder.**

2. **Open the window for your interface and double-click the** NSTextView.

   Make sure to double-click; a single click only selects its Scroll View container.

3. **Press ⌘+1 to open the Text View Attributes Inspector window.**

4. **In the Attributes section of the Info window, select the Undo check box, as shown in Figure 11-11.**

   Now, your users can undo any actions that they perform in the text view. You managed to add this useful functionality by clicking one check box.

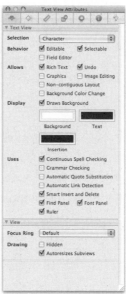

**Figure 11-11:**
Select the
Undo check
box to turn
on the Undo
functions for
an NSText
View.

## Manual editing

Sometimes you may want to alter the text in an NSTextView without using
the Pasteboard. Perhaps the most common editing task that you'll want
to perform is to change the text that appears in an NSTextView. You can
accomplish this task by using the setString method of the NSString class.
Create an NSString and assign a string to it:

```
NSString* someString = @"Cocoa says Hello!";
```

Note the @ character preceding the string. The @ character is an Objective-C
operator that tells the compiler to allocate a constant NSString object with
the stated value.

After you have an NSString, it's a simple matter to display it in an
NSTextView:

```
[textViewsetString:someString];
```

To see how it works, follow these steps:

1. **In Xcode, declare the** displayAsString **method by adding the
   following line to the MyTextController.h file.**

   ```
   - (IBAction)displayAString:(id)sender;
   ```

2. **Define the** `displayAsString` **method in MyTextController.m.**

   The code creates a string, `someString`, and then tells the `textView` to set its string to `someString`:

   ```
   - (IBAction)displayAString:(id)sender
   {
       NSString* someString = @"Cocoa says hello!";
       [textView setString:someString];
   }
   ```

3. **Double-click the MainMenu.xib file to open the project's interface in Interface Builder.**

4. **Add an** `NSButton` **to the window in your interface.**

5. **Change the button's Title Attribute in the Inspector window to display** `NSString`.

6. **Control+drag from the button to the** `MyTextController` **instance and connect it to the** `displayAString:` **action in the black connections list overlay that opens.**

   Notice that Interface Builder has read the MyTextController.h file on opening the interface and now an action named `displayAString:` is available in `MyTextController`.

Replacing specific text is another task that you might want to perform. To replace some portion of the text in an `NSTextView`, you must first define an `NSRange` variable. This range describes which part of the string you want to replace. In the preceding example, you used the string `"Cocoa says hello!"`. If you want to change *hello* to *goodbye,* you'd first find the location of that word in the string. Because the numbering begins at 0, the first letter of *hello* is the 11th character in the string. Further, the length of *hello* is 5. Thus, to make an `NSRange` for *hello,* you'd use code like this:

```
NSRange theRange;
theRange = NSMakeRange(11, 5);
```

To replace *hello* with *goodbye,* call the `replaceCharactersInRange` method of the `NSTextView`:

```
[textView replaceCharactersInRange:theRange
        withString:@"Goodbye" ];
```

Besides editing the text, you'll sometimes want to programmatically select portions of the text in an `NSTextView`. For example, suppose you want to perform a `Select All` operation. Create an `NSRange` representing the entire length of the text and then call the `setSelectedRange` method of the `NSTextView` to select the text:

```
NSRange theRange;
theRange = NSMakeRange(0, [[textView string] length]);
[textView setSelectedRange:theRange];
```

# Saving Text for a Rainy Day

Eventually, your users will want to save the text on which they've been working so hard. Cocoa lets you save text in two ways:

- ✔ **Plain:** Plain text is text without any formatting. You see this type of text in HTML and XML documents, and plain text files (such as when you press ⌘+Shift+T in the TextEdit application). When all you care about is the text data in a file and not its formatting, use the plain text format.

- ✔ **Rich:** Rich text conveys information about the formatting. You may recognize the rich text format from popular Microsoft applications, such as Word. The rich text file format saves formatting data, such as fonts, colors, and styles in the file along with the actual text data. If you're building a word processor or a similar type of application in which formatting matters, use the rich text format.

To see how these two file formats work with Cocoa, follow these steps:

1. **In Xcode, add the following lines of code to the MyTextController.h file to define two new actions:**

   ```
   - (IBAction)saveRichTextFile:(id)sender;
   - (IBAction)saveTextFile:(id)sender;
   ```

2. **Navigate to the MyTextController.m file and implement the two actions:**

   ```
   - (IBAction)saveTextFile:(id)sender
   {
       NSSavePanel *savePanel = [NSSavePanel savePanel];
       [savePanel setRequiredFileType:@"txt"];
       [savePanel setTitle:@"Save as Plain Text"];
       if ([savePanel runModal] == NSOKButton)
           {
           [[textView string] writeToFile:[savePanel
           filename] atomically:YES
           encoding:NSUTF8StringEncoding error:NULL];
           }
   }

   - (IBAction)saveRichTextFile:(id)sender
   {
   ```

```
NSSavePanel *savePanel = [NSSavePanel savePanel];
[savePanel setRequiredFileType:@"rtf"];
[savePanel setTitle:@"Save as Rich Text"];
if ([savePanel runModal] == NSOKButton)
{
[[textView RTFFromRange:
        NSMakeRange(0, [[textView string]
    length])]
writeToFile:[savePanel filename] atomically:YES];
}
}
```

3. **Open the MainMenu.xib file in Interface Builder.**

4. **To the existing** `Window` **object in your interface, add two** `NSButton`
   **controls and change their Title Attributes in the Inspector window to**

   - Save Plain Text

   - Save Rich Text

   Figure 11-12 shows these new buttons.

5. **Control+drag from each** `NSButton` **in the interface to the**
   `MyTextController` **instance in MainMenu.xib and then when you let
   go of the mouse, assign the appropriate action to that button with the
   black connections list overlay that appears.**

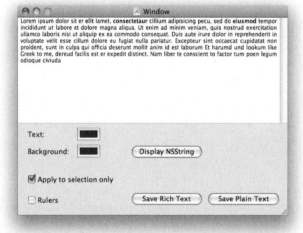

**Figure 11-12:**
Add two
NSButtons
that will
save rich
and plain
text files.

The code for both actions works similarly, with a few exceptions:

✔ Both actions display a SavePanel so that users can select the name and destination of the file they want to save.

✔ The two methods differ on the file type and title that they display in the SavePanel and the fact that plain text files need an encoding.

To display the panel, each method uses this line of code:

```
if ([theSavePanel runModal] == NSOKButton)
```

The runModal method of the SavePanel takes care of displaying the modal window. A *modal window* is one in which users are forced into a *mode* of operation — they must make a decision (saving a file or halting the operation) before proceeding any further.

When a user clicks a file and clicks the Save button in the SavePanel, the runModal function of the SavePanel returns a value. Instead of worrying about what numerical value it returns, Cocoa provides you with the constant NSOKButton indicating that the user clicked the Save button. The following code example checks for the Save button. Conversely, you could check for the Cancel button by using the appropriate constant for that button:

```
if ([theSavePanel runModal] == NSCancelButton)
```

If the users click Save in the SavePanel, the code writes the text from the TextView to a plain or rich text file.

For plain text files, this means using the writeToFile method of the NSString class:

```
[[textView string] writeToFile:[savePanel filename]
        atomically:YES encoding:NSUTF8StringEncoding
        error:NULL];
```

You retrieve the text from the text view as an NSString using the [text Viewstring] method. The text file is saved with the writeToFile method, passing it four parameters:

✔ **The name of the file that the user entered in the SavePanel.**

✔ **A Boolean value titled atomically:** If you pass YES as the atomically parameter, the writeToFile method first writes the data to a temporary file and renames that file after the write operation is finished. If it has a value of NO, writeToFile writes the data directly to the file returned by the filename method. Set the atomically parameter to YES.

✔ **An encoding:** The encoding is best set to UTF8, as it accounts for languages beyond English.

✔ **An error routine should something go wrong:** The error parameter can be set to NULL, as I won't trap errors in this demo.

The second method in the code listing saves the file to a rich text file. Much of the code in it is identical to the plain text version, with one big exception. Instead of retrieving text from text view with the string method of the NSString class, you use the RTFFromRange method for rich text. This has the effect of retrieving the text with its style information (bold, size, color, and so on) intact:

```
[[textViewRTFFromRange:
        NSMakeRange(0, [[textViewstring] length])]
        writeToFile:[theSavePanel filename]
        atomically:YES];
```

The only parameter of the RTFFromRange method is an NSRange value indicating the portion of text that you want to retrieve from text view. To retrieve all the text, you supply the method with the starting point of the text and the length of text to grab. In this instance, you grab all the text found in the text view, starting from position 0 (zero) and extending the length of the text in the text view:

```
NSMakeRange(0, [[textView string] length])
```

After you have NSString from TextView, writeToFile works the same as it does for plain text files, with a minor caveat. When you use the writeTo File method, the resulting plain text files have the .txt file extension and rich text files have the .rtf extension.

# *Retrieving Text*

Another important task that you'll likely need to perform regularly is opening text files. To open and read a text file, your code should do the following:

✔ Display an OpenPanel so users can choose which file they want to open.

✔ Read the text data from the file.

✔ Display that data in an NSTextView.

To add the capability to open and view plain and rich text files, add a few items to the interface:

1. **In Xcode, add the following lines of code to the MyTextController.h file to define these two actions:**

```
- (IBAction)openRichTextFile:(id)sender;
- (IBAction)openTextFile:(id)sender;
```

2. **Navigate to the MyTextController.m file and implement those two actions:**

```
- (IBAction)openTextFile:(id)sender
{
    NSOpenPanel *theOpenPanel = [NSOpenPanel
        openPanel];
    if ([theOpenPanel runModal] == NSOKButton)
    {
        NSString *theFileName = [theOpenPanel
        filename];
        NSString *theFileContents = [NSString
            stringWithContentsOfFile:theFileName];
      [textView setString:theFileContents];
    }
}

- (IBAction)openRichTextFile:(id)sender
{
    NSOpenPanel *theOpenPanel = [NSOpenPanel
        openPanel];
    if ([theOpenPanel runModal] == NSOKButton)
    {
     NSString *theFileName = [theOpenPanel filename];
        NSData *theRTFData = [NSData dataWithContentsO
        fFile:theFileName];
     [textView replaceCharactersInRange:
            NSMakeRange(0, [[textView string] length])
        withRTF:theRTFData];
}
}
```

3. **Open the MainMenu.xib file in Interface Builder.**

4. **To the existing window object in the XIB project window, add two additional NSButton controls and then change their Title Attributes in the Inspector window to Open Plain Text and Open Rich Text.**

Figure 11-13 shows the new buttons.

5. **Control+drag from each** NSButton **in the interface to the** MyText Controller **instance in MainMenu.xib and then when you let go of the mouse, assign the appropriate action to that button with the black connections list overlay that appears.**

In contrast to the examples from earlier in this chapter in which you saved text files, opening text files requires the use of the NSOpenPanel class. Opening files works in much the same manner as the NSSavePanel. In the two methods for opening text files, you aren't setting the title displayed in the NSOpenPanel (with setTitle) like you did for the NSSavePanel earlier. You certainly could, though.

Like the NSSavePanel, you display the NSOpenPanel with the runModal method:

```
NSOpenPanel *theOpenPanel = [NSOpenPanel openPanel];
```

If the user selects a text file and clicks OK to open it, runModal returns NSOKButton:

```
if ([theOpenPanel runModal] == NSOKButton)
```

From there, you open the text file, read its contents, and display them in an NSTextView. For plain text files, it's a straightforward process to read in a text file with the stringWithContentsOfFile method of NSString:

```
NSString *theFileName = [theOpenPanel filename];
NSString *theFileContents = [NSString
        stringWithContentsOfFile:theFileName];
```

To display the text in an `NSTextView`, you need only one line of code:

```
[textView setString:theFileContents];
```

After you're finished working with the `NSString` objects, don't forget to dispose of them:

```
[theFileName release];
[theRTFData release];
```

Reading rich text files requires a bit of extra work, but not too much. Instead of using an `NSString` to read text from a rich text file, you must use an `NSData` object. Call the `dataWithContentsOfFile` method of the `NSData` class to load stylized text from the file into the `NSData` object:

```
NSData *theRTFData = [NSData dataWithContentsOfFile:theFil
        eName];
```

To display it in the text view, use the `replaceCharactersInRange` method:

```
[textView replaceCharactersInRange:
        NSMakeRange(0, [[textView string] length])
        withRTF:theRTFData];
```

The `replaceCharactersInRange` method takes two parameters:

✔ **NSRange:** The location in the `NSTextView` where you want to display the text

✔ **NSData:** The rich text data that you read from the file

To test your code, choose Build⇨Build and Go in Xcode.

# Chapter 12

# Graphics

*F*rom the beautiful fonts in a word processor to the shiny Finder interface, the Mac OS has always prided itself on fantastic looking graphics. Mac OS X is no different. With its sophisticated Quartz graphics engine, Mac OS X can produce stunning graphics. Cocoa gives you direct access to these powerful features of Mac OS X.

This chapter covers the basics of working with graphics in Cocoa. You create a custom view for displaying your graphics and draw on it with a variety of colors, shapes, and images. You even write code to change the opacity of your graphics, giving them the coveted see-through look.

## Cocoa and the Art of Graphics

Before jumping head first into graphics, you need to familiarize yourself with a few important Cocoa data types: NSPoint, NSRect, NSSize, and NSColor. You need them to do any type of graphics programming in Cocoa, so they make a good starting point.

### Points

Just like in geometry, Cocoa uses points to designate positions on a square grid. To work with points in Cocoa, you use an NSPoint structure. NSPoint is a structure comprised of two floats (x and y, respectively). *Quartz,* the graphics engine on the Mac OS, defines the bottom-left corner of a view as the origin (0,0). The x value increases as you move to the right. The y value increases as you advance up.

The bottom-left origin is different than what you might be accustomed to in other programming environments, where the origin is in the top-left corner. This bottom-left arrangement comes from PostScript, upon which OS X's underlying PDF (Portable Document Format) graphics model is based.

The following structure shows how the Quartz framework defines a point:

```
typedef struct _NSPoint {
    float x;
    float y;
} NSPoint;
```

The x and y portion of the structure are the coordinates of the point that you want to represent. To use an NSPoint variable, you must first declare it like you would any other variable or structure:

```
NSPoint thePoint;
```

Then to assign values to the x and y members of an NSPoint structure, use the NSMakePoint function. This example creates an NSPoint at the location (100,100):

```
thePoint = NSMakePoint(100,100);
```

## Rects and sizes

Closely related to the NSPoint structure is the NSRect structure. An NSRect (*Rect* is short for *rectangle*) is a structure comprised of an NSPoint, the origin of the rectangle, and an NSSize, the size of the rectangle:

```
typedef struct _NSRect {
    NSPoint origin;
    NSSize size;
} NSRect;
```

To understand how this works, you also need to know about the NSSize structure:

```
typedef struct _NSSize {
    float width;
    float height;
} NSSize;
```

Thus, an `NSRect` is really a structure of four float values: two for the `NSPoint` and two for the `NSSize`. The `NSPoint` portion describes where the `NSRect` begins, and the `NSSize` variable describes the dimensions of the `NSRect`.

To create an `NSRect`, first declare the `NSRect` variable:

```
NSRect theRect;
```

Then initialize that variable with the `NSMakeRect` function. `NSMakeRect` takes four parameters: `x`, `y`, `width`, and `height`. For example, this line of code creates an `NSRect` with an origin at (100,100) and dimensions of 50 x 50:

```
theRect = NSMakeRect(100,100, 50, 50);
```

Later, if you want to find the origin or size of `theRect`, use code like this:

```
float theOriginX, theOriginY;
float theSizeW, theSizeH;

theOriginX = theRect.origin.x;
theOriginY = theRect.origin.y;

theSizeW = theRect.size.width;
theSizeH = theRect.size.height;
```

# Colors

Cocoa's AppKit includes the `NSColor` data type to help you work with color in your graphics projects. You have two ways of working with color.

## Using convenience colors

The easiest way to create and define an `NSColor` object is to use one of the color convenience methods. You'll recognize immediately the colors that each `NSColor` convenience method represents because it has a plain-English name. For example, to create an `NSColor` object that stores the color black, use code like this:

```
//Declare a pointer to an NSColor object
NSColor *aColor;

// assign the color black to it
aColor = [NSColor blackColor];
```

As you may have guessed, this technique works for many other colors too (blueColor, redColor, and so on). Table 12-1 lists common colors that you can use.

| Table 12-1 | Preset Color Components |
|---|---|
| *Preset Component* | *Color It Produces* |
| blackColor | Black |
| blueColor | Bright blue |
| brownColor | Brown |
| clearColor | Clear/transparent |
| cyanColor | Light blue |
| darkGrayColor | Dark gray (for the Canadians, dark grey) |
| grayColor | Medium gray |
| greenColor | Bright green |
| lightGrayColor | Light gray (you were expecting something else?) |
| magentaColor | Pinkish purple color . . . or is it a purple-ish pink color |
| orangeColor | Orange |
| purpleColor | Purple |
| redColor | Bright red |
| whiteColor | White |
| yellowColor | Bright and sunny yellow |

### Using device-dependent color spaces

Eventually, you'll want some colors that the convenience methods don't cover. In that case, you have to resort to some of the more sophisticated color methods in the AppKit. The AppKit has three kinds of color spaces that you can use to create colors:

✔ **Device dependent (or device):** When you use *device colors,* you can't be sure that you'll always see the same color across devices. You're probably most familiar with this kind of color because most home computer monitors and printers display it. Stand any two computer monitors next to each other, and you'll soon discover that they don't produce colors equally. Sure, it's good enough to view Web pages, play games, and even create graphics. It also works for many kinds of home-printing chores. It's not so good, however, for professional printing, color correction, and similar color tasks.

- ✔ **Device independent (or calibrated):** Computer and printer manufacturers began creating hardware and software solutions to calibrate their equipment. The idea was that you could see the same kind of output no matter what device you used. The calibration is supposed to account for the peculiarities of your particular device and adjust it to produce accurate colors.

- ✔ **Named:** This color space is for even more sophisticated work with color. You can disregard it for this book.

The *device-dependent* color space has three color spaces. A *color space* is just a fancy way of saying "ways of creating color." Normally, you create colors by mixing different amounts of specific base colors. The three mixing schemes that you can use in device-dependent color are

- ✔ **DeviceRGB:** Red, green, blue, and alpha components

- ✔ **DeviceCMYK:** Cyan, magenta, yellow, black, and alpha components

- ✔ **DeviceWhite:** White and alpha components

For the rest of this chapter, you have to worry only about DeviceRGB because it's the best choice for displaying graphics on a monitor. The colors that emanate from a monitor are produced by mixing varying amounts of red, green, and blue light, hence RGB. As you combine colors in RGB, the color approaches white. CMYK, on the other hand, is used for printing color. As you combine colors in CMYK, the color approaches black. After you get the hang of the DeviceRGB color space, it's easy to use the DeviceCMYK and DeviceWhite color spaces. You're not missing anything by forgetting about them for the time being because this chapter deals solely with color on a monitor, not a printer.

Now, it's time to get to the code. You define your own RGB (red, green, blue) colors with the colorWithDeviceRed function. The function takes four floats as parameters. These four numbers correspond to the three color channels (red, green, and blue) and the alpha channel. Each parameter can have a value between 0.0 and 1.0; 1.0 is fully on for that particular color channel. The alpha parameter dictates how opaque the color is. A value of 1.0 is completely opaque, and a value of 0.0 is fully transparent.

This numbering scheme contrasts with the colors used in familiar applications, such as Web pages and Photoshop documents, where the numbering usually has a range between 0 and 255. To correlate with the Cocoa way of doing things, add 1 to the value of each color component and divide by 256. For example, if you want to convert a Photoshop color with RGB values of (127,63,255) to the RGB values for an NSColor, perform this simple calculation:

```
127 + 1 = 128/256 = 0.5
63 + 1 = 64/256 = 0.25
255 + 1 = 256/256 = 1.0
```

To create an NSColor object in the DeviceRGB color space, use code like this:

```
//Declare a pointer to an NSColor object
NSColor* theColor;

//create the object
//and assign the color black to it
theColor = [NSColor  colorWithDeviceRed:(float)0.0
        green:(float)0.0 blue:(float)0.0
        alpha:(float)1.0];
```

Notice that the red, green, and blue parameters are all set to 0.0, which yields the color black. If you wanted to create a red color object, you'd use code like this:

```
//create the object
//and assign the color red to it
theColor = [NSColor  colorWithDeviceRed:(float)1.0
        green:(float)0.0 blue:(float)0.0
        alpha:(float)1.0];
```

The red parameter has a value of 1.0, and the green and blue components have a value of 0.0. By adjusting the alpha value, you can create different shades of the same color. I discuss color in more detail later in this chapter, in the "Painting with Lines and Shapes" section.

After you create a color object, the only other thing you need to do before working with it is to use the set function. This sets the graphics pen to your desired color:

```
[theColor set];
```

Yes, it's as easy as that. Again, you'll see more clearly how Cocoa colors work in the code examples in the remainder of this chapter.

# Building a Graphics Interface

To begin coding your graphics masterpiece, you need an interface in which to display graphics:

1. **Launch Xcode and choose File➪New Project to create a new Cocoa project, as shown in Figure 12-1.**

2. **Expand the Resources folder and double-click the MainMenu.xib file to open it in Interface Builder.**

3. **In Interface Builder, open the Library window by choosing Tools➪ Library and searching for** `Custom View`**, as shown in Figure 12-2.**

4. **Drag a** `Custom View` **control from the Library to the main window of the project's interface.**

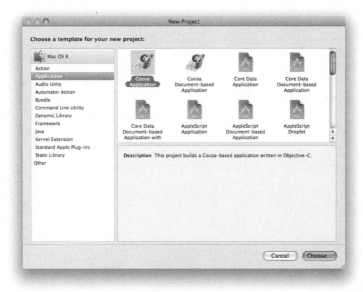

**Figure 12-1:**
Create a
new Cocoa
project.

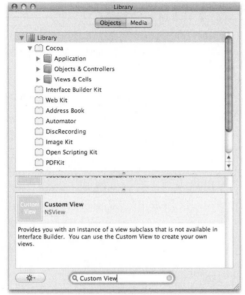

**Figure 12-2:**
Locate the
Custom
View
control.

5. **With the new control selected in the interface, press ⌘+6 to open the Identity Inspector and rename the class.**

For example, you can name it `MyCanvas`, as shown in Figure 12-3.

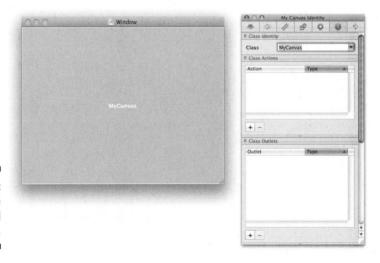

**Figure 12-3:**
Rename
the control
MyCanvas.

6. **Press ⌘+3 to change the Autosizing of the view.**

   The Autosizing properties affect how the view behaves when a user resizes the parent window.

7. **Click twice inside the Autosizing square to activate the horizontal and vertical arrows, as shown in Figure 12-4.**

   With the horizontal and vertical arrows activated within the Autosizing square, the view stretches with the parent window when a user resizes it.

8. **Select the `MyCanvas` view in the interface.**

9. **Choose File⇨Write Class Files to create and add the header and implementation files to your Xcode project.**

10. **Back in Xcode, change this line in MyCanvas.h:**

    ```
    @interface MyCanvas : /* Specify a superclass (eg:
          NSObject or NSView) */ {
    ```

    **to this:**

    ```
    @interface FileInfoController : NSView {
    ```

    In MyCanvas.m, you focus mainly on the `drawRect` method. This is where you put drawing commands to draw to the `MyCanvas` view. The MyCanvas.m file doesn't have the `drawRect` method defined, so you have to add it.

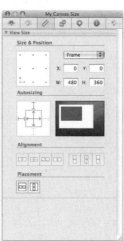

**Figure 12-4:**
Set the
horizontal
and vertical
Autosizing.

**11. Add the** `drawRect` **method to the MyCanvas.m file:**

```
- (void)drawRect:(NSRect)rect {
    // Drawing code here.
}
```

The drawing code appears in this method. The `drawRect` function takes care of redrawing your `Custom View` by automatically refreshing the view from your application's event loop.

# Painting with Lines and Shapes

With your interface and custom view ready for displaying graphics, you can now add some code to make it actually display something. Before you draw something, you have to define what that *something* is. When it comes to defining shapes in Cocoa, paths are the name of the game.

## Starting with Beziér paths

If you've ever played connect the dots, you're already well on your way to understanding how paths work. A *path* is a collection of points that together form the outline of a shape. For example, a square-shaped path has four points, an octagon-shaped path has eight points, and so on. Cocoa represents paths with the `NSBezierPath` type. Typically you begin working with paths by declaring a pointer to a `NSBezierPath`:

```
NSBezierPath *thePath;
```

Then you create a path. Your path might form a square, a circle, or some other shape. Because you'll want to create different shapes, Cocoa gives you several methods for creating paths.

One of the most common paths you'll create is the shape of a rectangle. For that, you can use the `bezierPathWithRect` method of the `NSBezierPath` class. The `bezierPathWithRect` method takes a `Rect` (which defines its origin and size) as its sole parameter. Because the `drawRect` function passes in a `Rect` that describes the dimensions of the `MyCanvas` object, you can easily create a rectangular path around `MyCanvas`:

```
- (void)drawRect:(NSRect)rect {

    NSBezierPath *thePath;
    thePath = [NSBezierPath bezierPathWithRect:rect];

}
```

Similarly, you can create an oval path within a bounding box by using the `bezierPathWithOvalInRect` method and passing it the `rect` you want to use as the bounding box:

```
- (void)drawRect:(NSRect)rect {
    // Drawing code here.

NSBezierPath *thePath;
thePath = [NSBezierPath bezierPathWithOvalInRect:rect];

}
```

Other times, you may not want to limit your `Rect` to the size of `MyCanvas`. In these instances, simply create a `Rect` structure and pass that to the `NSBezierPath` functions. The following example creates a 50 x 50 circular path in the bottom-right corner of the view:

```
NSRect theRect;
theRect = NSMakeRect(0, 0, 50, 50);

NSBezierPath *thePath;
thePath = [NSBezierPath bezierPathWithOvalInRect:theRect];
```

Just because you have a Beziér path doesn't mean you've drawn anything yet. Beziér paths strictly define the path that you'll fill or stroke later.

## Filling a path

After you create a path, filling it in with your color of choice is a simple matter. Send the path the `fill` message, and you're finished!

```
[thePath fill];
```

Of course, you'll want to create and set a color first. For example, to fill the entire background of the view with black, your code might look like this:

```
- (void)drawRect:(NSRect)rect {

  //create a path
  NSBezierPath *thePath = [NSBezierPath
          bezierPathWithRect:rect];

  //create a black color object
  NSColor *theColor = [NSColor blackColor];

  //set the color
  [theColor set];
```

```
//fill the path with the current color (black)
[thePath fill];

}
```

Figure 12-5 shows the results of this code.

**Figure 12-5:**
Fill the
entire view
with a solid
color.

You can use the same plan of attack to fill an NSRect that doesn't cover the entire background of the Custom View. For example, to draw a white rectangle at the top of the view, use this code:

```
- (void)drawRect:(NSRect)rect {

    //create and define an NSRect
    NSRect theRect = NSMakeRect(70, rect.size.height-235,
            120, 230);

    //define a rectangular path
    thePath = [NSBezierPath bezierPathWithRect:theRect];

    //define a white color object
    NSColor *theColor = [NSColor whiteColor];

    //set the color
    [theColor set];

    //fill the path with white
    [thePath fill];
}
```

Put the black and white together, and you'll see a result like the one shown in Figure 12-6.

**Figure 12-6:**
Fill the background in black and fill a white rectangle toward the top of the view.

You aren't limited to filling rectangular paths. Remember that oval-shaped path you created earlier in this chapter? Now is a good time to put it to use. By creating three oval paths and filling them with red, yellow, and green, respectively, you can create a simple traffic-light image. Add this code to the end of the drawRect function:

```
//**********************************
//      DRAW THE LIGHTS
//**********************************
  //create oval path
  theRect = NSMakeRect(100, rect.size.height-220, 60, 60);
  thePath = [NSBezierPath bezierPathWithOvalInRect:theRec
        t];

  //fill oval in green
  theColor = [NSColor  colorWithDeviceRed:(float)0.0
                  green:(float)1.0 blue:(float)0.0
        alpha:(float)1.0];
  [theColor set];
  [thePath fill];

  //create oval path
  theRect = NSMakeRect(100, rect.size.height-150, 60, 60);
  thePath = [NSBezierPath bezierPathWithOvalInRect:theRec
        t];
```

```
//fill oval in yellow
theColor = [NSColor  colorWithDeviceRed:(float)1.0
             green:(float)1.0 blue:(float)0.0
      alpha:(float)1.0];
[theColor set];
[thePath fill];

//create oval path
theRect = NSMakeRect(100, rect.size.height-80, 60, 60);
thePath = [NSBezierPath bezierPathWithOvalInRect:theRec
      t];

//fill oval in red
theColor = [NSColor  colorWithDeviceRed:(float)1.0
             green:(float)0.0 blue:(float)0.0
      alpha:(float)1.0];
[theColor set];
[thePath fill];
```

Figure 12-7 shows the results.

**Figure 12-7:**
Add a few
round ovals
to create an
image of
a simple
traffic light.

# Drawing a path

You don't have to fill all paths that you run across. You can also *stroke* a
path, which has the effect of drawing an outline around a path. Stroking a
path is just as simple as it is to fill one:

```
[thePath stroke];
```

You can also use a combination of `fill` and `stroke` for different effects. When you do, make sure to perform the `stroke` functions after the `fill` function so that the outline draws on top of the filled path. For example, suppose you wanted to draw a black ring around one of the traffic lights. Your code might look like this:

```
//stroke oval in black
theColor = [NSColor blackColor];
[theColor set];
[thePath stroke];
```

This code draws a thin outline around the light. If you'd prefer a thicker outline, use the path's `setLineWidth` function. The default line width is 1, so anything larger produces thicker lines:

```
[thePath setLineWidth: 5];
```

To draw an outline around each of the lights, adjust your `drawRect` function by adding the boldface code:

```
- (void)drawRect:(NSRect)rect
{

... code omitted ...

//*************************************
//      DRAW THE LIGHTS
//*************************************
  //create oval path
  theRect = NSMakeRect(100, rect.size.height-220, 60, 60);
  thePath = [NSBezierPath bezierPathWithOvalInRect:theRec
          t];

  //fill oval in green
  theColor = [NSColor  colorWithDeviceRed:(float)0.0
              green:(float)1.0 blue:(float)0.0
          alpha:(float)1.0];
  [theColor set];
  [thePath fill];

  //stroke oval in black
  theColor = [NSColor blackColor];
  [theColor set];
  [thePath setLineWidth: 5];
  [thePath stroke];
```

```
//create oval path
theRect = NSMakeRect(100, rect.size.height-150, 60, 60);
thePath = [NSBezierPath bezierPathWithOvalInRect:theRec
        t];

//fill oval in yellow
theColor = [NSColor  colorWithDeviceRed:(float)1.0
            green:(float)1.0 blue:(float)0.0
        alpha:(float)1.0];
[theColor set];
[thePath fill];

//stroke oval in black
theColor = [NSColor blackColor];
[theColor set];
[thePath setLineWidth: 5];
[thePath stroke];

//create oval path
theRect = NSMakeRect(100, rect.size.height-80, 60, 60);
thePath = [NSBezierPath bezierPathWithOvalInRect:theRec
        t];

//fill oval in red
theColor = [NSColor  colorWithDeviceRed:(float)1.0
            green:(float)0.0 blue:(float)0.0
        alpha:(float)1.0];
[theColor set];
[thePath fill];

//stroke oval in black
theColor = [NSColor blackColor];
[theColor set];
[thePath setLineWidth: 5];
[thePath stroke];
}
@end
```

Figure 12-8 shows the result of the code change.

## Creating fancy-pants paths

So far, you've worked with rectangular and oval paths. Paths need not conform to these two simple shapes, though. A path can be as simple or as complex as you want.

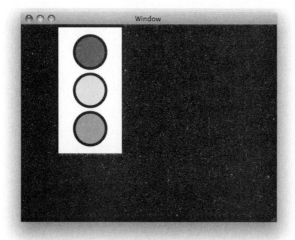

**Figure 12-8:**
Draw an
outline
around each
of the lights
for an added
effect.

Suppose that you want to display a stop sign next to your traffic-light graphic. A stop sign is an octagon. To create a stop-sign-shaped path, simply create eight NSPoint variables and populate them with points that represent the shape of a stop sign. Because tracking the various points in complex paths can get tedious, Cocoa gives you the ability to define paths relative to the last point in the path. That way, you can define the starting point with the actual coordinates and define the rest of the path relative to that point.

If you want to move that path to another location later, you have to change only one point — the first one. The rest of the path follows the first point without any other code changes.

The following code creates the points for a path in the shape of a stop sign. This code uses points that are relative to the first point:

```
//****************************************
//          DRAW A STOP SIGN
//****************************************

    // Create the eight points of an octagon (stop sign)
    NSPoint pt1,pt2,pt3,pt4,pt5,pt6,pt7,pt8;

    //Define the points
    pt1 = NSMakePoint(300, rect.size.height-220);
    pt2 = NSMakePoint(100, 0);
    pt3 = NSMakePoint(50, 50);
    pt4 = NSMakePoint(0, 100);
    pt5 = NSMakePoint(-50, 50);
    pt6 = NSMakePoint(-100, 0);
    pt7 = NSMakePoint(-50, -50);
    pt8 = NSMakePoint(0, -100);
```

The first point is relative to the origin of the view. Each of the last seven points has a value that's relative to the point that precedes it in the list.

Here's how to create a path with relative points:

1. **Define relative point positions for a path.**

   Use the following guidelines:

   - *Positive x value:* Path moves to the right.
   - *Negative x value:* Path moves to the left.
   - *Positive y value:* Path moves up.
   - *Negative y value:* Path moves down.

2. **After you define the various points on the path, create the** NSBezierPath **with the** bezierPath **class method of the** NSBezierPath **class.**

   ```
   // Create a stop sign path
   NSBezierPath *stopSign = [NSBezierPath bezierPath];
   ```

3. **Add the points to the path.**

   For the first point, use the moveToPoint function. For subsequent points, use the relativeLineToPoint function because you should position these points relative to the first point:

   ```
   [stopSign moveToPoint:pt1];
   [stopSign relativeLineToPoint:pt2];
   [stopSign relativeLineToPoint:pt3];
   [stopSign relativeLineToPoint:pt4];
   [stopSign relativeLineToPoint:pt5];
   [stopSign relativeLineToPoint:pt6];
   [stopSign relativeLineToPoint:pt7];
   [stopSign relativeLineToPoint:pt8];
   ```

4. **Close the path with the** closePath **function:**

   ```
   [stopSign closePath];
   ```

5. **With a path defined, you can apply the usual** color, fill, **and** stroke **commands to it.**

   For example, to fill in the stop sign with red and outline it in white, use code like this:

   ```
   // Draw the path
   [[NSColor redColor] set];
   [stopSign fill];

   // Draw the path
   [[NSColor whiteColor] set];
   [stopSign setLineWidth: 5];
   [stopSign stroke];
   ```

Combined, the code in this section produces result like those shown in Figure 12-9.

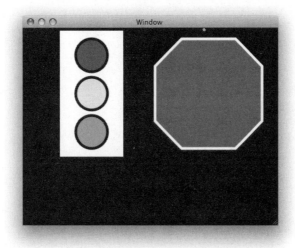

**Figure 12-9:**
Fill and
stroke the
path to see
the stop
sign appear
before your
eyes.

# Drawing Text

Besides shapes and paths, Cocoa is quite adept at displaying text in graphics. Before you start drawing text, you need to load that text into an `NSString` variable. For example, to add *STOP* to a stop sign, follow these steps:

1. **Create the `NSString` variable:**

```
NSString *theString;
theString = @"STOP";
```

2. **Determine the location in the view where you want to display the text and store that position in an `NSPoint`:**

```
NSPoint theTextPos;
theTextPos = NSMakePoint(275, rect.size.height-150);
```

3. **Draw the string with the `drawAtPoint` method, passing it the `NSPoint`:**

```
[theString drawAtPoint:theTextPos withAttributes:nil];
```

This line of code draws the text at the position determined by the `NSPoint`. When you run the example, you may be disappointed with the results, as shown in Figure 12-10. The *STOP* string appears in a tiny font, and the letters are black, the default text settings.

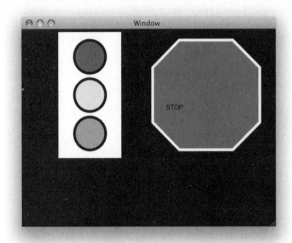

**Figure 12-10:**
So far, this doesn't look much like a stop sign.

Clearly, you want to define how the font looks. To accomplish this, pass something other than `nil` in the `withAttributes` parameter of the `drawAtPoint` function. The `withAttributes` parameter takes an `NSDictionary`, so you need to declare and create one of those.

An `NSMutableDictionary` is a container for a collection of items; in this case, a collection of text attributes. `NSMutableDictionary` is a subclass of `NSDictionary`, so it works in place of an `NSDictionary`. A *mutable* object is one that you can change sometime after you create it. An *immutable* object is one that you can't change after you create it. Mutable objects (such as `NSMutableDictionary`) have *mutable* in their names. Immutable objects (such as `NSDictionary`) don't.

Follow these steps to define your font:

1. **Create an** `NSMutableDictionary`**:**

   In this situation, you use a predefined set of attributes, so you can use an immutable dictionary.

   ```
   NSMutableDictionary *theAttributes;

   //create the NSDictionary object
   theAttributes = [[NSMutableDictionary alloc] init];
   ```

2. **Add objects to the** `NSMutableDictionary` **that represent some text attribute.**

For example, to set the font to Helvetica with a size of 62, use code like this:

```
[theAttributes setObject:
        [NSFont fontWithName: @"Helvetica" size: 62]
        forKey: NSFontAttributeName];
```

**3. Set the color of the text.**

This code adds a white text color attribute to the NSDictionary:

```
[theAttributes setObject:
        [NSColor whiteColor] forKey:
            NSForegroundColorAttributeName];
```

**4. When you finish adding text attributes to the** NSDictionary **object, pass the dictionary object in the** withAttributes **parameter of the** drawAtPoint **function:**

```
[theString drawAtPoint:theTextPos withAttributes:
        theAttributes];
```

**5. Dispose of the** NSDictionary:

```
[theAttributes release];
```

The combined code to draw the string on the stop sign looks like this. Note that theTextPos has a value of 267 for its first parameter instead of 275, to account for the larger Helvetica font.

```
//*************************************
//         DRAW STOP SIGN TEXT
//*************************************
    //Define a string
    NSString *theString;
    theString = @"STOP";

    //Position the text
    NSPoint theTextPos;
    theTextPos = NSMakePoint(267, rect.size.height-150);

    //Create the NSDictionary object
    NSMutableDictionary *theAttributes;
    theAttributes = [[NSMutableDictionary alloc] init];

    //Add attributes to the NSDictionary
    [theAttributes setObject:
        [NSFont fontWithName: @"Helvetica" size: 62]
        forKey: NSFontAttributeName];
```

```
[theAttributes setObject:
    [NSColor whiteColor] forKey:
        NSForegroundColorAttributeName];

//Draw the text
[theString drawAtPoint:theTextPos withAttributes:
        theAttributes];

//Dispose of the NSDictionary
[theAttributes release];
```

You can view the results in Figure 12-11.

**Figure 12-11:**
That's more
like it!

# Displaying an Image

Eventually, you'll grow tired of creating your own graphics and want to display an image file instead. The easiest way to display an image file in your Cocoa application is to add the file directly to the project. For example, if you were to drag a `face.jpg` image from Finder to Xcode, your project might look like Figure 12-12.

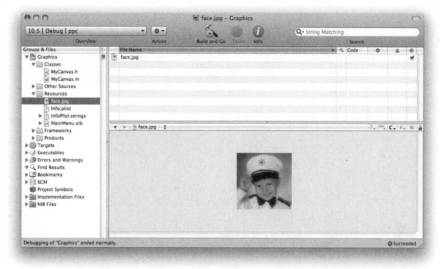

**Figure 12-12:**
Drag an
image from
Finder to
your project
for easy
access.

To draw this image in a view, you need to add only a few lines of code:

1. **Create an** NSPoint **to hold the coordinates for where you want to display the image.**

   This code creates an NSPoint for the lower-left corner of the view:

   ```
   NSPoint theImagePos;
   theImagePos = NSMakePoint(0, 0);
   ```

2. **Create an** NSImage **object and load the image into it.**

   ```
   NSImage* theImage;
   theImage = [NSImage imageNamed:@"face.jpg"];
   ```

3. **Display the image in the view by calling the** dissolveToPoint **function.**

   ```
   [theImage dissolveToPoint: theImagePos
           fraction:(1.0)];
   ```

   Figure 12-13 demonstrates the dissolveToPoint function in action.

The fraction parameter of the dissolveToPoint function represents the opacity of the image. The smaller the value you use for the fraction, the more transparent it is. A value of 1.0 indicates no transparency; a value of 0.0 denotes complete transparency. Figure 12-14 shows the effect of different opacity settings.

**Figure 12-13:**
Draw an image in a view by using the dissolve ToPoint function.

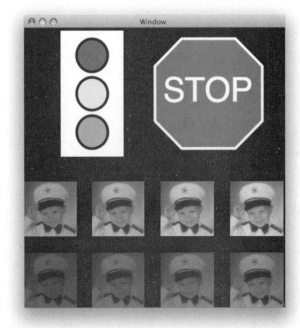

**Figure 12-14:**
Change the opacity of an image for different effects.

To see how opacity works, add this code to the end of your `drawRect` function:

```
NSPoint theImagePos;
theImagePos = NSMakePoint(0, 0);

NSImage* theImage;
theImage = [NSImage imageNamed:@"face.jpg"];

int i;
for (i=3; i<7; i++)
{
    [theImage dissolveToPoint: theImagePos
         fraction:(i*0.1)];
    theImagePos.x = theImagePos.x + 130;
}

theImagePos = NSMakePoint(0, 130);
for (i = 7;i<=10;i++)
{
    [theImage dissolveToPoint: theImagePos
         fraction:(i*0.1)];
    theImagePos.x = theImagePos.x + 130;
}
```

In this example, you used a literal value of 130 to position elements on the screen. This is simply for demonstration purposes to make the code easier to read, but don't do such things in the real world. Instead, base your values on the height and width of the view.

# Chapter 13

# Managing Your Files

. . . . . . . . . . . . . . . . . . . . . . . . . . . . . . . . . . . . . . . . .

. . . . . . . . . . . . . . . . . . . . . . . . . . . . . . . . . . . . . . . . .

Almost every device that Apple ships sports some kind of storage device. Whether it's the hard drive in your old iPod, a SuperDrive in your desktop Macintosh, or a flash drive in your MacBook Air, all storage devices share one common trait — they store data. To facilitate this storage, the Mac OS X operating system uses a hierarchical system of files.

Cocoa has a large array of functions that you can use to make your file manipulation tasks easier. With only a few lines of code, it's a cinch to open, copy, move, and delete any file or folder on your hard drive, assuming that you have adequate privileges for the file or folder. This chapter shows you how.

# About Files and Folders in Mac OS X

Mac OS X has several types of files. You are undoubtedly familiar with the most basic file type — a *document.* You use document files every time you save work in your favorite word processor. When you want to view the document, you simply reopen it with your word processor.

Documents aren't the only type of file on your Mac, however. Another important file type is the *application.* You're probably also very familiar with this file type because you use applications to surf the Web, send e-mail, draw pictures, or program with Xcode. In fact, the whole point of Cocoa programming is to create applications. Cocoa applications come in a special *directory* (or *bundle*) that the Finder treats as a single file. An application bundle contains directories and individual files that contain the executable and supporting files for your application. The idea here is that an application can store its resources (such as pictures, audio, and data) in the same bundle as the application. The accessory files are kept with the application, while also hiding them from the user. That way, users are less likely to delete files that are important to the operation of an application. Many documents also come as bundles, such as iMovie and iDVD projects, RTFD files from TextEdit, and iPhoto Library files.

To help you keep your documents and applications in order, Mac OS X organizes files in a hierarchical structure of folders. *Folders* are containers of files. A folder can hold documents, applications, or even other folders. Some folders contain your operating system; others are ones that you create and modify yourself.

Computer geeks also refer to folders as *directories.* This chapter uses the terms *folder* and *directory* interchangeably. Not content to keep things simple, geeks also refer to *applications* as *executables.* The two terms are synonyms, so whenever you hear someone say, "place the executable in the directory," you can be sure that he could also mean "place the application in the folder." To confuse naming matters even further, you'll also hear the terms *package* and *bundle* used to mean the same thing. Control-click a bundle in Finder, and you'll find a Show Package Contents menu item. Choosing it opens the bundle as a folder to reveal its contents.

For years, Macintosh users have happily navigated the files on their hard drives by double-clicking a folder icon to open it. With Mac OS X, most Mac users got their first taste of the command line by using the *Terminal,* which uses the strange and frightening world of paths. *Paths* are a textual method of describing where a file or folder resides on a drive. For example, the Mac OS X Fonts folder resides in the following location:

```
/Library/Fonts
```

Whenever you see the / character, think *folder* or *directory.* The preceding example reveals that the Fonts folder resides in the Library folder. If your username is Fred, your home folder is located at this path:

```
/Users/Fred
```

These two examples of paths assume that you're describing a file folder or file on your boot drive (assuming that the /Users file system mount point resides on the boot volume). The *boot* drive contains the operating system that you're using at any one time. If you have other drives connected to your machine, the path of a file or folder located on that machine is preceded by Volumes and the name of the drive. For example, if you have a

VacationPhoto.jpg image file that resides on a Drive2 drive, its path looks like this:

```
/Volumes/Drive2/VacationPhoto.jpg
```

# Opening and Using Files

The project for this chapter, File Demo, displays important information about any file or folder that a user selects. You'll be familiar with the information because it all appears in the Get Info window of Finder.

## Building the interface

The interface consists of a button and several NSTextField controls. Users click the button to select a file or folder, after which the application displays information about that file or folder in the various NSTextField controls. To create the interface for this project, perform these steps:

1. **Create a new Cocoa project in Xcode, name it File Info, and then after it opens, expand its Resources folder and double-click the MainMenu. xib file to open it in Interface Builder.**

2. **In Interface Builder, open the default window in the XIB project window and add six** NSTextField Label **controls from the Library window and one** Wrapping Label **control.**

    You can locate the controls by searching for Label from the Library window's search field.

    The wrapping label type is similar to the other labels, except that it's preset to be a multiple line label. The multiple lines help display long file paths.

    Starting with the wrapping label, these seven labels display the following information about a selected file or folder:

    - File path

    - Filename

    - File exists: Displays YES if it exists; NO, if it doesn't

    - File directory: Displays YES if the selection is a folder; NO, if it isn't

    - File creation date

    - File modification date

    - File size in bytes

3. **Change the Title attribute of each** NSTextField **to blank (that is, delete all the text in each field).**

   You'll use these controls to display information about a file or folder.

4. **Add seven more** NSTextField Label **controls to the window and change the Title attribute in the Identity Inspector window for each of these new** Labels **to match the descriptions in the previous step.**

   Figure 13-1 shows what the interface looks like at this point with all 14 NSTextField controls. Note that the wrapping label is taller than the other labels to give it some space to display long file paths. A large number of handles are around the border of each NSTextField to show you the position of each NSTextField, even though half of them are currently displaying nothing.

**Figure 13-1:**
Add 14
NSTextField
controls to
the window.

5. **Add an** NSButton **control to the window and with the Identity Inspector window, change the Title attribute of the button to Select File or Folder.**

   Figure 13-2 shows what the button now looks like.

6. **Add an** NSImageView Image Well **to the window and resize it to 128 x 128 with the Inspector window.**

   The *image well* is where you'll display a file's icon later in this chapter. You may have to move the File Path label and associated text field around to make room for the image well. Figure 13-3 shows the interface with the addition of the image well.

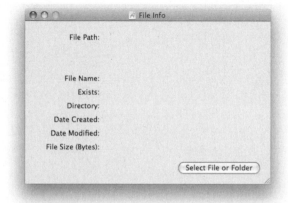

**Figure 13-2:**
Add an
NSButton
that users
click to
select a file
or folder.

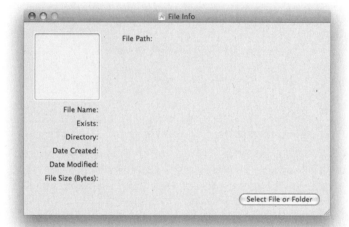

**Figure 13-3:**
Add an
image well
to the
interface.

# Creating a Controller class

When you have the interface in place, you need to create a Controller class.
Perform the following steps:

1. **Drag an** NSObject **from the Library window to the XIB project
   window to add a new controller.**

2. **Press ⌘+6 to open the Identity Inspector and change the class name to**
   FileInfoController, **as shown in Figure 13-4.**

**Figure 13-4:**
Name the
object
FileInfo
Controller.

3. **Add eight outlets to the** `FileInfoController` **class.**

   These eight outlets should have descriptive names that tell you the purpose of each. You'll connect seven of them to the `NSTextFields`. The eighth outlet connects to the `NSImageView`. Name them `fileCreated Display`, `fileDirDisplay`, `fileExistsDisplay`, `fileIconDisplay`, `fileModifiedDisplay`, `fileNameDisplay`, `filePathDisplay`, and `fileSizeDisplay`, as shown in Figure 13-5.

4. **Add an action to the class in the Identity Inspector window and name it** `selectTheFile:`.

5. **Wire the interface to the** `FileInfoController` **outlets:**

   a. *Control+drag from the* `FileInfoController` *instance to each of the* `NSTextFields` *in your interface's main window. Select the appropriate outlet from the black connections list overlay that appears after the Control+drag operation.*

   b. *Control+drag from the* `FileInfoController` *to the* `NSImageView` *control. Connect* `NSImageView` *to the* `fileIconDisplay` *outlet.*

6. **Connect the interface to the** `FileInfoController` **action.**

   Control+drag from the `NSButton` in the interface to the `FileInfo Controller` instance in the MainMenu.xib file window. Connect the `NSButton` to the `selectTheFile` action (see Figure 13-6).

**Figure 13-5:**
Add eight
outlets to
the class.

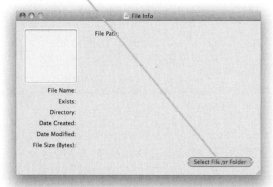

**Figure 13-6:**
Connect the
button in
your inter-
face to the
selectThe
File action.

7. **Create the files for the** `FileInfoController` **class:**

   a. *In the XIB project window, click the* `FileInfoController` *class.*

   b. *Choose File⇨Write Class Files to create the files for* `FileInfoController` *and to add them to the Xcode project.*

8. **In Xcode, assign an** `NSObject` **superclass to the FileInfoController.h file.**

   Change this line:

   ```
   @interface FileInfoController : /* Specify a
           superclass (eg: NSObject or NSView) */ {
   ```

   to this:

   ```
   @interface FileInfoController : NSObject {
   ```

# Open sesame . . . er, panel

When you have the interface built, you can add some code in Xcode to make the interface functional. Don't forget about the goal of this project — to select a file and report information about it. To display information about a specific file or folder, you use Cocoa's `OpenPanel` class. With the `OpenPanel` class, you can display an Open dialog that allows a user to select a file or folder. When you use an `OpenPanel`, you typically follow four basic steps:

1. Create an instance of `OpenPanel`.

2. Set the attributes of the `OpenPanel` instance.

3. Display the `OpenPanel` for the user and wait for the user to do something with it: Select a file and click OK or cancel the operation.

4. Perform a function with the file that the user selected.

To see how `OpenPanel` works in Cocoa, perform these four steps.

1. **Create an** `OpenPanel` **instance.**

   You do so in the same way that you create other objects in Cocoa:

   ```
   NSOpenPanel *openPanel = [NSOpenPanel openPanel];
   ```

2. **Alter the attributes of** `OpenPanel` **by calling one or more of its methods.**

   For example, to change the title of `OpenPanel`, use the `setTitle` method.

   ```
   [openPanel setTitle:@"Choose a File or Folder"];
   ```

The `setTitle` method of `OpenPanel` is a method provided by the `NSWindow` superclass. Because `OpenPanel` is a subclass of `NSWindow`, it can take advantage of the `NSWindow` methods.

The `OpenPanel` class also has methods of its own too, of course. For example, you'll want to tell `Open Panel` which files a user may open or select. By default, `Open Panel` lets users choose any document or application that they want, but they can't choose folders. You can remedy the situation by adding a call to the `setCanChooseDirectories` method of `OpenPanel`. This method takes one parameter: a Boolean. If you pass `YES`, users can select folders in `OpenPanel`. If you pass `NO` (or if you don't use this `setCanChooseDirectories` method at all), users can't choose folders in `OpenPanel`.

```
[openPanel setCanChooseDirectories:YES];
```

3. **Display** `OpenPanel`.

You have several options when it comes to displaying `OpenPanel`. The most basic way to display it is to use its `runModal` method, which returns an integer upon completion.

```
NSInteger i = [openPanel runModal];
```

The result of this line of code is the dialog, as shown in Figure 13-7.

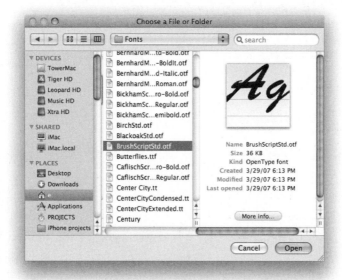

**Figure 13-7:**
Display an
OpenPanel
with the
runModal
method.

**4. Find out what the user did with the** OpenPanel.

To find out whether the user clicked OK or Cancel in the OpenPanel, you must examine the value that runModal returns. If the user clicked OK, the return value is NSOKButton, a constant that Cocoa provides for you. If the user cancels the open operation instead, the return value is NSCancelButton.

```
NSInteger i = [openPanel runModal];
if (i == NSOKButton)
{
    NSLog(@"The user clicked OK!");
}
```

Rather than create a new variable just to check the return value, wrapping the runModal command into the if statement is easier:

```
if ([openPanel runModal] == NSOKButton)
{
    NSLog(@"The user clicked OK!");
}
```

## Finding a file's path, name, and more

After you discover that a user has clicked OK in OpenPanel, you need to find out which file or folder the user selected. By using the filename method of the OpenPanel class, you can get the path to that file or folder in the form of an NSString:

```
NSString *theFilePath = [openPanel filename];
```

To display the path in the interface, call the setStringValue method of the filePathDisplay outlet:

```
[filePathDisplay setStringValue:theFilePath];
```

Besides the path of the file, you can discover all sorts of interesting information about a file with the NSFileManager class. Follow these steps:

**1. Create a new** NSFileManager **object using the** defaultManager **class method:**

```
NSFileManager *theManager = [NSFileManager
        defaultManager];
```

**2. Call the various** NSFileManager **methods to find out information about a file:**

- *To retrieve the filename from the selected file,* use the display NameAtPath method. Because the method returns an NSString, you can nest the call to display it in the interface. In this case, display it with the `fileNameDisplay` outlet:

```
[fileNameDisplay setStringValue:
[theManager displayNameAtPath:theFilePath]];
```

- *To know whether the file exists,* use the `fileExistsAtPath` method of the `NSFileManager`:

```
if ( [theManager fileExistsAtPath:theFilePath ] ) {
    [fileExistsDisplay setStringValue:@"YES"];
}
 else {
    [fileExistsDisplay setStringValue:@"NO"];
}
```

- *To find out whether the selected file is a directory,* use the alternate version of the `fileExistsAtPath` method. The alternate version has two parameters: the file's path and a pointer to a Boolean. After this call completes its execution, the Boolean value holds a value of YES if the file in the first parameter is a directory:

```
if ( [theManager fileExistsAtPath:theFilePath
    isDirectory:&isFolder] ) {
    [fileExistsDisplay setStringValue:@"YES"];
}
else {
    [fileExistsDisplay setStringValue:@"NO"];
}
```

You can also find out a fair amount about a file with the `fileAttributes AtPath` method:

```
NSDictionary *theFileAttributes = [theManager fileAttribut
        esAtPath:theFilePath traverseLink:YES];
```

Note that the `fileAttributesAtPath` method returns an `NSDictionary`. An `NSDictionary` is a data structure that holds a collection of different values. This `NSDictionary` returns a collection of data about a file or folder, including the following:

- **File size:** The size of a file or folder, measured in bytes

- **Creation date:** The date the file or folder was created

- **Modification date:** The date the file or folder was last modified

Use an `NSDictionary` instead of an `NSMutableDictionary` because you don't need to change the data in that dictionary. You're simply filling in the `NSDictionary` so you can read its contents.

To extract this data from the NSDictionary object, use the objectForKey method of the NSManager instance:

```
NSNumber *theFileSize;
NSDate *theModificationDate;
NSDate *theCreationDate;

if (theFileSize = [theFileAttributes
        objectForKey:NSFileSize])        [fileSizeDisplay
        setIntValue:(int)theFileSize];

if (theModificationDate = [theFileAttributes objectForKey:
        NSFileModificationDate]) {
    [fileModifiedDisplay setStringValue:(NSString*)
        theModificationDate];
}
if (theCreationDat = [theFileAttributes objectForKey:NSFil
        eCreationDate]) {
    [fileCreatedDisplay setStringValue:(NSString*)
        theCreationDate];
}
```

## Viewing a file's icon

The icon is another great feature of Finder. Without icons, you'd be stuck in the dark days of text-only interfaces like DOS. *Yikes!* Fortunately, it's easy to work with icons in Cocoa. But before you grab an icon from a file, you must create an NSFileWrapper. An NSFileWrapper is an object that stores a file's data in memory. For this example, though, you use it to load the file's icon into memory.

1. **Initialize the** NSFileWrapper **instance with this path to create it:**

   ```
   NSFileWrapper *theFileWrapper = [ [[NSFileWrapper
           alloc]
   initWithPath:theFilePath] autorelease];
   ```

2. **Extract the icon from the file with the** icon **method of the** NSFileWrapper.

   This call returns an NSImage, which you can then display in the NSImageView of the interface.

   ```
   NSImage *theIcon = [theFileWrapper icon];
   ```

3. **To view the icon at dimensions of 128 x 128, for example, stretch the icon to the size of the** NSImageView **with** setImageScaling **before displaying it:**

   ```
   [fileIconDisplay setImageScaling:NSScaleToFit];
   [fileIconDisplay setImage:theIcon];
   ```

NSScaleToFit is just one of a few scaling values that you can place in this parameter. To see the others, Option-double-click NSScaleToFit to view the online documentation for this call.

With your icon code in place, the complete code listing for the select TheFile action is as follows:

```
- (IBAction)selectTheFile:(id)sender
{
    NSOpenPanel *openPanel = [NSOpenPanel openPanel];
    [openPanel setTitle:@"Choose a File or Folder"];
    [openPanel setCanChooseDirectories:YES];


    if ([openPanel runModal] == NSOKButton)
    {
        NSString *theFilePath = [openPanel filename];

        //display the file path
        [filePathDisplay setStringValue:theFilePath];

        NSFileManager *theManager = [NSFileManager
        defaultManager];
        [fileNameDisplay setStringValue:[theManager di
        splayNameAtPath:theFilePath]];

        //does the file really exist at this path?
        if ( [theManager fileExistsAtPath:theFilePath
        ] ) {
            [fileExistsDisplay setStringValue:@"YES"];
        }
        else {
            [fileExistsDisplay setStringValue:@"NO"];
        }

        //is it a directory?
        BOOL isFolder;
        if ( [theManager fileExistsAtPath:theFilePath
        isDirectory:&isFolder] && isFolder ) {
            [fileDirDisplay setStringValue:@"YES"];
        }
        else {
            [fileDirDisplay setStringValue:@"NO"];
        }

        //GET FILE ATTRIBUTES
        NSNumber *theFileSize;
        NSDate *theModificationDate;
        NSDate *theCreationDate;

        NSDictionary *theFileAttributes =
        [theManager fileAttributesAtPath:theFilePath
        traverseLink:YES];
```

```
    if (theFileSize = [theFileAttributes
objectForKey:NSFileSize]) {
        [fileSizeDisplay setIntValue:(int)
theFileSize];
        }

    if (theModificationDate = [theFileAttributes o
bjectForKey:NSFileModificationDate]) {
        [fileModifiedDisplay
setStringValue:(NSString*)
theModificationDate];
        }

    if (theCreationDate = [theFileAttributes objec
tForKey:NSFileCreationDate]) {
        [fileCreatedDisplay
setStringValue:(NSString*)theCreationDate];
        }

    //display an icon
    NSFileWrapper *theFileWrapper
= [ [[NSFileWrapper alloc]
initWithPath:theFilePath] autorelease];
    NSImage *theIcon = [theFileWrapper icon];
    [fileIconDisplay setImageScaling:NSScaleToFit];
    [fileIconDisplay setImage:theIcon];

    }
}
```

**4. Choose Build⇨Build and Go to test your work.**

Figure 13-8 shows the result.

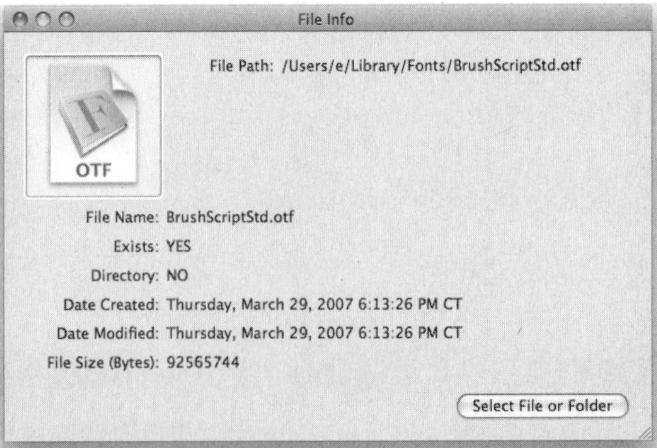

**Figure 13-8:**
With the
NSFile
Manager
and NSFile
Wrapper,
you can
easily
display a
variety of
information
about a file.

| | File Info |
| --- | --- |
| | File Path: /Users/e/Library/Fonts/BrushScriptStd.otf |

File Name: BrushScriptStd.otf
Exists: YES
Directory: NO
Date Created: Thursday, March 29, 2007 6:13:26 PM CT
Date Modified: Thursday, March 29, 2007 6:13:26 PM CT
File Size (Bytes): 92565744

Select File or Folder

## *Reading from and writing to documents*

Many types of files are on your hard drive. Each file type has its own format, whether it's text, graphics, fonts, or audio. Cocoa has built-in functions to deal with common file formats. For example, Cocoa is adept at working with text documents of all sorts. See Chapter 11 to get the scoop on working with text files.

Graphics is another place where Cocoa shines. Whether you need to view a PICT file, save a JPEG file, or convert a view to PDF, Cocoa and the underlying QuickTime engine of Mac OS X have you covered. You can find information about working with graphics files in Chapter 12.

Multimedia is yet another highlight of the Mac OS. Chapter 16 discusses the use of audio and video files in your applications. There, you'll find the code you need to view QuickTime movie files as well as play a variety of audio files.

# *Working with Files and Folders*

Copying and moving files are important functions that you may want to perform in your applications. To add these features to your project, follow these steps:

1. **Open your MainMenu.xib file in Interface Builder.**

2. **To your main window, add two new** NSButtons **and change their titles.**

   To follow along with the example, change the Title attribute of one button to Copy File to Desktop. As you may have guessed, when users click this button, they can select a file. The application then duplicates that file, placing it on the desktop.

   Change the Title attribute of the other NSButton to Move File to Desktop.

3. **Add a new action to the** FileInfoController **class in the Identity Inspector window.**

   To follow along with the example, name the action copyTheFile.

4. **Connect the action to the button.**

   To do so, Control+drag from the button to the FileInfoController instance in the NIB file.

5. **Save your interface and return to Xcode.**

6. **In Xcode, add the new actions to the FileInfoController.h file, placing them after the** selectTheFile **action.**

The resulting header file looks like this with the new actions in boldface:

```
/* FileInfoController */

#import <Cocoa/Cocoa.h>

@interface FileInfoController : NSObject {
    IBOutlet id fileCreatedDisplay;
    IBOutlet id fileDirDisplay;
    IBOutlet id fileExistsDisplay;
    IBOutlet id fileIconDisplay;
    IBOutlet id fileModifiedDisplay;
    IBOutlet id fileNameDisplay;
    IBOutlet id filePathDisplay;
    IBOutlet id fileSizeDisplay;
}
- (IBAction)selectTheFile:(id)sender;
- (IBAction)copyTheFile:(id)sender;
- (IBAction)moveTheFile:(id)sender;
- (IBAction)createAFolder:(id)sender;
@end
```

## Copying files and folders

To copy a file or folder, you need two things:

✔ **Source path:** The path to the file that you want to copy

✔ **Destination path:** Where you want the file copy to reside

You can get the source file from the OpenPanel class covered earlier in this chapter. You could do something similar for the destination with the SavePanel, but this time you know where you want the resulting file to appear: on the desktop. Therefore, you can create your own path that points to a new file on the desktop.

To do so, follow these steps:

1. **Gain access to the Desktop folder with the** NSHomeDirectory **function in the** Foundation **class.**

   ```
   NSString *theDestination = [ [NSHomeDirectory()
   ```

2. **Tack on additional parts of the path with the** stringByAppending PathComponent **method (say** *that* **five times fast!).**

```
stringByAppendingPathComponent:@"Desktop"]
stringByAppendingPathComponent:theFileName ];
```

3. **Copy the file by using the** `copyPath` **method of the** `NSFileManager`
   **class, pass it the source path, the destination path, and** `nil` **for the**
   **handler:**

```
[theManager copyPath:theFilePath
toPath:theDestination handler:nil];
```

The resulting `copyTheFile` action looks like this:

```
- (IBAction)copyTheFile:(id)sender
{
    NSOpenPanel *theOpenPanel = [NSOpenPanel openPanel];
    [theOpenPanel setTitle:@"Choose a File or Folder to
        copy"];
    [theOpenPanel setCanChooseDirectories:YES];

    if ([theOpenPanel runModal] == NSOKButton)
    {
        NSString *theFilePath = [theOpenPanel filename];
        NSFileManager *theManager = [NSFileManager
            defaultManager];
        NSString *theFileName = [theManager
            displayNameAtPath:theFilePath];

        NSString *theDestination = [ [NSHomeDirectory()
        stringByAppendingPathComponent:@"Desktop"]
          stringByAppendingPathComponent:theFileName ];
        [theManager copyPath:theFilePath
          toPath:theDestination handler:nil];
    }
}
```

## Moving files and folders

Moving a file is just as simple as duplicating one. In fact, the code is identical
to the `copyTheFile` action, except for one line. Instead of the `copyPath`
method, you use the `movePath` method. The code for the `moveTheFile`
action looks like this:

```
- (IBAction)moveTheFile:(id)sender
{
    NSOpenPanel *theOpenPanel = [NSOpenPanel openPanel];
    [theOpenPanel setTitle:@"Choose a File or Folder to
        move"];
    [theOpenPanel setCanChooseDirectories:YES];
```

```
if ([theOpenPanel runModal] == NSOKButton)
{
    NSString *theFilePath = [theOpenPanel filename];
    NSFileManager *theManager = [NSFileManager
        defaultManager];
    NSString *theFileName = [theManager
        displayNameAtPath:theFilePath];

    NSString *theDestination = [ [NSHomeDirectory()
        stringByAppendingPathComponent:@"Desktop"]
    stringByAppendingPathComponent:theFileName ];
    [theManager movePath:theFilePath
    toPath:theDestination handler:nil];
}
}
```

## Deleting files and folders

Sometimes you'll want to delete files from a drive. Rather than bore you with another identical code example, I'll simply tell you that the code to delete a file resembles the copyTheFile and moveTheFile except for the last command. Look up the removeFileAtPath method in the NSFileManager documentation. Doing so gives you experience in looking up calls in the documentation and provides you with an ample amount of time to consider why you'd want to use this call.

Delete a file, and it's gone! Permanently. Make sure that your users know that a deletion will occur and always give them a way out. One way to do this is to display an alert:

```
NSOpenPanel *theOpenPanel = [NSOpenPanel openPanel];
[theOpenPanel setTitle:@"Choose a File or Folder to
    Delete"];
[theOpenPanel setCanChooseDirectories:YES];

if ([theOpenPanel runModal] == NSOKButton)
{
    NSString *theFilePath = [theOpenPanel filename];
    NSFileManager *theManager = [NSFileManager
        defaultManager];

    NSInteger n;
    n = NSRunAlertPanel (NSLocalizedString(@"Are you
        sure you want to delete the file?",nil),

    NSLocalizedString(@"You cannot undo this
        deletion.", nil),
```

```
        NSLocalizedString(@"Yes",nil),
        NSLocalizedString(@"No",nil),
        nil);

    if (n == NSAlertDefaultReturn) {
            [theManager removeFileAtPath:theFilePath
        handler:nil];
        }
    }
```

The code asks the user which file to delete using the NSOpenPanel. After creating theFilePath and theManager objects, the code displays an Alert panel by calling the NSRunAlertPanel function. NSRunAlertPanel takes five parameters that correspond to the title of the alert, the message on the alert, the text on the default button, the text on the alternate button, and finally text for a third button, which you ignore this time by passing nil. If NSRunAlertPanel returns a value of NSAlertDefaultReturn, which corresponds to the default button in the alert, the code deletes the file with the removeFileAtPath method.

## Creating folders

To create a folder on your drive, use the createDirectoryAtPath method of the NSFileManager. You need to pass it two parameters:

✔ The first parameter is the path where you want to create the folder.

✔ The second parameter lets you set various attributes of the folder. You won't use this second parameter very often, so you can simply set it to nil.

To show the createDirectoryAtPath method in action, follow these steps:

1. **Add the following code to FileInfoController.m to create a MyNewFolder folder on the desktop:**

```
- (IBAction)createAFolder:(id)sender
{
    NSString *theDestination = [ [NSHomeDirectory()
        stringByAppendingPathComponent:@"Desktop"]
        stringByAppendingPathComponent:@"MyNewFolder"
        ];

    [theManager createDirectoryAtPath:theDestination
        attributes:nil];
}
```

If you use the `createAFolder` action, don't forget to define it in the header file:

```
- (IBAction)createAFolder:(id)sender;
```

2. **Add an action to** `FileInfoController` **and connect it to a new** `NSButton` **in Interface Builder.**

   Figure 13-9 shows the completed interface.

   Sometimes it's easiest to simply add actions and outlets to your project in Xcode and your NIB file in Interface Builder, rather than relying on those applications to talk to each other.

3. **To test your work, return to Xcode and press ⌘+R.**

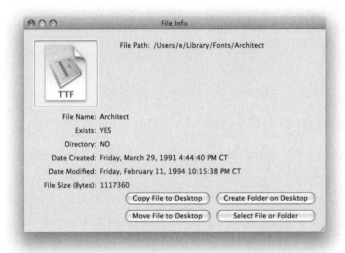

**Figure 13-9:** The completed Files project can display information about a file or folder as well as perform a variety of file tasks.

# Chapter 14

# Printing with Cocoa

. . . . . . . . . . . . . . . . . . . . . . . . . . . . . . . . . . . . . . . . . . . . . . . . . . . . . . . . . . .

. . . . . . . . . . . . . . . . . . . . . . . . . . . . . . . . . . . . . . . . . . . . . . . . . . . . . . . . . . .

Although Cocoa's on-screen display of graphics and text is world class, that doesn't mean Apple forgot about printing. Known for decades as one of the innovative adopting forces behind technologies, such as PostScript and laser printing, Apple continues in this tradition by adding easy-to-implement printing features to Cocoa. This chapter shows you how to add printing features to your Cocoa applications. Although printing has been a messy topic for programmers in the past, Cocoa makes it simple to implement some sophisticated printing features to your projects. You'll love the consistency that Apple provides you as a developer, and your users will love the professional printing results that your application implements.

To begin working with printing, copy the Start source code for this chapter to your hard drive. (To download the code, go to www.dummies.com/go/cocoafd.) The printing project for this chapter is based on the completed project from the end of Chapter 12. Because you can print using any view, you can use the graphics view from Chapter 12 as your printable canvas.

# How Printing Works in Cocoa

To help you achieve great results that address all your printing needs, Cocoa offers a collection of important classes for printing in Mac OS X. You use these classes together to add printing to your applications:

✔ **NSView:** Printing to a page is as simple as drawing text and graphics in an NSView. The examples in this chapter build on the graphics example in Chapter 12.

✔ **NSPageLayout:** This class is responsible for displaying the Page Setup panel. Typically applications display this panel when a user chooses File⇨Page Setup. Your users will invoke the Page Setup panel to choose the orientation of the printed page. They can also set the paper size in the Page Setup panel. When the user has finished adjusting the printing properties of the NSPageLayout object, the NSPageLayoutObject saves the results in an NSPrintInfo object.

✔ **NSPrintInfo:** NSPrintInfo is a storage class that holds the settings and options for printing. NSPrintInfo stores the settings from the Page Setup panel as well as the page count, margins, and other items that appear in the NSPrintPanel.

✔ **NSPrintPanel:** When you choose File⇨Print from most applications, you see an example of the NSPrintPanel. The NSPrintPanel is responsible for managing the settings of a print job. NSPrintPanel stores its settings in an NSPrintInfo object.

✔ **NSPrintOperation:** This class takes care of creating the printed page. It displays the Print panel and carries out the print job.

To help you envision how the printing process works in Cocoa, here's a brief rundown of the steps involved:

1. Draw text and graphics to a view.

   This drawing can occur in any view, whether it's a view in a graphics application, a word processor, or even the background of a window. Cocoa can print from them all.

2. The user chooses File⇨Page Setup.

   Your application displays the Page panel.

3. The user selects the format and scale of the print job.

   Figure 14-1 shows what the Page panel looks like.

4. The user dismisses the panel.

   Your application stores the settings in a PrintInfo object.

5. The user chooses File⇨Print.

   Your application displays the Print panel, where the user tweaks the settings for the print job. Figure 14-2 shows a typical Print panel. When the user finishes preparing the print job, he may dismiss the panel by clicking Cancel or start the print job by clicking OK.

6. The user prints the view.

Your application sets up the print operation with the Page and Print panel settings that you stored in the `PrintInfo` object. The view's `drawRect` takes care of drawing the graphics or text, just as it does on-screen.

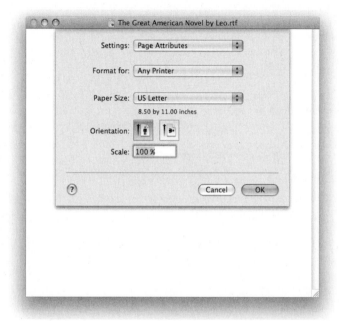

**Figure 14-1:**
Use the Page panel to adjust settings for the pages in your print job.

**Figure 14-2:**
Use the Print panel to adjust settings for the print job.

# *Tweaking the Page Settings*

The first step of your printing journey begins with the Page panel, where your users can select the scale and format of a project job.

If you have access to multiple printers, you can also choose a Format For option to get the dimensions of a printable area. The dimensions help you avoid cropping around the edges.

Open the Xcode project for this chapter. Double-click the MainMenu.xib file to open the interface XIB file for this project in Interface Builder. After the XIB file opens, follow these steps to add a print controller to the project:

1. **Create a new controller class:**

   a. *Open the Library window and search for* NSObject.

   b. *Drag a new object to the project window.*

   c. *Press ⌘+6 and name the new* NSObject MyPrintController.

   Figure 14-3 shows the newly named object.

**Figure 14-3:**
The MyPrint Controller object takes the printing tasks.

2. **Add an outlet and two actions to** `MyPrintController`.

   a. *Press ⌘+6 to open the Identity Inspector window and add a* `canvas View` *outlet to the* `MyPrintController` *class.*

   b. *Add two actions to the controller by clicking the + button beneath the Class Actions section of the Identity Inspector.*

   c. *Name the actions* `printOnePage:` *and* `showPagePanel:`.

   The `showPagePanel` action takes care of displaying the Page panel and storing its settings. The `printOnePage` action displays a Print panel and then executes a print job.

   Figure 14-4 shows the outlets and actions for `MyPrintController`.

3. **Connect the** `MyPrintController` **instance to the user interface.**

   a. *Control+drag from the* `MyPrintController` *instance to the view in the main window of your interface. Select the* `canvasView` *outlet in the small black connections list overlay that appears.*

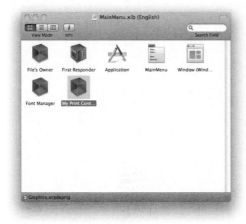

**Figure 14-4:**
The MyPrint Controller has one outlet and two actions.

b. *Connect the two actions to the menu items for this project: Control+drag from the Page Setup menu item in the MainMenu menu bar to the* MyPrintController *instance. Select the* showPagePanel *action in the small black connections list overlay that appears, listing the actions in* MyPrintController. *Repeat for the Print menu item and the* printOnePage *action.*

Figure 14-5 shows the MyPrintController outlet and action connections in the Identity Inspector window.

4. **Create the files for** MyPrintController.

Select MyPrintController in the XIB project window. Choose File➪Write Class Files to add the header and implementation files to your project in Xcode.

5. **Save your interface project by choosing File➪Save and quit Interface Builder by choosing Interface Builder➪Quit.**

6. **Return to Xcode and select the MyPrintController.h file to view its contents. Change your MyPrintController.h file to read as follows:**

```
/* MyPrintController */

#import <Cocoa/Cocoa.h>

@interface MyPrintController : NSObject
{
    IBOutlet id canvasView;
    NSPrintInfo *thePrintInfo;
}
```

**Figure 14-5:**
Connect the one outlet and two actions of the MyPrint Controller instance.

```
-  (IBAction)printOnePage:(id)sender;
-  (IBAction)showPagePanel:(id)sender;
@end
```

Besides defining `MyPrintController` as an `NSObject`, the only other addition is this line:

```
NSPrintInfo *thePrintInfo;
```

This line declares a pointer to an `NSPrintInfo` object as an instance variable to help you store settings that the user makes in the Page and Print panels.

7. **Select the MyPrintController.m file and change its code to read**

```
#import "MyPrintController.h"

@implementation MyPrintController

-  (IBAction)showPagePanel:(id)sender {

    int i;
    thePrintInfo = [NSPrintInfo sharedPrintInfo];
    NSPageLayout *pageLayout = [NSPageLayout
        pageLayout];
    i = [pageLayout runModalWithPrintInfo:(NSPrintInfo
        *)thePrintInfo];

}

@end
```

Here's how the code works:

1. The `showPagePanel` method first populates the `thePrintInfo` variable with the `NSPrintInfo` value, which is shared by all applications.

2. The code creates an `NSPageLayout` instance and displays it using the `runModalWithPrintInfo` method.

   By passing `thePrintInfo` to the `runModalWithPrintInfo` method, the Page panel retains its settings in `thePrintInfo` when the user dismisses it.

So far, this code is functional but not terribly interesting. You can run it and choose File⇨Page Setup to view and play with the settings in the Page panel.

# Setting Up the Print Job and Printing the View

To add printing, all you have to do is implement the `printOnePage` action that you defined as part of `MyPrintController` in the preceding section. Click the MyPrintController.m file in Xcode and change its code to read

```
#import "MyPrintController.h"

@implementation MyPrintController

- (IBAction)showPagePanel:(id)sender {

    int i;
    thePrintInfo = [NSPrintInfo sharedPrintInfo];
    NSPageLayout *pageLayout = [NSPageLayout pageLayout];
    i = [pageLayout
        runModalWithPrintInfo:(NSPrintInfo *)
            thePrintInfo];

}

- (IBAction)printOnePage:(id)sender
{

    thePrintInfo = [NSPrintInfo sharedPrintInfo];
    NSPrintOperation *thePrintOperation;

    thePrintOperation =
        [NSPrintOperation printOperationWithView:
            myCanvasView printInfo:thePrintInfo];

    [thePrintOperation setShowPanels:YES];
    [thePrintOperation runOperation];

}

@end
```

The `printOnePage` method takes care of running the Print panel and executing the print job in this way:

1. It creates an `NSPrintOperation` instance using the class method `printOperationWithView`.

2. You pass the `printOperationWithView` method a view to print and an `NSPrintInfo` instance.

3. The `printOperationWithView` method returns an instance of `NSPrintOperation`.

4. (Optional but typical in most applications) If you want to display the Print panel, call the `setShowPanels`, passing it a Boolean value of `YES`.

5. The `runOperation` method of the `NSPrintOperation` object runs the print job.

Cocoa takes care of everything else for you, including dismissing the Print panel and printing the view.

# *Printing to Places Other Than a Printer*

So far, you've implemented some pretty boring stuff. Printing is nice, but it's become a standard requirement on all applications and operating systems and it's not altogether exciting. When it comes to printing, Cocoa really shines in its capability to print directly to PDF (Portable Document Format) files. Instead of printing your view to a standard printer, you can ask Cocoa to save it to a PDF-formatted file instead. PDF is a standard format for publishing and printing documents. In the past, you had to rely on third-party solutions when creating PDF content on the fly. With Cocoa, it's as easy as adding a few lines of code to your project.

Before you begin adding PDF features to your project, you should know that you already have one form of PDF printing: The user can click the PDF button that's at the bottom of the Print panel.

Here's a more elegant solution if you don't like that users have to open the Print panel to print to PDF:

1. **Open the MainMenu.xib file in the project for this chapter.**

2. **Add a new push button to the existing interface by dragging one from the Library window.**

Figure 14-6 shows what the interface looks like.

**Figure 14-6:**
Add a new
button that
users click
to print to a
PDF file.

3. **Add a new action to the** MyPrintController **class.**

   Click MyPrintController in the XIB project window, press ⌘+6 to
   open the Identity Inspector window, and add a new printToPDF action,
   as shown in Figure 14-7.

**Figure 14-7:**
Add a new
printToPDF
action to the
MyPrint
Controller
class.

**4. Connect the new action to the interface.**

Control+drag from the new button in your interface to the
MyPrintController instance in the XIB project window. Select
printToPDF from the small black connections list overlay that appears.

**5. Return to Xcode and add the new** printToPDF **action to the
MyPrintController.h file:**

```
/* MyPrintController */

#import <Cocoa/Cocoa.h>

@interface MyPrintController : NSObject
{
    IBOutlet id myCanvasView;
    NSPrintInfo *thePrintInfo;
}

- (IBAction)printOnePage:(id)sender;
- (IBAction)showPagePanel:(id)sender;
- (IBAction)printToPDF:(id)sender;
@end
```

**6. Add the following code to implement the** printToPDF **method in the
MyPrintController.m file:**

```
- (IBAction)printToPDF:(id)sender
{
    NSRect theRect;
    NSData *theData;

    theRect = [myCanvasView bounds];
    theData = [myCanvasView dataWithPDFInsideRect:
        theRect];
    [theData
        writeToFile: [@"~/Desktop/MyView.pdf"
stringByExpandingTildeInPath]
        atomically: YES];
}
```

Just to keep matters simple, this method creates a PDF file on the desktop.

1. The code starts by getting the bounds of the NSRect that surrounds
   the view.

2. With those bounds, dataWithPDFInsideRect provides you with raw
   PDF data for use in a file.

3. The `writeToFile` method saves the data to a file.

   You can view the resulting PDF with popular PDF viewers, such as the Apple Preview application, the Adobe Acrobat Reader, or a Web browser like Safari.

Although this method doesn't exactly use printing classes, you can always print from your project with the Print panel. For this reason, PDF is part of the printing chapter.

# Chapter 15

# Cocoa on the Internet

· · · · · · · · · · · · · · · · · · · · · · · · · · · · · · · · · · · · · · · · · · · · · · · · · ·

## In This Chapter

▶ Loading a Web site with Cocoa

▶ Downloading files from the Internet

▶ Sending e-mails with only a few lines of code

· · · · · · · · · · · · · · · · · · · · · · · · · · · · · · · · · · · · · · · · · · · · · · · · · ·

The last two decades of personal computing have witnessed explosive growth in networking technologies. Consequently, the vast majority of personal computer owners use the Internet, many on a daily basis. Among the various means of communication available to a user on the Internet, the World Wide Web and e-mail stand out as the two main tools that everyone uses.

In this chapter, you explore the wild and wooly world of the Internet and see how it applies to Cocoa applications. The chapter starts by showing you how to load Web pages, download files, and render HTML (HyperText Markup Language) in your own projects. Later, you add e-mail features to your application as well. By the end of this chapter, you'll have a fully functional project that performs some important Internet functions. Although it's not necessarily the kind of application you'll want to use for your next best-selling killer app, it can serve as a handy reference for future projects.

## Interacting with the Web

Just over a decade ago, few were familiar with the Internet or the World Wide Web. Now, even your dog has a domain name, an e-mail address, and a MySpace account. Computer users have eaten up all that the Internet has to offer and in the process have become discerning consumers. They expect instant connectivity to any Web site in the world. Luckily, Cocoa has you covered. Perhaps the two most popular tasks on the Web are viewing Web pages and downloading files. With only a few lines of code, Cocoa gives you the ability to offer these important Internet functions in your own applications.

# Loading a Web page in a browser

Loading a URL (Uniform Resource Locator) into a Web browser is one of the most common Internet-related tasks that you'll want to perform. It comes in handy for directing users to online documentation, to a download page where they can get the latest version of your application, or even to your Web-based store to purchase software.

Because viewing Web pages is a task that you perform so frequently, Cocoa provides a class to handle the dirty work for you: NSWorkspace. The NS Workspace class gives you easy access to miscellaneous utilities. Every application has one, and only one, NSWorkspace object. By calling the openURL method of the NSWorkspace instance, you can load and view a URL with the default Web browser.

To use your application's NSWorkspace instance, and, more important, its openURL method, use code like this:

```
[[NSWorkspace sharedWorkspace] openURL:theURL]
```

This code snippet works by calling the sharedWorkspace class method of NSWorkspace. From there, it's a simple matter of calling the openURL method and passing it a valid URL in the form of an NSURL. The NSURL class lets you wrap a traditional URL in a Cocoa object. You can define an NSURL with a hard-coded URL:

```
NSURL *theURL = [NSURL URLWithString:@"http://www.wiley.
    com"];
```

If you want users to supply the URL in an NSTextField (with a theURL Field outlet) in your app's interface, you might do something like this instead:

```
NSURL *theURL = [NSURL URLWithString:[theURLField
    stringValue]];
```

Because openURL returns a Boolean value, you can determine whether the command executed successfully. For example, if you create a loadWebPage action, the code might look like this:

```
- (IBAction)loadWebPage:(id)sender
{
    NSURL *theURL = [NSURL URLWithString:[theURLField
        stringValue]];

    if ( [[NSWorkspace sharedWorkspace] openURL:theURL] )
        NSLog(@"URL Loaded");
}
```

If the `openURL` method performs as it should, the code displays a `URL Loaded` message on the screen.

## Downloading files

Another important feature that you may want to add to your Cocoa applications is the capability to download files from the Internet without using a browser. You can use download functionality for a variety of situations:

- ✔ Offer instant one-click access to the latest version of your application on the Web.
- ✔ Download and display HTML help files from your Web site.
- ✔ Retrieve a file from the Web that lists the current version of your application.

Cocoa makes it easy to offer all these features and more. With only two lines of code, you can download a file from the Web to your hard drive. This example loads the *For Dummies* home page:

```
NSURL *theURL = [NSURL URLWithString:@"http://www.dummies.
        com"];
NSData *pageData = [theURL resourceDataUsingCache:YES];
```

Like the browser code from earlier in this chapter, you first define an `NSURL`. In this example, the URL is hard-coded to `www.dummies.com`. Although hard-coding may suffice for some purposes, other times you'll want to be more flexible in your approach to creating a URL. Because the `URLWithString` parameter is an `NSString`, you can use any of the usual `NSString` functions with it, including retrieving the URL from the interface.

Don't forget that an `NSURL` doesn't necessarily have to point to a file somewhere on the Web. It can also point to a file on your local hard drive. For example, you can use the `initFileURLWithPath` method of `NSURL` to build a URL to a local file, based on its path. Check the built-in Cocoa documentation in Xcode to see the complete list of `NSURL` methods.

After you create and define an `NSURL`, call its `resourceDataUsingCache` method to begin downloading the file into memory. In the preceding code snippet, `pageData` points to data in memory. From there, transferring that data from memory to a file on your hard drive is a simple matter. For example, if you want to save a simple HTML document to your desktop, call the `writeToFile` method of the `NSData` class.

If you pass a relative path (for example, `~/Downloads/download.html`) to the `writeTofile` method, you must expand it into a full URL with the `stringByExpandingTildeInPath` method:

```
if ([pageData writeToFile:[@"~/Downloads/download.html"
        stringByExpandingTildeInPath]
        atomically:YES])
{
   NSLog(@"download successful");
}
```

One shortcoming of this download-and-save-to-disk approach is that it functions in a synchronous manner. Your application won't do anything else until the file has finished downloading. This may suffice for small downloads, but larger downloads become troublesome. The solution is to use the `loadResourceDataNotifyingClient` method instead of `resourceData UsingCache`:

```
[theURL loadResourceDataNotifyingClient:self
        usingCache:YES];
```

This method enables you to perform other functions while downloading the file. If you implement the `URLResourceDidFinishLoading` method, Cocoa notifies you when the download finishes, giving you the chance to access the data. For example, to save the download to an HTML file on the desktop, implement the `URLResourceDidFinishLoading` method like this:

```
- (void)URLResourceDidFinishLoading:(NSURL *)sender
{
   NSData *pageData = [sender resourceDataUsingCache:YES];
   if ([pageData writeToFile:[@"~/Downloads/download.html"
        stringByExpandingTildeInPath] atomically:YES])
      {
         NSLog(@"download successful");
      }
      else
      {
         NSLog(@"download failed");
      }
}
```

Just because you're downloading and saving an HTML file in this example doesn't mean that you're limited to HTML downloads. You can download any kind of file that you want. To download a JPG image, for instance, simply change the URL and name of the destination file to indicate that it's a JPG file:

```
NSURL *theURL = [NSURL
   URLWithString:@" http://purplee.net/images/cocoa_cover.
        jpg"];
...
```

```
if ([pageData writeToFile:[@"~/Downloads/download.jpg"
          stringByExpandingTildeInPath]
                              atomically:YES])
...
```

# Building a Web browser

You could use the code from earlier in this chapter to download an HTML file from the Web and display it with a Cocoa control. Doing so is possible, but it requires a lot of work. Fortunately, the WebKit Framework gives you the ability to load and display Web content very easily. So easily in fact, you can do so without writing a single line of code.

At the heart of the WebKit is the `WebView` control, which has built-in methods for a variety of Web-related functions that you'd find in a typical Web browser:

✔ Load a Web page

✔ Go back one page in the history

✔ Go forward one page in the history

✔ Reload a Web page

✔ Stop a Web page from loading

✔ Print a Web page

Are some of these functions sounding familiar? They should because not only are they the staple of most Web browsers, but they're used in Apple's own Safari Web browser. Safari uses the same exact rendering features that are available to you with WebKit. And because these functions are so common, WebKit has them ready to go without nary a line of code.

To see how the WebKit Framework works, create a new Cocoa application project in Xcode (see Chapter 2). Then, add the WebKit Framework to the project by following these steps:

1. **Control-click the Frameworks Group in the project window, as shown in Figure 15-1, and then choose Add⇨Existing Frameworks from the menu.**

2. **Navigate to** `/System/Library/Frameworks/WebKit.framework` **and click the Add button, as shown in Figure 15-2.**

   The WebKit Framework enables the powerful `WebView` control. Because the framework isn't used in most projects, it isn't part of a standard Cocoa project. Believe it or not, this is all you need to do in Xcode!

3. **Double-click the MainMenu.xib file in the Xcode project to open it in Interface Builder.**

**Figure 15-1:**
Add a
framework
to the Xcode
project.

**Figure 15-2:**
Select the
WebKit
Framework
to use the
WebView
control.

4. **Add a** `WebView` **control to the interface.**

   You can locate the `WebView` in the Library window by searching for `WebView`.

5. **Add a text field control to the interface.**

   Locate the text field by searching for `text field` or `NSTextField` in the Library window. This field is where users type Web addresses, just like on a Web browser.

   If you want to display a default Web site, double-click the control and enter a Web address.

6. **Add two buttons to the interface; double-click each button to change the text displayed on the buttons to Back and Forward, respectively.**

   You can use whichever button style you like. In Figure 15-3, I used the Textured Button control. The completed interface is shown in Figure 15-3.

7. **Connect the text field control to** `WebView`**.**

   Control+drag from the text field to the `WebView` control. Select the `take URLStringFrom` message from the black connections list overlay that appears, as shown in Figure 15-4. The `takeURLStringFrom` message means that the `WebView` control loads a URL based on the text in the text field.

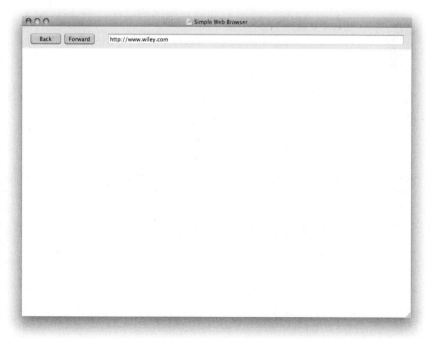

**Figure 15-3:**
The simple Web browser interface resembles common professional Web browsers.

**Figure 15-4:**
The take
URLString
message
loads a
URL in a
WebView.

8. **Connect the buttons to** `WebView`.

   Control+drag from each of the two buttons to the `WebView` control.
   Select `goBack` and `goForward`, respectively, from the black connections list overlay that appear.

   These two methods advance the Web browser one page forward or one
   page backward in the `WebView` history, just like Back and Forward
   buttons do in any other Web browser.

9. **Press ⌘+R to test the application in Interface Builder.**

   As you already know, Interface Builder lets you test your interfaces,
   but this one is special. Normally Interface Builder demonstrates what
   completed interfaces look like, but they don't really do anything. This
   time, however, it's different. Interface Builder demonstrates a fully functional application because all the functionality is provided by the built-in
   WebKit framework.

10. **Return to Xcode and choose Build⇨Build and Go to test your work.**

    The result looks like Figure 15-5, and you did it without writing a single
    line of code. Wow!

**Figure 15-5:** The finished product downloads and renders a URL just like other Web browsers.

# Sending E-Mail from a Cocoa Application

Downloading and displaying Web pages is just one of Cocoa's many networking skills. Cocoa is equally adept at e-mail. With a few simple lines of code, you can create an e-mail message in your favorite e-mail client. With a few more lines of code, you can take care of sending the e-mail too. E-mail features in an application are handy for several uses:

- Provide a contact e-mail in an About box
- Give users the opportunity to automatically send you bug reports
- Format an e-mail message in an existing client
- Send spam, but you wouldn't dare do that, would you? Would you?! I hope not!

In this section, you add e-mail features to the demo project that you created earlier in this chapter.

# *Sending e-mail from your favorite client*

When you click an e-mail link on the Internet, your Web browser instructs your e-mail client to open a new message, often with the To and Subject fields completed for you. Adding this kind of functionality to a Cocoa application is simple. In fact, if you followed along earlier when loading a URL in a browser, you're well on your way to creating an e-mail message.

The main difference between creating an e-mail message and loading a URL in a browser is the format of the URL. Whereas a typical URL in a browser looks like this:

```
http://www.wiley.com
```

an e-mail URL looks like this:

```
mailto:yourFriend@email.com
```

Otherwise, you handle the two URLs identically. To create an e-mail addressed to your friend, simply pass the e-mail URL for that friend to the `openURL` method of the `NSWorkspace` class. For example, to send your friend an e-mail, use code like this:

```
NSURL *theURL =
    [NSURL URLWithString:@"mailto:yourFriend@email.com"];
if ( [[NSWorkspace sharedWorkspace] openURL:theURL] )
        NSLog(@"Email Loaded");
```

If you know HTML, you've probably already guessed that it's possible to add other attributes to the e-mail address. If you want to attach a subject to an e-mail, simply tack it to the end of the e-mail URL preceded by `?subject=`, as follows:

```
mailto:yourFriend@email.com?subject=Important Message
```

If you want to e-mail more than one friend at a time, list additional addresses, with each separated by a comma:

```
mailto:yourFriend@email.com, anotherFriend@email.
            com?subject=Important Message
```

You can also CC and BCC your other friends with a simple e-mail URL. The following e-mail URL sends an e-mail to `yourFriend@email.com` with an

*Important Message* Subject heading. The same message also goes to your other friend (`otherFriend@email.com`):

```
mailto:yourFriend@email.com?subject=Important Message
    ?cc=otherFriend@email.com
```

Keep on tacking the new parameters to the end of the e-mail URL address to suit your needs. Just remember to always precede each parameter with a question mark. Pass this URL to the `openURL` method of the `NSWorkspace` to launch your e-mail client and create a new e-mail according to your specifications. Or, you can enter a `mailTo` address in a WebKit Web browser, as shown in Figure 15-6.

E-mail clients use the question mark character as a separator, so you can't use it as-is in a URL. Instead, you must use a hex character *encoding* if you want to include a ? in your subject. For example, to send an e-mail with the subject *Ready?,* convert the question mark to its hex equivalent by modifying the `mailto` URL as follows:

```
mailto:yourFriend@email.com?subject=Ready%3F
```

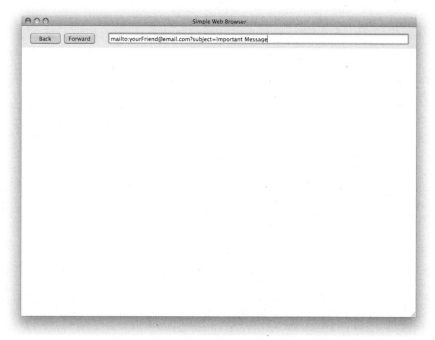

**Figure 15-6:**
Creating an e-mail is as easy as loading a Web page in your browser.

## *Sending e-mail from your own apps*

Giving your users a way to contact you by e-mail is a useful feature, but sometimes it may not fit your needs. This may be true for a variety of reasons, including the following:

✔ You're creating an e-mail application.

✔ You can't guarantee that your user has an e-mail client installed.

✔ You don't want to reply by using an additional e-mail client.

Cocoa offers you the opportunity to send e-mail from your own applications. Before you start sending e-mails *en masse,* though, you need to perform a preparatory step. E-mail functions aren't part of the frameworks that typically accompany the average Cocoa project. Instead, Apple stores the e-mail functions in the Message Framework. To use e-mail in your project, you must first add the Message framework to your project:

1. **Choose Project⇨Add Frameworks to add the Message Framework.**

2. **In the dialog that appears, select Message.framework, which you can find in the System directory:**

   ```
   /System/Library/Frameworks
   ```

   After you add the framework, it appears in the project window, as shown in Figure 15-7.

**Figure 15-7:**
Add the
Message
Framework
to your
project
to send
e-mails
from your
application.

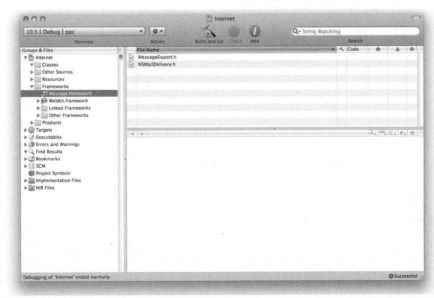

With the Message.framework in place, you can now send e-mail. You'll be amazed at just how easy it is to send an e-mail with Cocoa:

1. **Create a handful of** NSStrings **that represent different parts of an e-mail message:**

```
NSString *theEmailDest = @"youFriend@email.com";
NSString *theSubject = @"Important Message";
NSString *theBody = @"Hello there!";
```

2. **Call the** deliverMessage **method of the** NSMailDelivery **class.**

   Because deliverMessage is a class method, you don't have to create an NSMailDelivery object before using it. The deliverMessage method has parameters for the message, the subject of the e-mail, and the recipient. Furthermore, it returns a Boolean value, telling you whether the delivery occurred.

```
    if ( [NSMailDelivery
deliverMessage:theBody subject:theSubject
       to:theEmailDest] )
        NSLog(@"Email Sent");
    else
        NSLog(@"Email Not Sent");
```

That's all there is to it!

## Adding e-mail functions to the project

To see all these great e-mail functions in action, return to the project that you created earlier in this chapter. Open the MainMenu.xib file in Interface Builder and perform the following steps:

1. **Add two new buttons to the interface and label them.**

   For example, label them Send Email with Client and Send Email Manually, respectively.

2. **Add an** NSTextField **to the interface. Add a text label next to the** NSTextField **to let users know that this field is where they enter a destination e-mail address.**

   Figure 15-8 shows the interface.

**Figure 15-8:**
Add two
NSButtons
and an
NSTextField
to the
interface.

3. **Add a controller to the project.**

   Drag an NSObject from the Library window to the XIB project window. Press ⌘+6 and change the class name to InternetController in the Identity Inspector window.

4. **Add an outlet and two actions to the class.**

   In the Inspector window, add an emailField outlet, so you can retrieve the e-mail addresses that a user enters. Then add two new actions to the class names sendEmailManually and sendEmailWithClient. Figure 15-9 shows the Identity Inspector window, displaying the actions of the InternetController class.

5. **Connect the interface to the InternetController class:**

   a. *Control-drag from the Send Email with Client button to the* InternetController *class in the XIB project window. In the small black connections list overlay that opens, connect the button to the* sendEmailWithClient *action.*

   b. *Control-drag from the Send Email Manually button to the* Internet Controller *class. Connect the button to the* sendEmailManually *action.*

        *c. Connect the `emailField` outlet to the interface by Control-dragging from `InternetController` to the `NSTextField` in the main window of your interface.*

        *d. Click Connect in the Identity Inspector window to make the connection.*

**6. Click the `InternetController` class and then choose File↪Write Class Files to create and add the class files in Xcode.**

**7. Return to Xcode and change this line in InternetContoller.h:**

```
@interface InternetController : /* Specify a
        superclass (eg: NSObject or NSView) */ {
```

**to this**

```
@interface InternetController : NSObject {
```

**Figure 15-9:**
Add two actions and one outlet to the Internet Controller class for the e-mail functions.

**8. Add the following code to InternetController.m:**

Note the addition of `#import <Message/NSMailDelivery.h>` statement at the beginning of the code; this statement permits use of the
Message Framework:

```objc
#import "InternetController.h"
#import <Message/NSMailDelivery.h>

@implementation InternetController
- (IBAction)sendEmailWithClient:(id)sender
{

NSString *theURLString = @"mailto:";
theURLString =
  [theURLString stringByAppendingString:[emailField
        stringValue]];

NSURL *theURL = [NSURL URLWithString:theURLString];

if ( [[NSWorkspace sharedWorkspace] openURL:theURL] )
        NSLog(@"Email Loaded");

}

- (IBAction)sendEmailManually:(id)sender
{
    NSString *theEmailDest = [emailField stringValue];
    NSString *theSubject = @"Important Message";
    NSString *theBody = @"Hello there!";

    if ( [NSMailDelivery deliverMessage:theBody
        subject:theSubject to:theEmailDest] )
        NSLog(@"Email Sent");
    else
        NSLog(@"Email Not Sent");
}
@end
```

**9. To see the results of your hard work, choose Build⇨Build and Go.**

If your project sends the e-mail successfully, you see the *Email Sent*
message in the Console window. You can view the Console in Xcode by
choosing Run⇨Console.

# Chapter 16

# Multimedia

· · · · · · · · · · · · · · · · · · · · · · · · · · · · · · · · · · · · · · · · · · · · · · · · · · · · · · ·

· · · · · · · · · · · · · · · · · · · · · · · · · · · · · · · · · · · · · · · · · · · · · · · · · · · · · · ·

**W**orking with text and creating files are useful functions for your applications, but they aren't always the most exciting functions. Multimedia, on the other hand, *is* exciting. Cocoa continues the long Macintosh tradition of providing high-quality multimedia features for you to use in your projects.

In this chapter, you discover how easy it is to add sophisticated multimedia features to your applications. First, you explore audio by creating a simple application that plays audio files from a number of sources. Then you delve into the real fun — movies! By building a movie player application, you see how easy it is to add dynamic QuickTime content to your Cocoa projects. By changing only one line of code, you also see how to (dis)play many other kinds of media beyond QuickTime movies.

## Listening to Audio

The Macintosh has long been a popular machine with audio aficionados. Cocoa continues in this tradition, offering a complete set of tools for producing audio with your own applications. Some of the possibilities that Cocoa offers are

- Playing sounds that reside in your application's bundle
- Playing sounds that reside in the Mac OS X System folder
- Playing sounds from anywhere on your hard drive

Besides playing audio files that reside in a variety of locations, Cocoa can play many different audio file formats. In the past, you had to know about the various file formats to use them. Cocoa takes away this necessity and lets you play common audio file formats, such as AIFF, MP3, and WAVE, without knowing anything about them.

## Playing system sounds

Cocoa has a convenient method for playing sound in the NSSound class.

To play audio with the NSSound class, you typically follow a simple three-step process:

1. Create an object based on the NSSound class.
2. Load an audio file into the NSSound object.
3. Play the audio.

You usually combine the first two steps or even all three into one line of code. The easiest way to load an audio file is by using its filename. For example, drag and drop an AIFF file (for this example, banjo.aiff) into your Cocoa project. Then load it as an NSSound object by using the soundNamed class method:

```
NSSound *theSound = [NSSound soundNamed:@"banjo"];
```

You can omit the file extension.

Besides loading an audio file that you drag into your project, you can load sounds located in one of the three Mac OS X Sounds directories, located here:

```
/System/Library/Sounds
/Library/Sounds
~/Library/Sounds
```

For example, suppose you want to play the famous Sosumi alert that ships with Mac OS X. The code is identical to the previous example, except for a name change:

```
NSSound *theSound = [NSSound soundNamed:@"Sosumi"];
```

After you load a sound, it's a trivial matter to play it:

```
[theSound play];
```

To simplify matters further, you can combine everything into one line of sound-playing code:

```
[[NSSound soundNamed:@"Sosumi"] play];
```

## Loading and playing sound files

For some applications, playing sounds that reside in your project or in one of the library Sounds folder isn't sufficient. Suppose that you want your application to play any sound that a user selects. To accomplish this task, follow these steps:

1. **Create an array and fill it with all the sound file types that Cocoa recognizes by using the** `soundUnfilteredFileTypes` **class method:**

```
NSArray *audioFileTypes = [NSSound
        soundUnfilteredFileTypes];
```

If you're curious about which types of sounds Cocoa recognizes (and can play), you can display them in the console by looping through the elements in the `audioFileTypes` array and displaying each one in the console via `NSLog`. The following code snippet lists the file extensions of files that `NSSound` supports. Note that the list is case-sensitive, so you may see multiple instances of the same file type (for instance, mp3, MP3, Mp3):

```
int i;
for (i=0;i<[theFileTypes count];i++)
    NSLog([theFileTypes objectAtIndex:i]);
```

Figure 16-1 shows the available list of sound file types that a user can open.

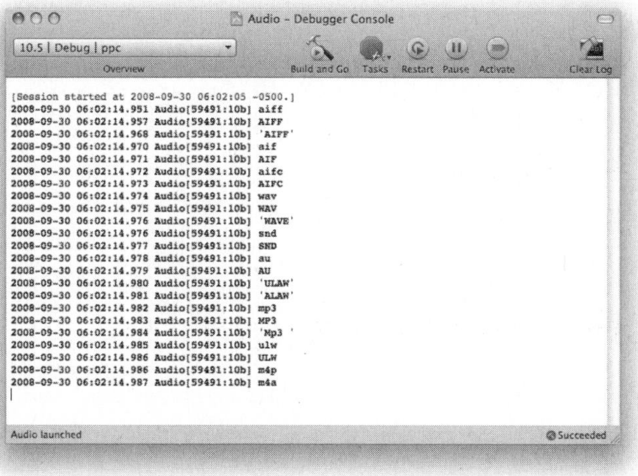

**Figure 16-1:** Cocoa can load and play many types of sound files.

2. **Display an** NSOpenPanel, **restricting the user's choices in that panel to the file types in your array.**

   In this instance, you aren't restricting the sound file types because you used soundUnfilteredFileTypes in Step 1, which populates the array with all possible sound file types. Limit the number of files a user can open in the NSOpenPanel to only one file:

   ```
   NSOpenPanel *theOpenPanel = [NSOpenPanel openPanel];
   [theOpenPanel setAllowsMultipleSelection:NO];
   result = [theOpenPanel runModalForTypes:theFileTypes];
   ```

3. **Use the** initWithContentsOfFile **method of** NSSound **to load the sound (represented by** theFileName**) that the user selected in** NSOpenPanel.

   Because you restricted the user to opening only one audio file, its path resides in the first element of the array that NSOpenPanel returns.

   ```
   theFiles = [theOpenPanel filenames];
   theFileName = [theFiles objectAtIndex:0];
   NSSound *theSound = [[NSSound alloc] initWithContentsO
           fFile:theFileName byReference:YES];
   ```

4. **Play the sound as usual:**

   ```
   [theSound play];
   ```

The preceding example limited the user to only one audio file selection in the NSOpenPanel. Depending on your application's needs, you may want to permit a user to select multiple audio files in the NSOpenPanel. To do so, you need to first permit multiple selections in theOpenPanel:

```
[theOpenPanel setAllowsMultipleSelection:YES];
```

After the user clicks the OK button in the NSOpenPanel, loop through all the selected audio files in the resulting theFiles array:

```
theFiles = [theOpenPanel filenames];
int i;
for (i=0;i<[theFiles count];i++) {
  theFileName = [theFiles objectAtIndex:0];
//do something with the file located at this path:
        theFileName
}
```

# Building a simple audio player

To see how audio playback works in a project, follow these steps:

1. **Create a new Cocoa project in Xcode by choosing File⟹New Project. After the project opens, double-click the MainMenu.xib file to edit the interface in Interface Builder.**

2. **In Interface Builder, add three `NSButton` controls to the main window of your interface. Resize the window and change the Title attributes of the three buttons to Play Application Sound, Play System Sound, and Play Sound File so that they look like Figure 16-2.**

   The first button plays a sound that's part of your application bundle. The second button plays a sound that resides in the System folder. The third button plays a sound file that the user selects.

**Figure 16-2:**
Add three buttons to the audio player interface.

3. **In the Attributes section of the Inspector window, deselect the Close and Resize check boxes for the window.**

   Figure 16-3 shows the position of the two attributes. By deselecting the Close check box, the window no longer has a Close button in the upper-left corner of the window. Because this is a one-window demo application, users might get confused when they close the window, and they can't reopen the window.

   By deselecting the Resize check box, users can't resize the window at run-time. If a user was permitted to resize the window, you'd have to account for this behavior by changing properties for the buttons and the window. Instead, it's simply easier to disallow window resizing.

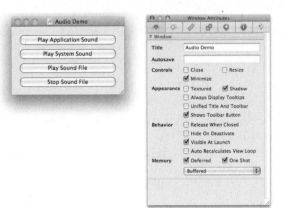

**Figure 16-3:**
Deselect the
Close and
Resize attri-
butes of the
audio player
window.

4. **Create a** `MyAudioController` **class.**

   a. *Open the Library, search for* `Object`, *and drag an* `NSObject` *sub-class instance to the project window.*

   b. *Press ⌘+6 and change the class name to* `MyAudioController`, *as shown in Figure 16-4.*

**Figure 16-4:**
Create a
new object
based on
NSObject.

5. **Select the** MyAudioController **class and open the Identity Inspector by choosing Tools⇨Identity Inspector. Add three actions to the** MyAudioController **class by clicking the + button at the bottom of the Class Actions section.**

   Name the actions playAppSound:, playSoundFile:, and play SystemSound:.

6. **Create the header and implementation files in Xcode.**

   Select the MyAudioController class and choose File⇨Write Class Files. Don't worry about connecting the actions in Interface Builder yet; you'll do that later.

7. **Return to Xcode and drag an AIFF file from Finder to your project.**

   Make sure that the AIFF file is banjo.aiff or modify the code to match whatever filename you choose.

8. **Navigate to the MyAudioController.m file and add the following code:**

```
#import "MyAudioController.h"

@implementation MyAudioController

- (IBAction)playAppSound:(id)sender
{
    //play a sound file that is part of the project
    NSSound *theSound = [NSSound soundNamed:@"banjo"];
    [theSound play];
}

- (IBAction)playSoundFile:(id)sender
{
    int result;
    NSArray *theFiles;
    NSString *theFileName;

    //fill an array with all
    //of the file types that Cocoa can use
    NSArray *theFileTypes = [NSSound
        soundUnfilteredFileTypes];

    //display the sound file types in the console
    int i;
    for (i=0;i<[theFileTypes count];i++)
        NSLog([theFileTypes objectAtIndex:i]);

    //create and display an open panel
    NSOpenPanel *theOpenPanel = [NSOpenPanel
        openPanel];
```

```
    //permit users to open only one file at a time
    [theOpenPanel setAllowsMultipleSelection:NO];
    result = [theOpenPanel
        runModalForTypes:theFileTypes];

    if (result == NSOKButton) {
        //which files did the user select - only one
        in this case
        theFiles = [theOpenPanel filenames];
        //get the path to the chosen file
        theFileName = [theFiles objectAtIndex:0];
        //create, load, and play the audio file
        NSSound *theSoundFile = [[NSSound alloc]
        initWithContentsOfFile:theFileName
        byReference:YES];
        [theSoundFile play];
    }
}

- (IBAction)playSystemSound:(id)sender
{

    //play a sound file that accompanies the operating
        system
    NSSound *theSound = [NSSound
        soundNamed:@"Sosumi"];
    [theSound play];
}
@end
```

*Note:* The code for playing the banjo.aiff sound file omits the `.aiff` file
extension. This omission of the file extension is both a convenience and
a requirement!

You might recognize most of the code in this listing. The `playAppSound` and
`playSystemSound` methods have identical code. They load a sound from
the project's bundle or from one of the system folders that contains sounds.
The `playSoundFile` method, on the other hand, permits users to open any
sound file for playback.

### Adding stop functionality

If you want to stop the playback of an audio file, call the `stop` method of the
`theSound` object, based on the `NSSound` class:

```
[theSound stop];
```

You have to make a few minor changes to your code if you want to add this
functionality to a new button, however. Because a `stop` function would pre-
sumably reside in a new method or action of the `MyAudioController` class
and need access to the `NSSound` object created in other actions, the first

change you should make is to declare the NSSound instance as a member of the class. The NSSound declaration shouldn't be in the playSoundFile method, as in the previous code listing. Thus, to implement a stop feature, follow these steps:

1. **Alter the MyAudioController.h file like this:**

```
/* MyAudioController */

#import <Cocoa/Cocoa.h>

@interface MyAudioController : NSObject
{
    NSSound *theSoundFile;
}
- (IBAction)playAppSound:(id)sender;
- (IBAction)playSoundFile:(id)sender;
- (IBAction)playSystemSound:(id)sender;
- (IBAction)stopSoundFile:(id)sender;

@end
```

   Note two things about the interface file:

   - A new stopSoundFile action is defined in the header.

   - MyAudioController is defined as an NSObject subclass.

2. **Return to the MyAudioController.m implementation file and change the second-to-last line of code in the** playSoundFile **method.**

   This line creates an NSSound object and loads it with the contents of a theFileName file.

```
theSoundFile = [[NSSound alloc] initWithContentsOfFile
        :theFileName byReference:YES];
```

3. **After you issue the** play **command, remember to release** theSound File **because you created it with the** alloc **method.**

```
[theSoundFile play];
[theSoundFile release];
```

4. **Implement the** stopSoundFile **action in MyAudioController.m.**

   This method stops any audio playback that playSoundFile started. Of course, you don't want to stop playback unless audio is playing already. To find out whether the sound file is currently playing, use the is Playing method of the NSSound class. The completed stopSoundFile method looks like this.

```
- (IBAction)stopSoundFile:(id)sender
{
    if ([theSoundFile isPlaying])
        [theSoundFile stop];
}
```

### Connecting the actions to the interface

Incidentally, you don't have to create actions in Interface Builder. Actions are just as valid if you declare them in Xcode. You still have to connect actions to their desired interface elements in Interface Builder, though, so do that now:

1. **Double-click the MainMenu.xib file in the Resources group of your project in Xcode to return to Interface Builder.**

2. **In the XIB project window of Interface Builder, select** `MyAudioController`.

3. **Choose File⇨Read Class Files and select MyAudioController.h at the prompt.**

   Interface Builder checks the header files for any changes. Because you added a new `stopSoundFile` action in Xcode, Interface Builder updates the MainMenu.xib NIB file, adding the new action as shown in Figure 16-5.

4. **Add a new button to the main window of your interface by dragging one from the Library window and labeling it Stop Sound File.**

   Figure 16-6 shows the result.

**Figure 16-5:**
If you add actions or outlets in Xcode, Interface Builder can find them in the header files and update the NIB file accordingly.

**Figure 16-6:**
Add a new
button to the
interface for
halting play-
back of a
sound file.

5. **Connect the new button to the** `stopSoundFile` **action.**

   Control+drag from the new button to the `MyAudioController` instance in the XIB project window. Select `stopSoundFile` from the black connections list overlay that opens.

6. **Control+drag from the three other buttons to the** `MyAudioController` **class and connect each one to its corresponding action.**

7. **Choose File⇨Save to save the MainMenu.xib file.**

8. **Return to Xcode and choose Build⇨Build and Go to test your work.**

   When testing, initiate playback of an audio file that has a long duration with the Play Sound File button. While the file plays, click the Stop Sound File button to cease playback.

# *Watching Movies with Cocoa*

Unless you've been living under a rock, you know that Mac OS X is a whiz at playing other kinds of multimedia content as well. *QuickTime* is a cross-platform multimedia engine that enables users to view, edit, and create all sorts of multimedia content. Chief among the various multimedia formats is the QuickTime movie. By using the QTKit framework in Cocoa, it's easy to add movie playback functions to your applications.

To work with QuickTime content in your projects, Cocoa provides you with five important classes:

✔ **QTMovie:** A movie that you want to view, edit, or create.

✔ **QTTrack:** Movies are composed of one or more tracks. `QTTrack` helps you to work with the individual tracks in a movie.

- ✔ **QTMedia:** Each track in a movie is composed of media. QTMedia lets you get and set information media in a track.

- ✔ **QTDataReference:** QuickTime is multifaceted and permits you to load movies from files, the Internet, or even straight from memory. QTDataReference is the QuickTime class that you use when you need this level of access.

- ✔ **QTMovieView:** A movie player you use to play a QTMovie.

Because the QTKit framework is so vast, and in certain cases, somewhat advanced, I show you two classes: QTMovie and QTMovieView. With these two classes, you can load a movie and display it in a fullyfunctional player.

## QTMovie

QTMovie is a class that represents a QuickTime movie. QTMovie can load movies into from files, Uniform Resource Locators (URLs), data references, or even the Pasteboard (Clipboard). For this section, I show you how to use the movieWithFile class method of the QTMovie class to load a movie from a file.

Earlier in this chapter, you loaded a sound file with an NSOpenPanel. Then you used the result from that NSOpenPanel to open the file using a traditional file path. You can follow a similar methodology for movies, but you have to expand the functionality a bit by filtering which files a user can select in the NSOpenPanel. To do this, you must pass an array to the runModal ForType method of NSOpenPanel:

1. **Create an array that defines which file types a user can open.**

   The last item in the array is always nil. For example, to define an array for .mov and .mp4 files, your code might look like this:

   ```
   NSArray *fileTypes = [NSArray arrayWithObjects:@"mov",
           @"mp4",nil];
   ```

2. **Pass the array to** runModalForType:

   ```
   if ([openPanel runModalForTypes:fileTypes] ==
           NSOKButton){
     // code to load a movie goes here
   }
   ```

3. **Pass the file path to the** movieWithFile **class method to create a** QTMovie.

   ```
   QTMovie *movie = [QTMovie movieWithFile:theFilePath
           error:nil];
   ```

# QTMovieView

After you load a movie, use the `QTMovieView` class to play it. You can find the `QTMovieView` control in the Library window of Interface Builder (see Figure 16-7) by searching for Movie View via the search field at the bottom of the Library window.

**Figure 16-7:** Find the QTMovie View by searching for Movie View.

`QTMovieView` has several attributes that you can set manually in Interface Builder — see Figure 16-8 — or programmatically with code.

**Figure 16-8:** The QTMovie View attributes in Interface Builder.

Here are the attributes you can set in Interface Builder:

- **Display color:** Control the color of the QTMovieView when no movie is loaded. The default color is black, but you can change it to whatever color you desire.

- **Show controller:** Toggle the display of the built-in QuickTime controller, which appears at the bottom of the QTMovieView control when you load a movie into it. You'll be familiar with the QuickTime controller if you've ever viewed a QuickTime movie in a Web browser or in the QuickTime Player application. The controller lets users control the playback of QuickTime content using a set of familiar buttons. Besides starting and stopping playback, you can rewind and fast forward through portions of the movie as well as adjust the volume during playback. Figure 16-9 shows a typical QuickTime movie controller.

- **Editable:** By default, Editable has a value of NO (that is, it's deselected in the Inspector window). The QuickTime controller appears, as shown in Figure 16-9. When you set Editable to YES by selecting the Editable check box in the Inspector window of Interface Builder and then loading a movie in code, you see a controller that looks like Figure 16-10.

  The Editable attribute causes a QTMovieView to display a slightly different QuickTime controller. You can use this type of controller for different purposes, such as to select some portion of the movie. As you can see in Figure 16-11, Shift-clicking permits you to select some or all the movie in the QTMovieView.

- **Volume:** Toggle the display of the volume button control that appears at the left edge of the QTMovieView. When you set this attribute to YES by clicking the Volume check box in the Inspector window, the volume button displays. When NO (deselected), the volume button doesn't display.

**Figure 16-9:**
The standard QuickTime controller offers simple playback interface elements.

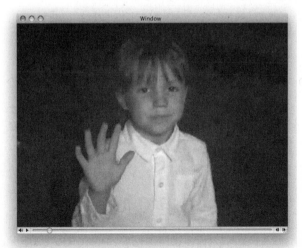

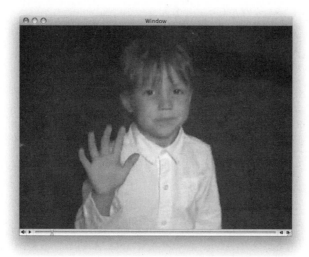

**Figure 16-10:**
The Editable attribute toggles between playback and editing interface elements.

**Figure 16-11:**
Shift-click the controller to select some section of a movie in a QTMovie View.

After you set the desired `QTMovieView` attributes in Interface Builder, add some code to Xcode to play a movie. Assuming you've already loaded a movie into memory using the `QTMovie` class, display that movie in the `QTMovieView`, by adding the following code:

```
[moviePlayer setMovie:theMovie];
```

You can set many other aspects of playback using code. Besides the attributes that you found in Interface Builder, you can set the volume of the movie during playback. A volume of 1.0 is *full* volume, as defined by the maximum system volume level. Thus, a volume of 0.5 is half the maximum system volume level.

```
[moviePlayer setVolume:1.0];
```

Alternatively, if you prefer, you can mute the sound:

```
[moviePlayer setMuted:YES];
```

## Building a simple movie player

The easiest way to see how movie playback in Cocoa works is to build a player. Follow these steps:

1. **Launch Xcode and create a new Cocoa application project by choosing File⇨New Project. Double-click the MainMenu.xib file in Xcode to open it with Interface Builder.**

2. **From the MainMenu.xib file window, open the main window for your interface and then open the Inspector for the window by choosing Tools⇨Inspector.**

3. **In the Inspector window, change the Title field for the window to something appropriate. Add a** QTMovieView **control and an** NSButton **from the controls from the Library window (as shown in Figure 16-12).**

**Figure 16-12:**
Add a
QTMovie
View and a
button to the
interface.

**4. Create a controller class for this interface.**

Drag an NSObject from the Library window to the XIB project window. Press ⌘+6 and name the new object MyMovieController. Figure 16-13 shows the new class.

**Figure 16-13:** Create a controller class for the project.

**5. Add an outlet and an action to the new controller class in the Inspector window.**

Name the outlet moviePlayer and name the action loadMovie.

**6. Connect the MyMovieController instance to the interface:**

   a. *Control+drag from the new* MyMovieController *instance to the* QTMovieView *that you added to the window earlier.*

   b. *Select the* moviePlayer *outlet in the black connections list overlay that appears.*

   c. *Control+drag from the push button to* MyMovieController *and connect it to the* loadMovie *action.*

**7. After you design the interface, select the** MyMovieController **instance in the XIB project window and choose File➪Write Class Files.**

Write the class files and add them to the Xcode project.

**8. In Xcode, change the code in the MyMovieController.h interface file to look like this:**

```
#import <Cocoa/Cocoa.h>

@interface MyMovieController : NSObject {
    IBOutlet id moviePlayer;
}
- (IBAction)loadMovie:(id)sender;
@end
```

9. **Add the following code to the MyMovieController.m implementation file:**

```
#import "myMovieController.h"
#import <QTKit/QTKit.h>

@implementation MyMovieController

- (IBAction)loadMovie:(id)sender {
    NSOpenPanel *openPanel = [NSOpenPanel openPanel];
    [openPanel setTitle:@"Choose a Movie"];
    [openPanel setCanChooseDirectories:NO];

    NSArray *fileTypes = [NSArray arrayWithObjects:@"m
        ov",@"mp4",nil];

    if ([openPanel runModalForTypes:fileTypes] ==
        NSOKButton)
    {
        NSString *theFilePath = [openPanel filename];
    [moviePlayer setMovie:[QTMovie
        movieWithFile:theFilePath error:nil]];
    }
@end
```

The code starts out by defining an array of file types that a user can open. In this case, you're restricting users to only .mov and .mp4 movies:

```
NSArray *theFileTypes = [NSArray
        arrayWithObjects:@"mov", @"mp4", nil];
```

Then, the code presents a standard NSOpenPanel where users can select a movie file. After they choose a file, the code loads the movie into a QTMovie:

```
NSString *theFilePath = [openPanel filename];
[moviePlayer setMovie:[QTMovie
        movieWithFile:theFilePath error:nil]];
```

10. **Choose Build⇨Build and Go to test the project.**

## When a movie isn't a movie

Playing movies is useful, but QuickTime can do much more. Everyone knows that a traditional movie is a sequence of movie pictures coupled with sounds, but fewer people know that in QuickTime, this is only one kind of movie. QuickTime treats all media types as movies.

For example, if you open your favorite audio files as QuickTime movies, QuickTime dutifully plays the audio file. Because audio files don't have a visual component, there's no need to display any part of the QTMovieView other than the controller. Figure 16-14 shows an audio file loaded into a QTMovieView.

**Figure 16-14:**
QuickTime
can play
audio files.

Some of the possible media file types that you can load into a QTMovie follow:

- **Audio:** AIFF, MP3, M4A, WAVE
- **Video:** MOV, AVI, MPEG-1
- **Graphics:** JPEG, TIFF, PNG, BMP
- **3D:** QTVR
- **Animation:** Flash

To give a user the option of loading other types of media, simply add them to theFileTypes array in the "Building a simple audio player" section from earlier in this chapter. For example, if you want to offer the option of loading a QuickTime movie or a TIFF file, change the code as follows:

```
NSArray *theFileTypes = [NSArray arrayWithObjects:@"mov",@
        "tiff", nil];
```

Cocoa (and subsequently QuickTime) treats both file types equally: as a QTMovie. This means you can load and play (or load and display if it's an image) many kinds of media without special code. This is one of the most powerful features of QuickTime, so use it often! Figure 16-15 shows the QTMovieView with an image loaded into the QTMovie.

**Figure 16-15:**
QuickTime
can also
display
images.

# Part IV
# Advanced Cocoa Topics

The 5th Wave                    By Rich Tennant

"We're much better prepared for this upgrade than before. We're giving users additional training, better manuals, and a morphine drip."

## In this part . . .

Cocoa affords you the ability to easily program simple projects, but can it handle other tasks? You betcha! Part IV takes you beyond simple Cocoa programming and into the realm of super geeks. You discover how to write applications that use multiple windows as well as how to harness the power of the Mac OS X command line. Part IV concludes with a discussion of how to take advantage of the super-powered Core Data framework in your Cocoa applications.

# Chapter 17

# Document-Based Applications

*T*hroughout this book, you create simple one-window applications to see how various aspects of Cocoa work. One-window applications are okay for testing your skills as you become familiar with Cocoa. But after you're comfortable working with Cocoa, you'll want to venture out on your own and create an honest-to-goodness application. Creating demo projects is one thing, but creating full-fledged applications is quite another.

When you create an application, you have to worry about much more than managing a single window. Many applications use a document-based approach whereby a user creates a document and adds some kind of content to it. If you've ever used a word processor or a drawing program, you're probably familiar with this kind of application. In document-based applications, a user might also save a document, open it later, or print it. All these features require a lot of work when you implement them on your own. Fortunately, Xcode helps by providing a full-featured, document-based project for you to use as a starting point for your own doc-based application.

This chapter guides you through the steps required to build a document-based application. Along the way, you'll implement many different features without doing much work.

## Creating a Document-Based Project

To begin working with document-based applications, create a new project in Xcode as follows:

1. **Choose File➪New Project and select Application on the left and Cocoa Document-Based Application on the right, as shown in Figure 17-1.**

**Figure 17-1:**
Choose
Cocoa
Document-
Based
Application
in the New
Project
window.

2. **Click the Choose button and save the new project in a location where you can find it later.**

When the new project opens, you notice a big difference from other projects throughout the rest of this book. This project contains a MyDocument class, as shown in Figure 17-2.

**Figure 17-2:**
A
document-
based
project
comes
equipped
with a My
Document
class.

**3. Click the MyDocument.h file to view its contents:**

```
#import <Cocoa/Cocoa.h>

@interface MyDocument : NSDocument
{
}
@end
```

The interface file defines MyDocument as a subclass of the NSDocument class. This is where you add outlets and actions.

**4. Click the MyDocument.m file to view its contents:**

```
#import "MyDocument.h"

@implementation MyDocument

- (id)init
{
    self = [super init];
    if (self) {

        // Add your subclass-specific initialization
        here.
        // If an error occurs here, send a [self
        release] message and return nil.

    }
    return self;
}

- (NSString *)windowNibName
{
    // Override returning the nib file name of the
        document
    // If you need to use a subclass of
        NSWindowController or if your document
        supports multiple NSWindowControllers, you
        should remove this method and override
        -makeWindowControllers instead.
    return @"MyDocument";
}

- (void)windowControllerDidLoadNib:(NSWindowController
        *) aController
{
    [super windowControllerDidLoadNib:aController];
    // Add any code here that needs to be executed
        once the windowController has loaded the
        document's window.
}
```

```
- (NSData *)dataOfType:(NSString *)typeName
      error:(NSError **)outError
{
    // Insert code here to write your document to data
       of the specified type. If the given outError
       != NULL, ensure that you set *outError when
       returning nil.

    // You can also choose to override
       -fileWrapperOfType:error:,
       -writeToURL:ofType:error:, or -writeToURL:ofTy
       pe:forSaveOperation:originalContentsURL:error:
       instead.

    // For applications targeted for Panther
       or earlier systems, you should use the
       deprecated API -dataRepresentationOfType:.
       In this case you can also choose to override
       -fileWrapperRepresentationOfType: or
       -writeToFile:ofType: instead.

    if ( outError != NULL ) {
    *outError = [NSError errorWithDomain:NSOSStatusErro
       rDomain code:unimpErr userInfo:NULL];
    }
    return nil;
}

- (BOOL)readFromData:(NSData *)data ofType:(NSString
       *)typeName error:(NSError **)outError
{
    // Insert code here to read your document from
       the given data of the specified type.  If the
       given outError != NULL, ensure that you set
       *outError when returning NO.

    // You can also choose to override -re
       adFromFileWrapper:ofType:error: or
       -readFromURL:ofType:error: instead.

    // For applications targeted for Panther or
       earlier systems, you should use the deprecated
       API -loadDataRepresentation:ofType. In
       this case you can also choose to override
       -readFromFile:ofType: or -loadFileWrapperRepre
       sentation:ofType: instead.
```

```
    if ( outError != NULL ) {
                                *outError = [NSError
    errorWithDomain:NSOSStatusErrorDomain
    code:unimpErr userInfo:NULL];
    }
    return YES;
}

@end
```

The MyDocument.m file has five methods where you add code to make
your application functional. Cocoa is even nice enough to give you full
comments on how to use each method.

5. **Press ⌘+R to build and run the project.**

When the project launches, you see a single document window, as
shown in Figure 17-3.

**Figure 17-3:**
The new
document-
based
project
already
does
something:
It makes
documents.

6. **Choose File⮕New to create a new document.**

The application creates a new document and adds it to the Window
menu. You can continue creating new windows as long as you want.

Note that the application has many other features, such as a full suite of
menus and an About Panel, which you had to add manually to your project
in Chapter 5. At this point, however, you can't save or open a document
because you haven't implemented that functionality yet.

# Building the Interface for a Document-Based Project

You need to make a decision about what kind of document-based application you want to create. It could be a word processor, a graphics application, or a checkbook program. In this chapter, you create a simple text editor.

Follow these steps:

1. **Return to Xcode and double-click the MyDocument.nib file to open it in Interface Builder.**

   A generic document opens (refer to Figure 17-3).

2. **Design the interface for this project:**

   a. *Delete the text label that stands at the center of your document window.*

   b. *Add an* NSTextView *control from the Library window to the document window in MyDocument.nib.*

   c. *Resize the* NSTextView *to your liking.*

   Figure 17-4 shows the new interface.

 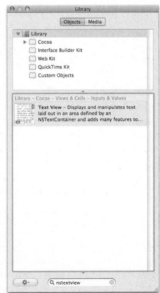

**Figure 17-4:**
The text editor interface.

**3. Add an outlet to the** MyDocument **class.**

*a. Select File's Owner in the project window and press ⌘+6 to open the Identity Inspector, labeled My Document Identity.*

*b. Add a new outlet to the Identity Inspector and name it* myTextView, *as shown in Figure 17-5.*

You use this outlet to get and set text in the NSTextView of the document.

**Figure 17-5:**
Select the
File's Owner
and add an
outlet to it.

**4. Connect the** myTextView **outlet to the** NSTextView **in the interface by Control+dragging from the File's Owner icon to the** NSTextView **in your document window.**

Make sure that you connect to the NSTextView and not its Scroll View parent. The NSTextView control is embedded within an NSScrollView control (which handles the scrolling, as you might have guessed). You may have to drag toward the top of the text view for it to become highlighted.

Figure 17-6 shows the outlet connection.

**Figure 17-6:**
Control+
drag from
the File's
Owner
icon to the
NSText-
View in the
interface.

5. **Choose File⇨Save to save the NIB file and then return to Xcode.**

   The outlet is added to the MyDocument.h file.

6. **Expand the Target group in the Groups & Files list and select the default application.**

7. **Click the Info button in the window's toolbar to open the Target Info window.**

8. **Click the Properties tab to display the list of document types in this application and click the + button at the bottom of the Info window.**

9. **Add rich text as a new document type that the application can use, as shown in Figure 17-7:**

   a. *In the Extensions box, type* **rtf** *(without quotation marks).*

   b. *Enter* **text/rtf** *in the MIME Types field.*

   c. *In the OS Types box, type* **"RTF "** *(this time use a double-tick mark, followed by RTF, a space, and another closing double-tick mark) in the OS Types field.*

   d. *Enter* **MyDocument** *in the Class field and choose Binary as the Store Type.*

      If you add an icon file (with the `.icns` extension) to your project and define it in the icon column, your application uses the custom icon when saving this file type. Chapter 5 details how to assign an icon to your application.

TIP

Feel free to remove the default DocumentType entry by selecting it and pressing the Delete key.

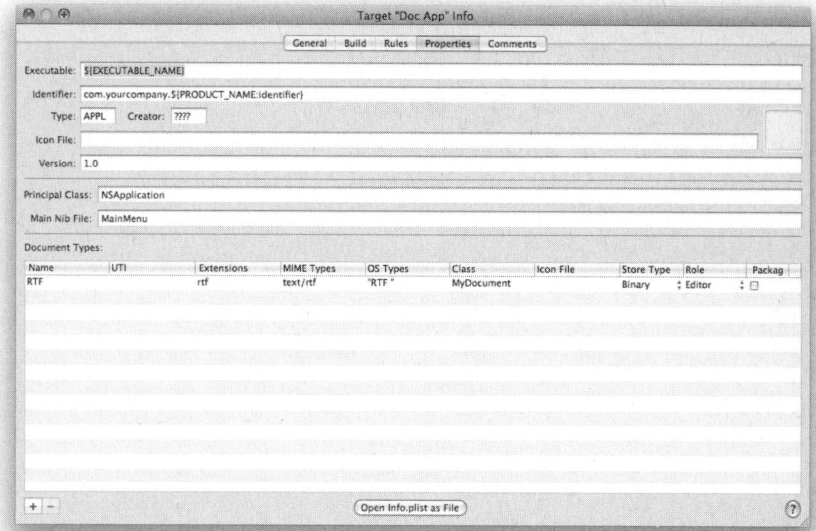

**Figure 17-7:**
Add RTF
to your
project as a
document
type.

# Adding the Code

Now that you've set up the interface and classes in Interface Builder and added the RTF document type in Xcode, you can add some code to your project. The MyDocument.h and MyDocument.m files were added to the document by default when you created the project. You need to add code to these two files to make the application work.

1. **In Xcode, add an outlet and an NSData pointer to your MyDocument.h interface file by entering this code:**

```
#import <Cocoa/Cocoa.h>

@interface MyDocument : NSDocument
{
    IBOutlet id myTextView;
    NSData *fileContents;
}
@end
```

The NSData object holds the contents of your rich text file. The IBOutlet is the outlet that you already added to File's Owner in Interface Builder.

2. **Navigate to your MyDocument.m implementation file and change its code to read as follows:**

```
#import "MyDocument.h"

@implementation MyDocument

- (id)init
{
  self = [super init];
  if (self) {
      // Add your subclass-specific initialization
        here.
      // If an error occurs here, send a [self
        release] message and return nil.
  }
  return self;
}


- (NSString *)windowNibName
{
  return @"MyDocument";
}

- (void)windowControllerDidLoadNib:(NSWindowController
        *) aController
{
  [super windowControllerDidLoadNib:aController];
  [myTextView replaceCharactersInRange:NSMake
        Range(0,[[myTextView string] length])
        withRTF:fileContents];
}

- (NSData *)dataOfType:(NSString *)typeName
        error:(NSError **)outError
{
  [fileContents release];
  fileContents = [[myTextView RTFFromRange:NSMakeRange
        (0,[[myTextView string] length])] retain];
  return fileContents;
}

- (BOOL)readFromData:(NSData *)data ofType:(NSString
        *)typeName error:(NSError **)outError
{
  fileContents = [data retain];
  return YES;
}
```

```
-(void)dealloc {
  [fileContents release];
  [super dealloc];
}

@end
```

The big changes in this file are in dataOfType, readFromData, and windowControllerDidLoadNib:

- The dataOfType method takes care of saving the file.

  The dataOfType method doesn't really have anything to do with files. Instead, it returns the data that the application should save to the file. The application actually takes care of the rest!

- The readFromData and windowControllerDidLoadNib methods handle the task of opening a rich text file. The readFromData method receives the incoming data from the file and lets the application know whether it's successful. Then the windowController DidLoadNib method takes care of displaying the text in the NSData instance named fileContents.

**3. Press ⌘+R to test your work.**

You can open and save rich text files just like those created with TextEdit or Microsoft Word. When you open a file, your application displays its contents in a new window. Notice that the application's other menus work, too. You can close a window by pressing ⌘+W or even use the spell-check on a document.

The beauty of using a Cocoa document project is that Cocoa takes care of a lot of the work for you. You don't have to do much work to implement a large assortment of features. Besides making it easy on you, Cocoa makes it easier on your users. By using the default behaviors that Cocoa document-based apps provide you, your users will be familiar with their operation.

# Chapter 18

# Cocoa Bindings

*W*henever you create a Cocoa application the traditional way, you implement a Model class that manages data, an interface that users interact with, and a Controller class that ties the two together. This is all well and good, but Objective-C saves you from a substantial bit of coding and hassle by permitting you to bypass the Controller class altogether.

Bindings let you bridge items in your interface directly to data in your Model classes. This is handy because Objective-C handles the tasks of keeping your interface updated and, more importantly, you don't have to. That means less coding work for you and less chance of creating bugs.

This chapter explains what bindings are and why you use them. Then, it describes some of the technology behind bindings (namely KVC and KVO). KVC and KVO are two complementary technologies that you can use to generically get and set the values of instance variables. Finally, you create a project that uses bindings instead of code to control an interface in your application.

Bindings is an advanced topic that is also voluminous, and as such, you have to do some exploration on your own to master the wild and wooly world of bindings. This chapter only scratches the surface of what you can do with bindings. You can bind all sorts of elements in your interface to many different keys in your classes to affect how the application behaves when it runs.

# What Are Bindings?

The Model-View-Controller (MVC) design pattern is the preferred method for writing Cocoa applications (see Chapter 7). Part of what makes the design so great is that it separates data (the *Model*) from the interface (the *View*). In between the data and the interface sits an intermediary object, the *Controller*. When the Controller changes the view (for example, when a user makes a move), you have to write code. For example, this line of code changes the display (an outlet connected to an `NSTestField`) any time a user deposits or withdraws money from the account:

```
[display setFloatValue:[account balance]];
```

This code also appears in the `awakeFromNib` method so the field displays an initial value on launch. With a MVC design, you set the text field in three different places.

Imagine what a chore all this coding becomes when your application starts expanding. Soon, things can become quite unruly. You might have to toggle the enabled state of particular controls depending on the state of the application. Or, maybe you need to display values in other fields too. Each time you have to change the interface via code, you increase your workload (and the resulting spaghetti code) by leaps and bounds. Surely, there must be a better way. And indeed there is — bindings!

*Bindings* is a technology in Cocoa that consists of some classes that help you keep data and an interface in sync. Instead of updating the interface each time a user changes the balance value in the bank account application, you can instead tell the interface to bind the balance value to the `NSTextField`. Then, whenever your application changes the balance value, the interface updates automatically. You can eliminate the three instances when you have to update the interface in the MVC design. And, because you used an outlet to update the interface, you can remove that too!

Bindings help you prune down your code significantly. Less code usually means fewer bugs.

# Starting a Project with Bindings

To see how bindings work, launch Xcode and create a new project:

1. **Choose File⇨New Project and select Application on the left and the Cocoa Application on the right, as shown in Figure 18-1. Click the Choose button and name the new project whatever you wish.**

   I named it the same as the Chapter 7 project: Bank Account.

**Figure 18-1:**
Create a
new Cocoa
application.

2. **Choose File⇨New File, select Cocoa and then Objective-C Class, as shown in Figure 18-2. Click the Next button, name the new class** `AccountController`, **and create the AccountController.m and AccountController.h files.**

   To simplify matters, you don't have a separate Account class. The `AccountController` class keeps track of the balance.

**Figure 18-2:**
Add a new
class to the
project.

3. **In the AccountController.h file that you created in Step 2, enter this code:**

```
#import <Cocoa/Cocoa.h>

@interface AccountController : NSObject {
  float balance;
}

- (IBAction)deposit:(id)sender;
- (IBAction)withdraw:(id)sender;

-(float)balance;
-(void)setBalance:(float)aBalance;
@end
```

The interface file has one instance variable, `balance`. That's followed by two actions for depositing and withdrawing money from the account. There are also two methods for setting and getting the balance value.

This application behaves identically to the bank account application with an MVC design (see Chapter 7), but the amount of code that you write is significantly smaller.

Why are you going to the trouble of creating accessor methods (`balance` and `setBalance`) if you could just query the value of the instance variable `balance`? That's a good question! And one that I answer in the next section.

# Making Your Bindings Work: KVC and KVO

*KVC* (Key-Value Coding) and *KVO* (Key-Value Observing) are conventions whereby you can get, set, and observe properties of a class by name.

In a typical class, you might retrieve an instance variable with an accessor method like this:

```
theBalance = [account balance];
```

With KVC, you can retrieve that value like this instead:

```
theBalance = [account valueForKey:@"balance"];
```

You retrieve the value generically by using the `valueForKey` method and passing the *name* of the key instead of accessing its accessor method directly. This might not seem like it makes sense, but it's what makes bindings work. When you call `valueForKey`, Cocoa tries to find a method with the same name as the key. So, it searches until it finds the accessor method that you defined and retrieves the value from it:

```
-(float)balance;
```

With KVC, you can also set values generically by key. For example, to set the balance, you'd do this:

```
[account setValue:115 forKey:@"balance"];
```

This time Cocoa searches for a `setBalance` method. It then uses that accessor method to set the value of `balance` to `115`.

```
-(void)setBalance:(float)theBalance;
```

Use set*X* as the name of the setter method, where *X* is the capitalized name of the instance variable. It might not make sense why you have to follow this convention, but bindings rely on it, so name your accessors this way!

So, Cocoa has a way to get and set values of instance variables by key name. If you adhere to the conventions of KVC, you can also observe the values of variables by key name. KVO lets your application register observe a value based on key name. Then, whenever the value of the key changes, your application is notified of the value change. For example, if you want the register to observe the `balance` variable, you'd do something like this (perhaps in `awakeFromNib`):

```
[account addObserver:self forKeyPath:@"balance" options:0
        context:NULL];
```

The `account` class is now an observer of the `balance` variable. Don't worry about the `options` and `context` parameters. They're for advanced users, and you'll know what they mean when you reach that level. For now, set `options` to `zero` and `context` to `NULL`. Whenever the value of the variable changes, the class, as an observer, gets a message letting it know that the value has changed. There, your code does something to respond. But where would this message arrive? It arrives in an `observeValueForKeyPath` method, which you must implement, like so:

```
-(void)observeValueForKeyPath:(NSString *)keyPath
        ofObject:(id)object change:(NSDictionary *)
        change
    context:(void *)context {

}
```

Because `observeValueForKeyPath` is generic and fires for all observed values, you have to check the `keyPath` to see if the incoming value is one you care about:

```
if ( [keyPath isEqualToString:@"balance"] ) {
  //do something here with regards to the value of balance
}
```

The reason KVC and KVO are so important is that the bindings technology uses them to perform its magic. That's not to say that you can't use KVC and KVO in your own applications separate from bindings. You can! And when you do, you also get bindings support for free.

# Implementing Bindings

To see how all this KVC and KVO stuff works, return to the project that you started in the "Starting a Project with Bindings" section. Your interface for `AccountController` has two actions for when the user clicks one of the buttons in the interface, and it has two accessor methods: `balance` and `SetBalance` (which follow the KVC naming conventions). If you're not sure how to name the KVC, see the previous section.

Click the AccountController.m file in your Xcode project and add the following code:

```
#import "AccountController.h"

@implementation AccountController

-(void)awakeFromNib {
  [self setBalance: 100];
}

- (IBAction)deposit:(id)sender {
  [self setBalance: [self balance]+20];
}

- (IBAction)withdraw:(id)sender {
  [self setBalance: [self balance]-5];
}

-(float)balance {
  return balance;
}

-(void)setBalance:(float)aBalance {
  balance = aBalance;
}

@end
```

Here's how the code works:

- ✔ The class starts off with `awakeFromNib`, where you set the value of `balance` to `100` for an initial balance.
- ✔ The code defines the two actions that execute when a user clicks one of the two buttons in the interface (`deposit` and `withdraw`).
- ✔ The accessor methods are defined.

Pretty standard stuff. But where's all that code you need for the MVC design that updated the interface? It's gone! That's because Cocoa bindings handle that dirty work for you.

Now, it's time to set up the bindings in Interface Builder:

1. **Double-click MainMenu.xib to open it in Interface Builder.**

2. **Create an interface with two** `NSTextField` **controls (called** `Label` **in the Library window) and two push buttons.**

If you need help creating the interface, see Chapter 7. Figure 18-3 shows the interface with the two controls and push buttons.

**Figure 18-3:**
Create the
interface.

3. **Choose File⇨Read Class Files and select the AccountController.h file, as shown in Figure 18-4.**

   When you read the interface file, seemingly nothing happens, but behind the scenes, Interface Builder is reading the interface file and is now cognizant of the class.

4. **Open the Library window in Interface Builder by choosing Tools⇨ Library and search for** `Object`. **Drag a new object to the project window, as shown in Figure 18-5.**

5. **Press ⌘+6 to open the Inspector window and change the Class to** `AccountController`. **Add** `deposit:` **and** `withdraw:` **actions.**

   See Figure 18-6.

**Figure 18-4:**
Read the
Account-
Controller.h
file.

**Figure 18-5:**
Drag an
Object from
the Library
to the
project
window.

**Figure 18-6:**
Change the
Object class
to Account
Controller
and add two
actions.

6. **Connect the two actions to the corresponding buttons in the interface by Control+dragging from the buttons to the** `AccountController` **class in the project window.**

   Figure 18-7 shows the connection being made to the `deposit` action.

**Figure 18-7:**
Connect the
two actions
to the
Account
Controller
class.

7. **Select the empty** `NSTextField` **control in the interface and press ⌘+4 to open the Bindings Inspector for that control. The Bindings Inspector has the title Text Field Bindings.**

   Figure 18-8 shows the Bindings Inspector.

8. **Expand the Value section of the Bindings Inspector. Select Account Controller from the pop-up menu and type** balance **in the Model Key Path field and press Return.**

   Instantly the Bindings Inspector selects the Bind To: check box and sets a couple check boxes (Allows Editing Multiple Values Selection and Raises for Not Applicable Keys) for you, as shown in Figure 18-9. Congratulations! You've just set your first binding.

**Figure 18-8:**
Select the
empty text
field and
open the
Bindings
Inspector.

**Figure 18-9:**
Select
Account
Controller
from the
pop-up
menu and
enter
balance in
the Model
Key Path.

**9. Save MainMenu.xib and return to Xcode where you can test your work by choosing Build➪Build and Go.**

The result looks something like Figure 18-10.

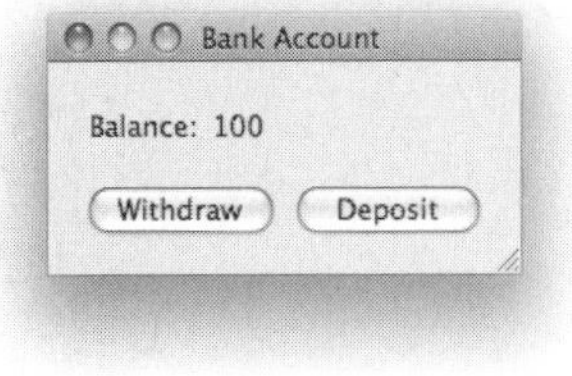

**Figure 18-10:**
Test your
work to see
the bindings
in action.

**Bank Account**

Balance: 100

( Withdraw )  ( Deposit )

**10. Click the Deposit button to deposit $20.**

The balance increases, as shown in Figure 18-11.

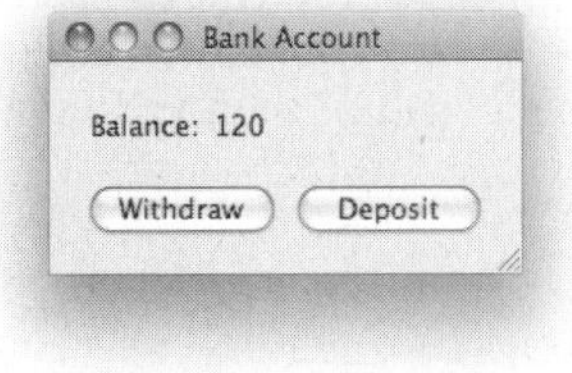

**Figure 18-11:**
Click the
Deposit
button to
increase the
balance.

**Bank Account**

Balance: 120

( Withdraw )  ( Deposit )

By jumping through these hoops, your application now displays the correct balance value in the interface, and you didn't write any code that actually set the value in the interface. Instead, by binding the balance value to the text field, Cocoa is observing that value (via KVO) behind the scenes. When the value changes, the binding updates the display. The reason that it knows the value is all thanks to you implementing the accessor methods following the KVC naming conventions.

This might not be super impressive, but as your applications increase in scope, the time savings is substantial. And you can avoid all kinds of buggy code in the process.

# Chapter 19

# Core Data

* * * * * * * * * * * * * * * * * * * * * * * * * * * * * * * * * * * * * * * * * * * * * * * * * * * *

## In This Chapter

▶ Discovering the greatness of Core Data

▶ Creating your Core Data project

▶ Defining your model

▶ Building your interface

* * * * * * * * * * * * * * * * * * * * * * * * * * * * * * * * * * * * * * * * * * * * * * * * * * * *

After you have some experience programming applications for the Macintosh, you soon realize that you spend an inordinate amount of time doing some of the same tasks over and over. One aspect in particular that you find yourself repeating is handling data. Many applications help users with data management. For example, a recipe application might help users organize information like ingredients, steps in a recipe, and special cooking instructions. Other applications — for example, iTunes — might assist users in organizing, sorting, and managing media files like music and video.

So many applications helping users with data aren't a surprise. Computers are exceedingly good at managing data, and lots of it. What might be surprising though is that programmers usually have to do all the hard work of writing code to handle all this data — until now. In this chapter, I show you how Cocoa makes adding data management to your projects easy with Core Data.

# What's So Great about Core Data Anyway?

Core Data is a relative newcomer to the Cocoa programming scene, but don't let its youth and inexperience dissuade you from unleashing its talents. *Core Data* is a framework of around a dozen pre-made classes that allows you to easily add data management to your applications. And oftentimes, Core Data can do so without you even writing a single line of code!

Core Data is handy for a number of reasons:

- ✔ Core Data helps you define data in a structured fashion.
- ✔ Core Data handles a lot of the messy (and boring) programming work for you, so you don't have to do it.
- ✔ Core Data can save and open data files for you automatically.
- ✔ Core Data can even build a functional interface for you.
- ✔ You might not even have to write a lick of code to take advantage of it!

When you're writing Cocoa applications for personal use, sometimes all you want is a quick-and-dirty hack to fulfill your needs. In these cases, you probably don't mind how the interface works or what additional applications the Cocoa project requires. All you care about is the functionality of your application.

Core Data gives your Cocoa project instant access to all these powerful features that are inherent to a variety of applications. Data management is an important aspect for a wide range of applications, and Core Data can help you achieve your goals more smoothly and accomplish things faster.

Core Data isn't just good at juggling data for you. It also helps you write cleaner, more structured software. Furthermore, it often can do so without you writing any code. Less code means less bugs. And less support. And less headaches. That's right, Core Data even has the healing power of aspirin! Just kidding on that last part, but you'll be so amazed at how much Core Data can assist your programming efforts that you might be able to forego a trip or two to the pharmacy.

# Creating a Core Data Project

To begin working with Core Data in a Cocoa application, follow these steps:

1. **Create a new Cocoa application project.**

   Launch Xcode and choose File⇨New Project.

2. **From the list of project templates, choose Application on the left side, then Core Data Application on the right, as shown in Figure 19-1, and then click the Choose button.**

Be careful here. You see three kinds of Core Data templates listed. For now, you don't have to worry about the Core Data Document-Based Application templates. This application uses only one window, so a document-based application won't help you here.

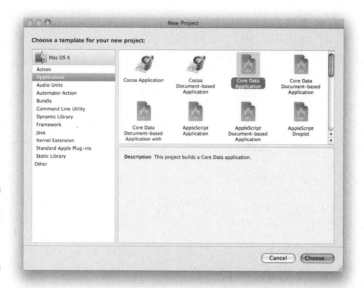

3. **Name the project Core Data and click the Save button to finish creating the new project.**

A Core Data project looks much like other Cocoa projects with Classes, Resources, and Frameworks folders as you've seen in other projects. However, Core Data projects also have one additional folder: Models. The Models folder contains a single data model by default. You'll use this model to design data storage for your application. You can add other models later if you need them, but for now, you need only this one. Figure 19-2 shows the Data Model file in a new project. Its name varies depending on the name you chose for the project.

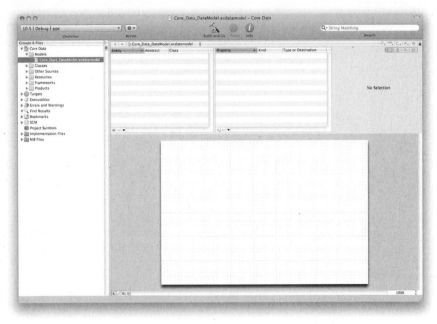

**Figure 19-2:**
The Models
folder
holds —
you
guessed
it — the
Core Data
model for
the project.

# Defining the Model

Although it's not technically true, it can be helpful to think of your core data model as a database. More specifically, the data model contains a definition for the data that your application will be managing. Much like creating a new database, you define the various data elements that make up the data model with Xcode's data modeler. For this chapter, imagine an application that helps you keep track of your book collection. A book application might help you track information, such as

✔ Title

✔ Author

✔ Page count

✔ Category: fiction or non-fiction

✔ Synopsis

✔ ISBN

In Core Data parlance, a book in this application is an *entity* and information about a book (title, author, and so on . . .) is a *property,* or more specifically an *attribute.* The Xcode data modeler helps you define entities, properties, and their relationships.

To create the data model for the book application, follow these steps:

1. **Open the Models folder and select the default data model to display the data modeler.**

   If you want more elbow room, you can double-click the model to open the data modeler in a separate window.

   The data modeler consists of four panes (not pains!): a list of entities, a list of properties, a pane that displays information about entities and attributes (currently displaying No Selection), and a big pane at the bottom that looks like graph paper. Refer to Figure 19-2.

   The graph paper–looking section at the bottom of the data modeler gives you a visual representation of the data model when you have entities and attributes in the model.

2. **Click the + button at the bottom of the Entity pane to create a new entity.**

   A new entity appears in the Entity pane, as shown in Figure 19-3.

3. **Change the entity name to** Book **by double-clicking its name in the Entity pane or by changing its name in the far-right pane of the data modeler.**

   The Book entity, as you might have already guessed, keeps track of your books.

**Figure 19-3:** Create a new Book entity.

**4. Create** `Author` **and** `Category` **entities, respectively.**

The author and category of a book might both be considered properties of a book, and in fact, you could define them that way. However, in this application, define both the `Category` and `Author` as entities instead (see Figure 19-4). That way, you can alter the author names and categories later without changing the author and category for each book in the collection.

TIP

If the three entities appear on top of one another on the graph paper–looking pane, move them by clicking and dragging each entity so you can see them better.

**Figure 19-4:**
Create the
Author and
Category
entities.

**5. Select the** `Book` **entity and then click the + button at the bottom of the Property pane to add an attribute to the** `Book` **entity.**

There are three kinds of properties: attributes, fetched properties, and relationships, which all appear in the pop-up menu that opens when you click the + button in the Property pane. For now, you need only concern yourself with the attributes property type.

**6. Name the new attribute** `title` **and make it a non-optional** `String` **type.**

Deselect the Optional check box for the `title` attribute and select String from the Type drop-down list, as shown in Figure 19-5. The title attribute will store the name of the book as a string of characters, which is why you selected the string type. Contrary to an entity name, an attribute name isn't capitalized (for example, use `title`, not `Title`).

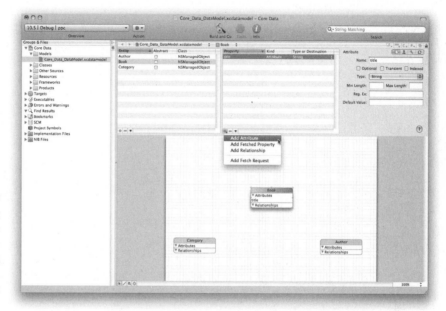

**Figure 19-5:**
Add a new title attribute to the Book entity.

7. **Add a** `pages` **attribute to the** `Book` **entity and choose Integer 16 from the Type drop-down list.**

   The `pages` attribute tracks the page count of a book. The `Integer 16` data type represents a 16-bit integer, large enough to store values as high as 65,536. That number should suffice for most books — even *War and Peace!* Figure 19-6 shows the `Book` entity with two attributes: `title` and `pages`.

8. **Add a third attribute,** `synopsis`, **and give it a** `String` **type.**

   This new attribute tracks the synopsis of the book. The attribute uses the String type because you want to store a string of text.

9. **Add a fourth attribute,** `isbn`, **and designate it as a** `String` **type.**

   Figure 19-7 shows the `Book` entity and its four attributes. The `isbn` attribute is a string instead of an integer because some users might enter the ISBN with hyphens separating the numbers, thus making it a string of characters. Also, some books don't have an ISBN and might use a different numbering system that requires text data.

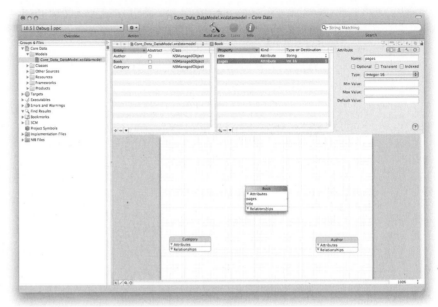

**Figure 19-6:**
Add a pages attribute to track page count for each book.

**Figure 19-7:**
Add synopsis and isbn attributes to the Book entity.

10. **Select the** `Author` **entity from the Entity pane on the left and add an attribute,** `name`, **to it and assign a** `String` **type. Deselect its Optional check box.**

11. **Select the** `Category` **entity from the Entity pane on the left and add an attribute,** `name`, **to it and assign a** `String` **type. Deselect its Optional check box.**

Figure 19-8 shows the completed `Category` entity.

**Figure 19-8:**
Add a name attribute to the Category entity.

12. **Select the** `Book` **entity, add a relationship,** `author`, **to it in the Property pane, select Author from its Destination pop-up menu, and select the To-Many Relationship check box.**

Like attributes, relationship names are lowercase.

A relationship is a different kind of property than an attribute. Instead of storing data like an attribute does, a relationship defines a link between two entities. To find the name of an author, the `Book` entity links to the `Author` entity. The To-Many Relationship check box is selected because some books have multiple authors. The arrow also has two heads at the `author` end.

The `Book` entity is now linked to the `Author` entity, showing their relationship. See Figure 19-9.

13. **Add a second relationship to the** `Book` **entity and name it** `category`. **Select Category from its Destination pop-up menu and select the To-Many Relationship.**

The `category` relationship gleans category information from the `Category` entity.

**Figure 19-9:**
Define an author relationship as part of the Book entity.

The Book entity is now linked to the Category entity, as shown in Figure 19-10. Because a book might belong to multiple categories, the To-Many Relationship check box is selected. Because of the To-Many relationship, the arrow has two heads.

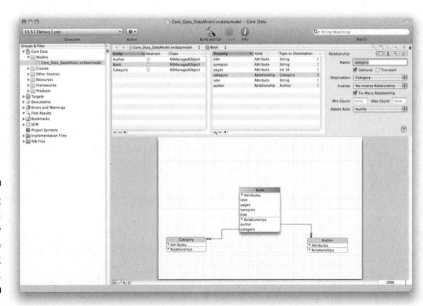

**Figure 19-10:**
Add a category relationship to the Book entity.

You could end your data modeling here, but you have one small additional detail to address. The Book entity knows about the Author and Category entities thanks to the relationships, but the Author and Category entities don't know about the Book entity. So, return to the data modeler and follow these steps to assign relationships in reverse:

1. **Add a relationship,** books, **to the** Author **entity. Select Book from its Destination pop-up menu and select the To-Many Relationship check box.**

   A two-headed arrow connects the Author entity to the Book entity, as shown in Figure 19-11, because one author might have written multiple books.

   A one-headed arrow indicates the two entities have a one-to-one relationship. A two-headed arrow indicates a one-to-many relationship.

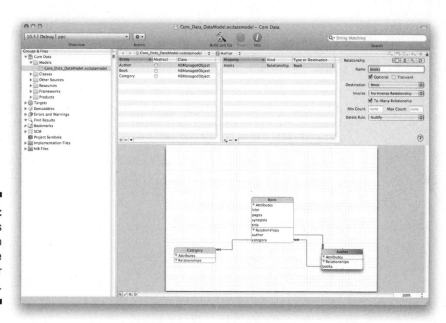

Figure 19-11: Add a books Relationship to the Author Entity.

2. **In the** books **relationship, select Author in the Inverse pop-up menu.**

   Because the Book and Author entities point at each other, the data modeler helps you clean up things by merging the two arrows, as shown in Figure 9-12. One end of the arrow has two heads. The opposite end has one head. The Book entity has a one-to-one relationship with the Author entity (one book is written by one author), but the Author entity has a one-to-many relationship with the Book entity (one author can write many books).

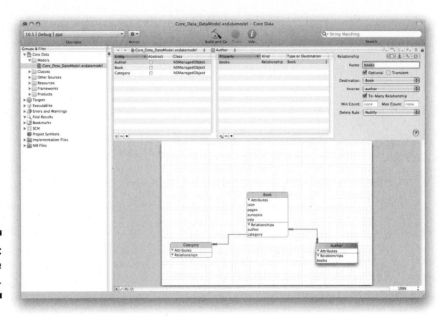

**Figure 19-12:**
Inverse the
relationship.

3. **Add a relationship,** `books`, **to the** `Category` **entity, select Book from its Destination pop-up menu, select the To-Many Relationship check box, and select Category from the Inverse pop-up menu.**

   The `Category` and `Book` entities now have a two-way relationship, as shown in Figure 19-13. A book can belong to multiple categories, and a category can have multiple books, so the arrow has two heads on each end.

4. **Add an attribute to the** `Author` **entity and the** `Category` **entity, assign the String type to both attributes, name both attributes** `name`, **and deselect the Optional check box for both.**

   See Figure 19-14.

   You've now completed building the data model for this book application, so save the project. Now, it's time to build an interface.

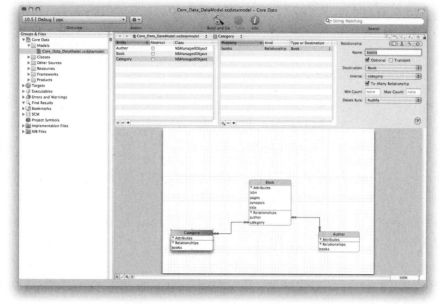

**Figure 19-13:**
Link the
Category
entity and
the Book
entity with
an inverse
relationship.

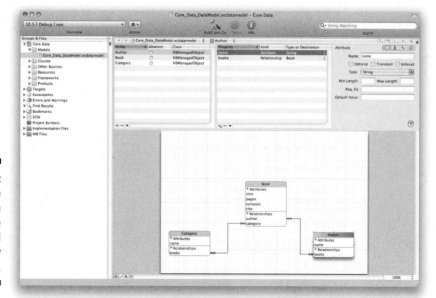

**Figure 19-14:**
Add a name
attribute
to both the
Author and
Category
entities.

# Building the Interface

This is where all your hard work pays off! Sure, you could go about creating an interface, adding buttons and tables 'til the cows come home, but why bother? Xcode can do all the hard work for you! Yes, you read that right. Xcode can actually create a full interface for you based on the data model alone! And what's more, it can even add complete functionality to the interface as well. Follow these steps:

1. **In Xcode, move the project window to the right side of your screen.**

   You'll need the extra room because you need to work with Xcode and Interface Builder at the same time.

2. **Double-click MainMenu.xib in the Resources folder to open Interface Builder, and in Interface Builder, open your project's main interface window so that it's visible.**

   Interface Builder opens and displays the typical items in a default interface file.

   Drag the window to one side of the screen, so you can see it and the Xcode project window at the same time.

3. **Return to Xcode and Option-drag the `Book` entity from the graph paper–looking pane to the interface window in Interface Builder.**

   This step can be a little tricky to master, so don't fret if you can't get it to work on your first try. You can drag the graphical representation of the `Book` entity, not the one in the Entity pane.

4. **Return to Interface Builder and choose Master/Detail View in the New Core Data Entity Interface window, as shown in Figure 19-15.**

5. **Select the Search Field, Details Fields, and Add/Remove check boxes and then click the Next button.**

6. **Accept the defaults (see Figure 19-16) and click the Finish button.**

7. **Return to Xcode again and Option-drag the `Category` entity from the graph paper–looking pane to the interface window in Interface Builder.**

**Figure 19-15:**
Choose
Master/
Detail
View and
select all
the check
boxes.

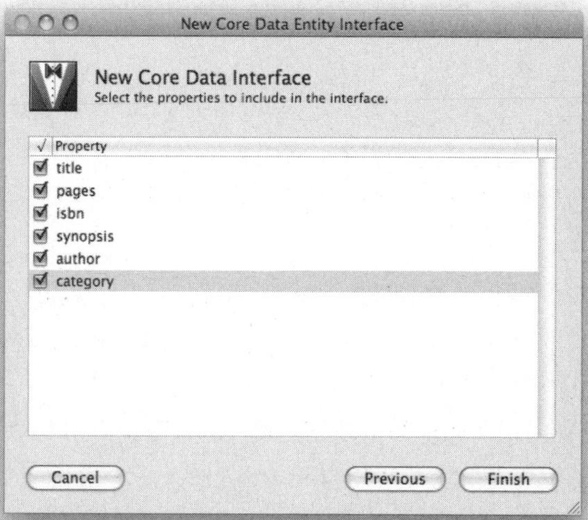

**Figure 19-16:**
Click the
Finish
button to
complete
the inter-
face for the
Book entity.

8. **Back in Interface Builder, choose Master/Detail View in the New Core Data Entity Interface window. Select the Detail Fields and Add/Remove check boxes, as shown in Figure 19-17; click Next.**

   This time, leave the Search Field check box deselected. To give you a little more room in the interface, this omits the search field.

**Figure 19-17:** Click the Next button to complete the interface for the Category entity.

9. **Deselect the Books check box and leave the Name check box selected. Click the Finish button to add the** Category **entity to the interface.**

10. **Return to Xcode and Option-drag the** Author **entity to the interface window in Interface Builder.**

11. **Return to Interface Builder and choose Master/Detail View in the New Core Data Entity Interface window and click Next.**

    Again, select all the check boxes, except the Search Field check box.

12. **Deselect the Books check box and leave the Name check box selected. Click the Finish button to add the** Author **entity to the interface.**

13. **Rearrange the interface to suit your preferences.**

    Figure 19-18 shows a sample interface. You may need to resize the window and move things to make everything fit.

**14. Save the interface and quit Interface Builder.**

**15. In Xcode, choose Build⟳Build and Go to test your hard work.**

You see a working application like that shown in Figure 19-19.

The completed application has an astounding array of features:

- ✔ It displays a complete working interface.
- ✔ You can remove authors and categories.
- ✔ You can add and remove a book and assign an author and a category to the book.
- ✔ The application saves all the data upon closing.
- ✔ It reloads all the data the next time you run the application.
- ✔ It fully supports Undo, which is no small feat to add on your own.
- ✔ The list of books is fully searchable based on title, ISBN, page count, and synopsis.
- ✔ It even has spell-checking!

This is an amazing feat and not only that, you didn't have to write a single solitary line of code to make it happen. Outstanding!

Granted, this may not be the interface you want, but it does give you a tremendous head start on creating your own interface for the application. This interface also gives you a significant number of clues about how Core Data works with interface and, in particular, bindings. In this project, bindings take care of updating your interface to match the data model. You can read more about bindings in Chapter 18.

Note that the interface project window now has new controller objects in it that represent the three entities. Note also that if you select one of those controllers and press ⌘+5, you can view all the various bindings that cause the interface to react with the data model. You can find out a lot about how Core Data works just by investigating these bindings on your own.

# Part V
# The Part of Tens

The 5th Wave          By Rich Tennant

## In this part . . .

To help make your experience more fulfilling, Part V gives you important tips that speed up your Cocoa development as well as Web locations for Cocoa code, demos, and assistance.

# Chapter 20

# Ten Tips to Make Cocoa Programming Easier

· · · · · · · · · · · · · · · · · · · · · · · · · · · · · · · · · · · · · · · · · · · · · · · · ·

## In This Chapter

▶ Use keyboard shortcuts

▶ Read the documentation

▶ Use Class Browser

▶ Adjust the window count

▶ Use drag and drop

▶ Use init and awakeFromNib

▶ Don't forget the methods of the superclass

▶ Position items with Cocoa coordinates

▶ Use guidelines in Interface Builder

▶ Reuse code

· · · · · · · · · · · · · · · · · · · · · · · · · · · · · · · · · · · · · · · · · · · · · · · · ·

*A*s you familiarize yourself with Objective-C and the Cocoa frameworks, you're bound to run across various tips and tricks that you'll want to remember. This chapter attempts to reduce the amount of time you have to wait until you discover some of those tips and tricks.

## Use Keyboard Shortcuts

One of the easiest ways to speed up your Cocoa programming is to take advantage of the multitude of keyboard shortcuts available to you in Xcode and Interface Builder. Table 20-1 lists some of the common keyboard shortcuts that Xcode and Interface Builder share.

| Table 20-1 | Keyboard Shortcuts Shared by Xcode and Interface Builder |
|---|---|
| **Shortcut** | **What It Does** |
| ⌘+S | Saves a file |
| ⌘+O | Opens a file |
| ⌘+M | Minimizes a window to the Dock |
| ⌘+? | Displays help for Xcode or Interface Builder |
| ⌘+N | Creates a new file in Xcode or a new NIB file in Interface Builder |
| ⌘+Q | Quits the application |
| ⌘+R | Runs a project or an interface |

Besides the run-of-the-mill keyboard shortcuts, you can help your Cocoa programming along by using the keyboard shortcuts of the pros. Table 20-2 lists some keyboard shortcuts that give a decided advantage.

| Table 20-2 | Keyboard Shortcuts Used by the Pros |
|---|---|
| **Shortcut** | **What It Does** |
| Option-double-click *keyword* | In Xcode, looks up the keyword's definition in the Xcode documentation |
| ⌘+Z | Goes back in time whenever you make a mistake. Xcode and Interface Builder offer multiple Undos |
| ⌘+Shift+F | Finds all instances of your search term in the Cocoa documentation |
| Control-click | Control-click (or right-click if you have a multi-button mouse) anywhere in Xcode or Interface Builder to reveal a large menu of context-sensitive functions |

# Read the Documentation

It seems too much of a cliché to say it, but your best bet for accelerating your Cocoa programming is to read the manual. Some documentation explains how the Developer Tools work; other documentation details the various classes and methods of Cocoa. You can view the built-in documentation by choosing Help⇨Documentation. You can also read the documentation by visiting the Apple Developer Connection Web site:

```
developer.apple.com/techpubs/macosx/macosx.html
```

# Use Class Browser

In addition to using the standard documentation that's part of Xcode, you can browse the various classes in Cocoa with Class Browser, although the Class Browser isn't Cocoa-specific. Choose Project⇨Class Browser in Xcode to display the Class Browser window. The Class Browser displays all the classes in Cocoa in a structured fashion. You have one-click access to the definitions of Cocoa classes in the interface files.

# Adjust the Window Count

Setting up your work environment to best suit your needs is another quick way to improve your Cocoa programming experience. Xcode can operate with a different number of windows, and it's up to you to set the number of windows with which you feel most comfortable.

Throughout this book, I use the default setting in the General Layout section of the Preferences window. Some people don't appreciate having all the various components of Xcode in one window and like to stretch out a bit. For them, Xcode offers a few other settings that force various Xcode functions to appear in different windows.

Choose Xcode⇨Preferences and click the General button on the toolbar to adjust the window count setting.

# Use Drag and Drop

Drag and drop has long been an attractive feature of the Macintosh operating system. Xcode and Interface Builder continue in this tradition, offering many different drag-and-drop features.

You can add files to Xcode from Finder by dragging them into your project window. These files include source code files, frameworks, image files, HTML (HyperText Markup Language) documents, rich text documents, and .icns icon files.

When you create classes in Xcode, you can let your XIB file know about them by dragging the header files for those classes from Xcode to the Interface Builder NIB file window.

In Interface Builder, drag and drop is, perhaps, the most important interface operation. You use drag and drop to create the entire interface.

# Initialize and Awaken!

When your application loads its NIB file, Cocoa creates the objects in that file and calls the init methods. Next, your application sets the outlets for your interface and calls the awakeFromNib method. Because the application sets the outlets after the init method, you can't use any methods that rely on outlets in the init method. Because awakeFromNib loads after the outlets are set, you can use code that replies on outlets.

As a basic rule, try to add initialization code to the init method of your object. If it doesn't work properly or yields a compiler error, move that initialization code to the awakeFromNib method for that object. After you get the hang of Cocoa programming, you know which method to use and when.

# Remember the Superclass

One of the great features of object-oriented programming is the fact that it has a hierarchical structure. This has a wonderful benefit — *inheritance.* Because every class in Cocoa (with the exception of NSObject) is a subclass of some other class (or classes) above it in the class hierarchy, every class has more methods than those listed for its particular type. This can be confusing at first for some beginners.

Consider this example. The NSTextField and NSTextView controls in Cocoa seem like they should work in a similar fashion because they both display text. By taking a quick look at the documentation, however, you find that they're very different controls. The NSTextView control doesn't have a method for setting its text. The documentation for NSTextView shows that it's a subclass of NSText. NSText, on the other hand, does have a method for setting the text of the view: setString. You may be tempted to use the setString method with an NSTextField control. It's a good guess but an incorrect one.

Like the NSTextView, the NSTextField control has no direct method for setting its text. Because it's a subclass of the NSControl class, you can use the setStringValue method from that class. The lesson here is that if you expect a control to have some kind of method and it doesn't, check one of the superclasses of that class to see whether one of them has the function you need.

# Position Items with Cocoa Coordinates

Programmers who are migrating to Cocoa from other frameworks may be surprised to discover that Cocoa bases all its coordinate measurements on a different coordinate system. Whereas many frameworks define the upper-left corner of a view as the origin, Cocoa drawing designates the bottom-left corner as the origin. You may remember this arrangement as Quadrant I from your high school trigonometry class.

If you're familiar with PDF (Portable Document Format) and PostScript, you can skip this tip. You're already living in an upside-down world. PDF and PostScript use the same coordinate system that Mac OS X uses — and this is no accident. NeXT based its image model on Display Postscript. Mac OS X also uses this model.

# Use Guidelines in Interface Builder

When it comes to building interfaces, Apple insists that you follow many human interface rules to ensure the best experience. There are so many human interface rules that it can be difficult to keep them all straight sometimes. To help you with this, Interface Builder offers a great feature in the form of guidelines. When you drag controls around your interface, Interface Builder displays lines in the interface to help you align controls and place them according to the Human Interface Guidelines.

Pay attention to these interface suggestions! They make it a snap to follow the stringent interface guidelines in Mac OS X and help you create software that follows the Apple standards. Doing so results in software that's easier to use by more people. If you follow your own rules, you're bound to hear complaints. Macintosh users expect a certain user experience. If you stray from it, your users won't be happy.

Consider reading the Apple Style Guide, located on the Apple developer Web site. This guide describes the interface rules and helps you know what terms to use in your application's Help and other documentations.

# Reuse Your Code

The guiding principle of object-oriented programming is code-reuse, and Cocoa is no different. In fact, many programmers claim that Cocoa code is some of the *most* reusable code around because Cocoa programmers separate form from function through the Model-View-Controller paradigm.

To reuse a NIB file, simply drag it into your project in Xcode. To reuse a class, drag its implementation (.m) and header (.h) files into your project in Xcode. It's as simple as that!

# Chapter 21

# Ten Great Web Sites for Cocoa Developers

*T*he Internet is a virtual treasure chest for Cocoa developers. On the Web, you find scores of sites offering Cocoa source code, demo projects, tutorials, instructions, and even personal assistance. This chapter touches on ten important Web sites that will improve your Cocoa experience by offering help and insight into how to program most effectively in Cocoa. You'll find links to professional Cocoa development companies as well as individual Web sites.

Many of these sites also support RSS feeds, so you can set up a subscription and avoid manually checking the sites for new information.

# Apple Developer Connection

developer.apple.com

It makes obvious sense that Apple's Developer Connection would be your first stop in search of Cocoa information. Apple's site offers online documentation (in addition to the built-in documentation in Xcode), tutorials, reference materials, and tons of sample source codes. Further, Apple hosts several user forums where you can ask questions from the professionals or simply read answers to thousands of questions that other developers have posted to the forums. If you visit only one Web site for Cocoa help, this is it.

# Borkware Quickies

www.borkware.com/quickies

The Borkware Quickies site offers dozens of useful code snippets that pertain mostly to Cocoa. These snippets rarely offer much additional discussion; that's okay! Here you find brief descriptions of how the snippets work, and the site does a good job of anticipating the common questions and requests of most developers working with Cocoa. If you find yourself lost in Apple's documentation, give Borkware Quickies a try, and you might be surprised to find that it's already documented the same exact solution you need.

# Cocoa Is My Girlfriend

www.cimgf.com

Cocoa is My Girlfriend is a Cocoa-related blog written by Marcus Zarra and Matt Long. This blog has a couple good things going for it. For starters, the posts are always interesting and well written. Combine that with the fact that most entries are very practical in nature. The authors usually explain how they figure out how something Cocoa-related works. You get to go along for the ride.

# Theocacao

theocacao.com

Another Cocoa blog, this one is run by Scott Stevenson. Scott is very involved in the Cocoa community, so don't be surprised if you hear him speak one day at a convention or a get-together for coders. He also covers these events on his blog, so you won't miss anything if you don't attend these events. The blog also covers popular Cocoa topics with a fair amount of depth, provides interviews with Cocoa luminaries, and offers the occasional rant.

# Call Me Fishmeal

wilshipley.com/blog

Wil Shipley is well-known among the Cocoa community, largely because of his outstanding business success writing Cocoa software and because he was the founder of The Omni Group, one of the seminal NeXT developers, and a major developer since the beginning of OS X. His site offers Wil's musings on a variety of subjects, including Cocoa, Macintosh, iPhone development, fast cars, Microsoft, software design, and product design in general. He's an opinionated bloke, but you can tell that his remarks are always well thought out and that he believes his stance strongly. One of the more popular Cocoa items on the blog is the Pimp My Code series, where Wil accepts a reader-submitted code submission and then explains how to fix and/or improve the code. It's immensely interesting watching how a professional approaches real-life code.

# Domain of the Bored

boredzo.org/blog

With a subtitle of "The personal Weblog of Peter Hosey," this blog has a significant amount of Cocoa materials. Between in-depth explanations of Cocoa concepts and anecdotes about his development experiences with his Growl framework, Peter's site is one not to miss. You have to do some digging on his site, but you come out with some useful gems. He also likes to tout the Macintosh platform as well as other kinds of programming, so you're never bored here.

# Dan Wood: The Eponymous Weblog

`http://gigliwood.com/weblog`

Dan Wood offers a lot of useful Cocoa discussions based on his real-world experience developing software. Sometimes he talks about his experiences releasing products, other times he riffs on software localization. Whatever the topic, you leave his site a better programmer.

# Apple Forums

`www.cocoabuilder.com`

This site provides archives of Apple's forums for Cocoa and Xcode development. With a quick search, you have instant access to thousands of posts by Cocoa developers from around the world. Mainly these come in the form of questions and requests for help, and the replies tend to come from Cocoa professionals. The answers are sometimes terse, but the information is always spot on. If a Cocoa developer has thought of it, it's appeared on this site at one time or another (or more likely — multiple times).

# Cocoa Dev Central

`cocoadevcentral.com`

Cocoa Dev Central hosts a couple dozen Cocoa tutorials. The tutorials are in-depth and very well done. Besides having a beautifully polished appearance, the tutorials are easy to follow and cover topics that aren't always available elsewhere. The tutorials are usually geared toward beginners, but pros will find something beneficial here too.

# CocoaDev

`cocoadev.com`

CocoaDev is a fantastically useful site that covers many different aspects of Cocoa development. Here you find all sorts of advice about Cocoa programming in a nice condensed format (just the facts, ma'am!). The site has a large user base, so you can be sure that the advice comes from a variety of developers. You also find on this site an enormous list of Cocoa blogs.

# Index

**• E •**

**• F •**

# BUSINESS, CAREERS & PERSONAL FINANCE

**Accounting For Dummies, 4th Edition***
978-0-470-24600-9

**Bookkeeping Workbook For Dummies†**
978-0-470-16983-4

**Commodities For Dummies**
978-0-470-04928-0

**Doing Business in China For Dummies**
978-0-470-04929-7

**E-Mail Marketing For Dummies**
978-0-470-19087-6

**Job Interviews For Dummies, 3rd Edition*†**
978-0-470-17748-8

**Personal Finance Workbook For Dummies*†**
978-0-470-09933-9

**Real Estate License Exams For Dummies**
978-0-7645-7623-2

**Six Sigma For Dummies**
978-0-7645-6798-8

**Small Business Kit For Dummies, 2nd Edition*†**
978-0-7645-5984-6

**Telephone Sales For Dummies**
978-0-470-16836-3

# BUSINESS PRODUCTIVITY & MICROSOFT OFFICE

**Access 2007 For Dummies**
978-0-470-03649-5

**Excel 2007 For Dummies**
978-0-470-03737-9

**Office 2007 For Dummies**
978-0-470-00923-9

**Outlook 2007 For Dummies**
978-0-470-03830-7

**PowerPoint 2007 For Dummies**
978-0-470-04059-1

**Project 2007 For Dummies**
978-0-470-03651-8

**QuickBooks 2008 For Dummies**
978-0-470-18470-7

**Quicken 2008 For Dummies**
978-0-470-17473-9

**Salesforce.com For Dummies, 2nd Edition**
978-0-470-04893-1

**Word 2007 For Dummies**
978-0-470-03658-7

# EDUCATION, HISTORY, REFERENCE & TEST PREPARATION

**African American History For Dummies**
978-0-7645-5469-8

**Algebra For Dummies**
978-0-7645-5325-7

**Algebra Workbook For Dummies**
978-0-7645-8467-1

**Art History For Dummies**
978-0-470-09910-0

**ASVAB For Dummies, 2nd Edition**
978-0-470-10671-6

**British Military History For Dummies**
978-0-470-03213-8

**Calculus For Dummies**
978-0-7645-2498-1

**Canadian History For Dummies, 2nd Edition**
978-0-470-83656-9

**Geometry Workbook For Dummies**
978-0-471-79940-5

**The SAT I For Dummies, 6th Edition**
978-0-7645-7193-0

**Series 7 Exam For Dummies**
978-0-470-09932-2

**World History For Dummies**
978-0-7645-5242-7

# FOOD, GARDEN, HOBBIES & HOME

**Bridge For Dummies, 2nd Edition**
978-0-471-92426-5

**Coin Collecting For Dummies, 2nd Edition**
978-0-470-22275-1

**Cooking Basics For Dummies, 3rd Edition**
978-0-7645-7206-7

**Drawing For Dummies**
978-0-7645-5476-6

**Etiquette For Dummies, 2nd Edition**
978-0-470-10672-3

**Gardening Basics For Dummies*†**
978-0-470-03749-2

**Knitting Patterns For Dummies**
978-0-470-04556-5

**Living Gluten-Free For Dummies†**
978-0-471-77383-2

**Painting Do-It-Yourself For Dummies**
978-0-470-17533-0

# HEALTH, SELF HELP, PARENTING & PETS

**Anger Management For Dummies**
978-0-470-03715-7

**Anxiety & Depression Workbook For Dummies**
978-0-7645-9793-0

**Dieting For Dummies, 2nd Edition**
978-0-7645-4149-0

**Dog Training For Dummies, 2nd Edition**
978-0-7645-8418-3

**Horseback Riding For Dummies**
978-0-470-09719-9

**Infertility For Dummies†**
978-0-470-11518-3

**Meditation For Dummies with CD-ROM, 2nd Edition**
978-0-471-77774-8

**Post-Traumatic Stress Disorder For Dummies**
978-0-470-04922-8

**Puppies For Dummies, 2nd Edition**
978-0-470-03717-1

**Thyroid For Dummies, 2nd Edition†**
978-0-471-78755-6

**Type 1 Diabetes For Dummies*†**
978-0-470-17811-9

---

\* Separate Canadian edition also available
† Separate U.K. edition also available

Available wherever books are sold. For more information or to order direct: U.S. customers visit www.dummies.com or call 1-877-762-2974.
U.K. customers visit www.wileyeurope.com or call (0)1243 843291. Canadian customers visit www.wiley.ca or call 1-800-567-4797.

 WILEY

## INTERNET & DIGITAL MEDIA

**AdWords For Dummies**
978-0-470-15252-2

**Blogging For Dummies, 2nd Edition**
978-0-470-23017-6

**Digital Photography All-in-One Desk Reference For Dummies, 3rd Edition**
978-0-470-03743-0

**Digital Photography For Dummies, 5th Edition**
978-0-7645-9802-9

**Digital SLR Cameras & Photography For Dummies, 2nd Edition**
978-0-470-14927-0

**eBay Business All-in-One Desk Reference For Dummies**
978-0-7645-8438-1

**eBay For Dummies, 5th Edition\***
978-0-470-04529-9

**eBay Listings That Sell For Dummies**
978-0-471-78912-3

**Facebook For Dummies**
978-0-470-26273-3

**The Internet For Dummies, 11th Edition**
978-0-470-12174-0

**Investing Online For Dummies, 5th Edition**
978-0-7645-8456-5

**iPod & iTunes For Dummies, 5th Edition**
978-0-470-17474-6

**MySpace For Dummies**
978-0-470-09529-4

**Podcasting For Dummies**
978-0-471-74898-4

**Search Engine Optimization For Dummies, 2nd Edition**
978-0-471-97998-2

**Second Life For Dummies**
978-0-470-18025-9

**Starting an eBay Business For Dummies, 3rd Edition†**
978-0-470-14924-9

## GRAPHICS, DESIGN & WEB DEVELOPMENT

**Adobe Creative Suite 3 Design Premium All-in-One Desk Reference For Dummies**
978-0-470-11724-8

**Adobe Web Suite CS3 All-in-One Desk Reference For Dummies**
978-0-470-12099-6

**AutoCAD 2008 For Dummies**
978-0-470-11650-0

**Building a Web Site For Dummies, 3rd Edition**
978-0-470-14928-7

**Creating Web Pages All-in-One Desk Reference For Dummies, 3rd Edition**
978-0-470-09629-1

**Creating Web Pages For Dummies, 8th Edition**
978-0-470-08030-6

**Dreamweaver CS3 For Dummies**
978-0-470-11490-2

**Flash CS3 For Dummies**
978-0-470-12100-9

**Google SketchUp For Dummies**
978-0-470-13744-4

**InDesign CS3 For Dummies**
978-0-470-11865-8

**Photoshop CS3 All-in-One Desk Reference For Dummies**
978-0-470-11195-6

**Photoshop CS3 For Dummies**
978-0-470-11193-2

**Photoshop Elements 5 For Dummies**
978-0-470-09810-3

**SolidWorks For Dummies**
978-0-7645-9555-4

**Visio 2007 For Dummies**
978-0-470-08983-5

**Web Design For Dummies, 2nd Edition**
978-0-471-78117-2

**Web Sites Do-It-Yourself For Dummies**
978-0-470-16903-2

**Web Stores Do-It-Yourself For Dummies**
978-0-470-17443-2

## LANGUAGES, RELIGION & SPIRITUALITY

**Arabic For Dummies**
978-0-471-77270-5

**Chinese For Dummies, Audio Set**
978-0-470-12766-7

**French For Dummies**
978-0-7645-5193-2

**German For Dummies**
978-0-7645-5195-6

**Hebrew For Dummies**
978-0-7645-5489-6

**Ingles Para Dummies**
978-0-7645-5427-8

**Italian For Dummies, Audio Set**
978-0-470-09586-7

**Italian Verbs For Dummies**
978-0-471-77389-4

**Japanese For Dummies**
978-0-7645-5429-2

**Latin For Dummies**
978-0-7645-5431-5

**Portuguese For Dummies**
978-0-471-78738-9

**Russian For Dummies**
978-0-471-78001-4

**Spanish Phrases For Dummies**
978-0-7645-7204-3

**Spanish For Dummies**
978-0-7645-5194-9

**Spanish For Dummies, Audio Set**
978-0-470-09585-0

**The Bible For Dummies**
978-0-7645-5296-0

**Catholicism For Dummies**
978-0-7645-5391-2

**The Historical Jesus For Dummies**
978-0-470-16785-4

**Islam For Dummies**
978-0-7645-5503-9

**Spirituality For Dummies, 2nd Edition**
978-0-470-19142-2

## NETWORKING AND PROGRAMMING

**ASP.NET 3.5 For Dummies**
978-0-470-19592-5

**C# 2008 For Dummies**
978-0-470-19109-5

**Hacking For Dummies, 2nd Edition**
978-0-470-05235-8

**Home Networking For Dummies, 4th Edition**
978-0-470-11806-1

**Java For Dummies, 4th Edition**
978-0-470-08716-9

**Microsoft® SQL Server™ 2008 All-in-One Desk Reference For Dummies**
978-0-470-17954-3

**Networking All-in-One Desk Reference For Dummies, 2nd Edition**
978-0-7645-9939-2

**Networking For Dummies, 8th Edition**
978-0-470-05620-2

**SharePoint 2007 For Dummies**
978-0-470-09941-4

**Wireless Home Networking For Dummies, 2nd Edition**
978-0-471-74940-0

## OPERATING SYSTEMS & COMPUTER BASICS

**Mac For Dummies, 5th Edition**
78-0-7645-8158-9

**Laptops For Dummies, 2nd Edition**
978-0-470-05432-1

**Linux For Dummies, 8th Edition**
78-0-470-11649-4

**MacBook For Dummies**
78-0-470-04859-7

**Mac OS X Leopard All-in-One Desk Reference For Dummies**
78-0-470-05434-5

**Mac OS X Leopard For Dummies**
978-0-470-05433-8

**Macs For Dummies, 9th Edition**
978-0-470-04849-8

**PCs For Dummies, 11th Edition**
978-0-470-13728-4

**Windows® Home Server For Dummies**
978-0-470-18592-6

**Windows Server 2008 For Dummies**
978-0-470-18043-3

**Windows Vista All-in-One Desk Reference For Dummies**
978-0-471-74941-7

**Windows Vista For Dummies**
978-0-471-75421-3

**Windows Vista Security For Dummies**
978-0-470-11805-4

## SPORTS, FITNESS & MUSIC

**Coaching Hockey For Dummies**
78-0-470-83685-9

**Coaching Soccer For Dummies**
78-0-471-77381-8

**Fitness For Dummies, 3rd Edition**
78-0-7645-7851-9

**Football For Dummies, 3rd Edition**
78-0-470-12536-6

**GarageBand For Dummies**
978-0-7645-7323-1

**Golf For Dummies, 3rd Edition**
978-0-471-76871-5

**Guitar For Dummies, 2nd Edition**
978-0-7645-9904-0

**Home Recording For Musicians For Dummies, 2nd Edition**
978-0-7645-8884-6

**iPod & iTunes For Dummies, 5th Edition**
978-0-470-17474-6

**Music Theory For Dummies**
978-0-7645-7838-0

**Stretching For Dummies**
978-0-470-06741-3

---

# Get smart @ dummies.com®

- Find a full list of Dummies titles
- Look into loads of FREE on-site articles
- Sign up for FREE eTips e-mailed to you weekly
- See what other products carry the Dummies name
- Shop directly from the Dummies bookstore
- Enter to win new prizes every month!

---

eparate Canadian edition also available
eparate U.K. edition also available

ailable wherever books are sold. For more information or to order direct: U.S. customers visit www.dummies.com or call 1-877-762-2974.
. customers visit www.wileyeurope.com or call (0) 1243 843291. Canadian customers visit www.wiley.ca or call 1-800-567-4797.

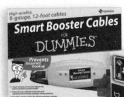
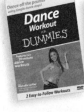